RACE AND POLICING IN AMERICA

Race and Policing in America is about relations between police and citizens, with a focus on racial differences. It systematically examines Americans' opinions, preferences, and personal experiences regarding the police. Guided by group-position theory and using both existing studies and the authors' own quantitative and qualitative data from a nationally representative survey of whites, blacks, and Hispanics this book examines the roles of personal experience, knowledge of others' experiences, mass media reporting on the police, and neighborhood conditions in structuring citizen views in four major areas: overall satisfaction with police in one's city and neighborhood, perceptions of several types of police misconduct, perceptions of police racial bias and discrimination, and evaluations of and support for a variety of reforms in policing.

Ronald Weitzer is professor of sociology at George Washington University. His books include *Current Controversies in Criminology* (2003), *Deviance and Social Control* (2002), *Sex for Sale: Prostitution, Pornography, and the Sex Industry* (2000), *Policing Under Fire: Ethnic Conflict and Police-Community Relations in Northern Ireland* (1995), and *Transforming Settler States: Communal Conflict and Internal Security in Northern Ireland and Zimbabwe* (1990).

Steven A. Tuch is professor of sociology and of public policy and public administration at George Washington University. His published work has appeared in such journals as *American Sociological Review, American Journal of Sociology, Social Forces, Social Problems, Criminology, Social Psychology Quarterly, Public Opinion Quarterly,* and *Sociological Quarterly,* among others. He is coeditor of *Racial Attitudes in the 1990s: Continuity and Change* (1997) and *The Other African Americans: Contemporary African and Caribbean Families in the United States* (forthcoming).

CAMBRIDGE STUDIES IN CRIMINOLOGY

Editors

Alfred Blumstein, *School of Public Policy and Management, Carnegie Mellon University,*

David Farrington, *Institute of Criminology*

Other Books in the Series:

Life in the Gang: Family, Friends, and Violence, by Scott Decker and Barrik Van Winkle

Delinquency and Crime: Current Theories, edited by J. David Hawkins

Recriminalizing Delinquency: Violent Juvenile Crime and Juvenile Justice Reform, by Simon I. Singer

Mean Streets: Youth Crime and Homelessness, by John Hagan and Bill McCarthy

The Framework of Judicial Sentencing: A Study in Legal Decision Making, by Austin Lovegrove

The Criminal Recidivism Process, by Edward Zamble and Vernon L. Quinsey

Violence and Childhood in the Inner City, by Joan McCord

Judicial Policy Making and the Modern State: How the Courts Reformed America's Prisons, by Malcolm M. Feeley and Edward L. Rubin

Schools and Delinquency, by Denise C. Gottfredson

Delinquent-Prone Communities, by Don Weatherburn and Bronwyn Lind

White Collar Crime and Criminal Careers, by David Weisburd and Elin Waring, with Ellen F. Chayet

Sex Differences in Antisocial Behavior: Conduct Disorder, Delinquency, and Violence in the Dunedin Longitudinal Study, by Terrie Moffitt, Avshalom Caspi, Michael Rutter, and Phil A. Silva

Delinquent Networks: Youth Co-offending in Stockholm, by Jerzi Sarnecki

Criminality and Violence among the Mentally Disordered, by Sheilagh Hodgins and Carl-Gunnar Janson

Corporate Crime, Law, and Social Control, by Sally S. Simpson

Companions in Crime: The Social Aspects of Criminal Conduct, by Mark Warr

Series list continues following the index.

Race and Policing in America

Conflict and Reform

Ronald Weitzer

George Washington University

Steven A. Tuch

George Washington University

CAMBRIDGE
UNIVERSITY PRESS

CAMBRIDGE UNIVERSITY PRESS
Cambridge, New York, Melbourne, Madrid, Cape Town, Singapore, São Paulo

Cambridge University Press
40 West 20th Street, New York, NY 10011-4211, USA

www.cambridge.org
Information on this title: www.cambridge.org/9780521851527

First published 2006

Printed in the United States of America

A catalog record for this publication is available from the British Library.

Library of Congress Cataloging in Publication Data

Weitzer, Ronald
Race and policing in America : conflict and reform / Ronald Weitzer, Steven A. Tuch.
  p.   cm. – (Cambridge studies in criminology)
Includes bibliographical references and index.
ISBN-13: 978-0-521-85152-7 (hardback)
ISBN-10: 0-521-85152-1 (hardback)
ISBN-13: 978-0-521-61691-1 (pbk.)
ISBN-10: 0-521-61691-3 (pbk.)
1. Police – United States – Public opinion.   2. Minorities – United States – Attitudes.
3. Police-community relations – United States.   4. Discrimination in law
enforcement – United States.   5. Racism – United States.   6. Police misconduct –
United States.   I. Tuch, Steven A.   II. Title.   III. Series: Cambridge
studies in criminology (Cambridge University Press)
HV8139.W45   2006
363.2089'00973 – dc22   2006000759

ISBN-13   978-0-521-85152-7 hardback
ISBN-10   0-521-85152-1 hardback

ISBN-13   978-0-521-61691-1 paperback
ISBN-10   0-521-61691-3 paperback

Contents

List of Tables and Figures   *page* ix

Acknowledgements   xi

1 : Police-Minority Relations in America   1
  The Nature of Police Work   3
  Race, Policing, and Public Opinion   5
  Theoretical Issues   7
  Key Policing Issues   25
  Overview of the Book   38

2 : Police Misconduct   39
  Overall Satisfaction with the Police   39
  Police Misconduct   45
  Perceptions and Experiences of Misconduct   50
  What Shapes Views of Misconduct?   58
  Observations of Misconduct   65
  Conclusion   70

3 : Racially Biased Policing   74
  Perceptions and Experiences of Racially Biased
    Policing   78
  Explaining Citizen Views of Racialized Policing   89
  Is Officers' Race Important?   95
  Conclusion   119

4: Reforming the Police   124
    Major Types of Reform   126
    Popular Support for Reform   139
    What Influences Reform Preferences?   152
    What Other Reforms are Desired?   161
    Conclusion   173

5: Conclusion: The Continuing Racial Divide   178

Appendix: Data and Methods   191

References   205

Index   221

List of Figures and Tables

FIGURES

2.1 Police Misconduct in City   *page* 51
2.2 Personal Experience in City   53
2.3 Personal Experience in City, Young Males   54
2.4 Vicarious Experience in City   55
3.1 Opinions on Racial Profiling   83
3.2 Experiences of Biased Policing   85
3.3 Experiences of Biased Policing, Young Males   86
3.4 Experiences of Racial Profiling   87
3.5 Experiences of Racial Profiling, Young Males   88
3.6 Perception that Officers' Race Affects Their Behavior   97
3.7 Preferred Type of Officers in Neighborhood   111
4.1 Support for Racial Diversification   139
4.2 Support for Greater Monitoring   145
4.3 Support for More Accountability   147
4.4 Support for Community Policing   150
4.5 Support for Intensified Policing   151

TABLES

2.1 Satisfaction with Local Police   41
2.2 Satisfaction with Police   43
2.3 Perceptions of Police Misconduct   60
3.1 Perceptions of Police Bias   90
4.1 Reform Preferences   154

A.1 Knowledge Networks' and Census Data for the Top 25
     Metropolitan Areas   194
A.2 Demographic Characteristics of Knowledge Networks
     Panel   195
A.3 Descriptive Statistics and Mean Difference Tests on All
     Study Variables   197

Acknowledgements

This book would not have been possible without the generous financial support of the National Institute of Justice, grant number 2001-IJ-CX-0016. This support provided the means for us to conduct a nationwide study of citizen attitudes toward the police, collecting both quantitative and qualitative data. The arguments and conclusions in the book do not necessarily reflect the views of the National Institute of Justice, but we expect that our findings will be of value to NIJ and to other officials, including police chiefs, involved in formulating standards and policies regarding policing.

We are also grateful to the Columbian College of Arts and Sciences at George Washington University for its support of our project. In 2003–2004, we received Columbian Research Scholar awards that provided release time to complete our research and work on the book.

Sandra Hanson, Lee Sigelman, and Gregory Squires read portions of the book and provided extremely helpful suggestions for revision. We also benefited greatly from two workshops sponsored by the National Institute of Justice on "Minority Trust and Confidence in the Police." We thank the participants in the workshop for their feedback on our research project: Geoffrey Alpert, Roger Dunham, Darnell Hawkins, Robert Kaminski, Dennis Rosenbaum, Chris Stone, and Tom Tyler.

CHAPTER ONE

Police-Minority Relations in America

Americans are ambivalent about the police. We are fascinated by them, as evident in the popularity and proliferation of police shows on television – from dramas such as *NYPD Blue* and *Law and Order* to reality programs such as *COPS*. These shows typically present the police in a sympathetic light, even when they act aggressively or improperly against citizens. Programs such as *COPS* appear to present the "reality" of everyday patrolling, but with a camera crew present the featured officers are obviously on their best behavior.

On the negative side, Americans' opinions of the police are periodically shaken by revelations in the media of serious incidents of police misconduct (such as brutality) or more entrenched and ongoing problems (such as corruption). Most people were appalled at the gratuitous beating of Rodney King in Los Angeles, as reflected in the massive drop in public approval of the Los Angeles Police Department (LAPD) in the wake of the beating. Just two weeks after the beating, black and Hispanic confidence in the LAPD fell a whopping 50 percentage points – from 80 to 31 percent among Hispanics and from 64 to 14 percent among blacks – according to a *Los Angeles Times* poll on March 20, 1991. Approval among whites also fell, but less dramatically (from 74 to 41 percent). The killing of Amadou Diallo in February 1999 – after New York City cops fired 41 bullets at him – created a furor in the city, with daily protests outside police headquarters. Corruption scandals take place with some frequency. In 1999, for instance, the Rampart Division of the LAPD was engulfed in a major crisis. Rampart officers were accused of a litany of abuses – including falsifying police reports, stealing drugs from suspects, framing people, lying in court testimony, and shooting unarmed suspects without cause. More than 200 law-suits and claims were filed against the city by people who claimed that they were victimized by officers, over 100 tainted criminal convictions have been overturned, and eight officers were convicted of corruption-related crimes. Of the 214 lawsuits, 179 resulted in settlements totaling $70 million (Glover and Lait 2005).

When asked in opinion polls about their general impressions of the police, most Americans appear to hold favorable views. The majority say they are "satisfied" with, have "confidence" in, or "trust" the police. For instance, when asked in 1997 about the level of trust people have in their local police department, 46 percent said they trusted the department "a lot," 32 percent said "some," 12 percent "only a little," and 8 percent "not at all" (Pew 1997). Although the meaning of such general attitudes is not entirely clear, they do seem to reflect basic approval or even the legitimacy of the police as an institution.

These general, overarching attitudes tell only part of the story, how-ever. When studying citizen views of the police, it is equally important to examine perceptions about specific issues and police practices. Studies that do so consistently find that people harbor some fairly critical views of the police, and this is especially true for minority group members. For example, when asked about the scope of police "racism against blacks," 4 out of 10 blacks said it was very common and another 30 percent believed it was fairly common (Gallup 1995). Moreover, a fair number of blacks and Hispanics report that they have been the victims of some kind of mistreatment by a police officer, whether it is verbal abuse, excessive force, or an improper stop.

Negative perceptions and adverse personal experiences with police officers can alienate citizens from the police. Such poor relations may contribute to altercations on the street, lower officer morale, make citizens reluctant to report crimes and come forward as witnesses, increase the danger of police work, and hamper recruitment of new officers. Distrust of the police also can increase anxiety among citizens. A recent poll, for example, reveals that a substantial number of blacks and Hispanics were "sometimes afraid that the police will stop and arrest you when you are completely innocent": 4 out of 10 Hispanics and blacks but only one-sixth of whites expressed such fear (Harris 2002).

No one doubts that there is room for improvement in the ways police officers relate to citizens, but because citizens have rarely been questioned about specific kinds of reforms, we know little about which changes are most strongly supported. Still, it is likely that a fairly large segment of the American public would support changes in the way the police operate. In addition to examining several serious problems with police treatment of citizens, and particularly minority citizens, this book also examines the prospects for reforms that might improve police-citizen relations.

Before turning to the issue of how Americans view and experience the police, we briefly describe some aspects of police work that illuminate how officers perceive the public.

THE NATURE OF POLICE WORK

Key features of police work shape how officers perceive and treat citizens. Included here are the low visibility of police work, officers' immense discretionary authority, the problems they face on a daily basis, and the values and beliefs ingrained in the police subculture. The *low visibility* of police work means that the behavior of patrol officers is largely hidden from the public (most officers work alone) and is not systematically monitored by supervisors (Goldstein 1960). This autonomy affords cops great *discretion* in deciding how to handle problems, improvise solutions, and enforce the law. Police are asked to "maintain order," but this fairly vague mandate is open to interpretation and discretionary action. Regarding law enforcement, it is simply impossible for officers to enforce the law in all cases that come to their attention. One study found that police made arrests on only about half of the occasions in which they had legal grounds to do so (Black 1971). Selective enforcement is the norm, particularly with respect to minor offenses (Goldstein 1963). This is just one area that lends itself to friction between officers and the public. Some citizens press officers not to enforce the law against them and become angry when their appeal is ignored, whereas others (e.g., victims and other complainants) become incensed when an officer decides not to take action against an offender.

Police work has been called "dirty work." Officers routinely confront *problem citizens*, who are difficult to handle – including victims who are emotional or traumatized, suspects who are unruly or violent, bystanders who attempt to interfere with police actions, and motorists who behave in an uncivil manner toward an officer. Some citizens construe police intervention as harassment or as an infringement of rights, prompting a belligerent response from the recipient. Other citizens interpret officers' curt and authoritarian demeanor, which is standard practice among officers, as a personal affront or as racial animus (Sykes and Clark 1975). Police claim that they have good reasons for being brusque and withholding information from citizens. For example, an officer typically is "reluctant to reveal his reasons for stopping people because he sees his cues as private knowledge which, if it were generally known, would aid criminals and make his work even harder than it is" (Rubenstein 1973:264). Such unresponsiveness is unsettling to many citizens.

For their part, police frequently complain that citizens not only fail to understand police work, but also do not respect them or defer to their authority (Baker 1985). In Chicago, for instance, half the officers surveyed in one study believed that most people do not respect the police, and two-thirds felt that citizens do not understand the problems police face (Skogan and Hartnett 1997:79). This, in turn, may influence how officers treat citizens. In a recent Police Foundation survey of 121 police departments across the country, half of the officers interviewed stated that police are likely to arrest someone simply because he or she displays a "bad attitude" toward an officer (Weisburd and Greenspan 2000).

Because street cops deal mostly with problem citizens, not the general population, they develop an "us versus them" orientation toward the public. This adversarial outlook is one ingredient in the *police subculture* – a distinct set of values and beliefs that shape officer behavior. A related part of that subculture is the very mission of the police institution: Officers hold a lofty sense of their mission, seeing themselves as a "thin blue line" between order and chaos (Skolnick and Fyfe 1993:92–93). This high calling, coupled with officers' social distance from the public, combine to insulate the police and reinforce a third aspect of their subculture: group loyalty and a protective "code of silence" that shields cops from scrutiny. As one officer remarked, "It is basically a non-written rule that you do not roll over – tell on – your partner" (Christopher Commission 1991:169). Doing so will lead to ostracism. The Police Foundation survey found that fully two-thirds of cops agreed with the statement: "An officer who reports another officer's misconduct is likely to be given the cold shoulder by his or her fellow officers" (Weisburd and Greenspan 2000).

The police subculture influences how officers treat citizens. On the job, officers learn to trust only fellow officers and to distrust members of the public, to deal forcefully with people who question their actions, to skirt at least some legal restrictions on their behavior, and to administer summary "street justice" to suspicious or troublesome people (Baker 1985; Skolnick and Fyfe 1993). These practices depend in part on fellow officers' tacit support and silence and are made possible by the low visibility and high discretion characterizing police work. In short, *the aspects of police work described here have the net effect of driving a wedge between police officers and many of the citizens they encounter*. If officers regard citizens as antagonists, the insular police subculture only reinforces this us-versus-them mentality. Some see all citizens in this light, whereas others believe that minority group members are cops' main adversaries.[1]

RACE, POLICING, AND PUBLIC OPINION

Despite decades of research, much remains to be known about police-citizen relations. We do know that race plays a major role in shaping citizens' attitudes and experiences with the police in the United States and other multiracial societies. Whites and blacks tend to perceive the criminal justice system in America in strikingly different terms. Indeed, race is one of the strongest predictors of attitudes toward the courts and police. Blacks are more inclined than whites to believe that the police abuse citizens, treat minorities more harshly than whites, and are not held accountable for misconduct. At the same time, large numbers of

---

[1] Of course, not all officers are equally influenced by the police subculture. Officers differ, at least to some extent, in the degree to which subcultural values are internalized. Our brief discussion of the subculture outlines its general features, without assuming that it is universally salient.

blacks, particularly those living in communities with high crime rates, believe their neighborhoods receive inadequate law enforcement and demand an intensification of police protection and services. Whites are, on the whole, much more satisfied with the police than other groups. Little is known about Hispanics' and Asians' relations with the police.

Most studies that highlight the importance of race and ethnicity in shaping police-citizen relations fail to analyze different groups separately. Analyses of pooled samples may mask important race-specific determinants of perceptions. Thus, we know that race matters, but much less is known about the *factors that shape each racial group's outlook* on the police. It is possible, for example, that some factors influence whites, blacks, and Hispanics equally, whereas others are salient for one or two groups only. Minorities seem to have more contentious face-to-face encounters with the police than is true for whites, and minority neighborhoods tend to have more serious crime problems than white neighborhoods – both of which may be important predictors of relations with the police for blacks and Hispanics but less so for whites. Our comparative examination of the three groups will help address an important question in the literature on police-minority relations – the relative orientations, and perhaps distinctive concerns, of Hispanics, blacks, and whites.

The lack of information on Hispanics is particularly acute in light of their growing presence in many American cities, and they make up the majority in some cities. Some of the literature is overly anecdotal and makes unsubstantiated assertions (Mirande 1987; Escobar 1999). In other work, the number of Hispanics studied is often too small for statistical analysis, while some polls are limited by focusing on Hispanics alone (Mirande 1981; Carter 1985), by comparing them only to whites (Holmes 1998), or by lumping Hispanics and blacks together into a "nonwhite" category. Few studies systematically compare blacks, whites, and Hispanics (e.g., Webb and Marshall 1995; Tuch and Weitzer 1997; Reitzel, Rice, and Piquero 2004), and this literature is too sparse to draw definitive conclusions.

Anecdotal evidence suggests that Hispanics, and particularly immigrants, may face some unique obstacles when interacting with the police: namely, language and cultural barriers, fear of deportation among illegal immigrants, and an ingrained suspicion of police imported from immigrants' home countries, where police are often thoroughly corrupt or a paramilitary arm of an oppressive regime. But, again, scholars have not explored the degree to which Hispanics hold distinctive perceptions, experiences, or concerns that set them apart from other groups. If Hispanics and blacks differ in their opinions and experiences, this finding would run counter to the commonly held assumption that minorities are treated similarly by the police and that they are monolithic in their evaluations of police. There are four possible patterns:

- The conventional wisdom holds that Hispanics and blacks share a "minority-group perspective" toward the police that is distinct from a white "majority-group perspective";
- Hispanics might be closer in their perceptions to whites than to blacks;
- Hispanics may take an intermediate or a unique position – so that group perceptions are organized in a white–Hispanic–African American "racial hierarchy"; or
- the Hispanic-black pattern may be issue-specific: On some issues most Hispanics and blacks may be in agreement, whereas on other issues, most members of the two groups may disagree.[2]

THEORETICAL ISSUES

We do not fully understand *why* racial differences exist in citizen perceptions and experiences of the police. What accounts for these differences? The conventional wisdom holds that members of each group are treated differently by the police and, consequently, view police differently. But this may be only part of the explanation and, by itself, is atheoretical. Unfortunately, most of the research on police-minority relations is not grounded within any theoretical perspective. The following section addresses this issue.

[2] Even less is known about variations *within* the Hispanic population along the lines of national origin. Do Puerto Ricans, Cubans, Mexicans, and other Hispanic subgroups differ in their relations with the police? Virtually no studies address this question. Although the primary focus of the book is a comparison of whites, blacks, and Hispanics, intra-Hispanic patterns are also examined. However, this part of our analysis is limited by the low sample size of some of the Hispanic nationality groups.

The Group-Position Thesis: Interests and Threats

Our analysis is informed by the *group-position thesis* and the related power-threat thesis in the fields of race relations and criminology. Both theses are derived from conflict theory. The group-position thesis depicts racial attitudes not simply as free-floating positive feelings, stereotypes, or animus but, instead, as a reflection of intergroup competition and conflict over material rewards, power, and status in a multiracial society. In the group-position model, prejudice is rooted in a collective "sense of group position," and *group interests* are the driving force underlying contentious intergroup relations and racial attitudes. Thus, "racial feelings point to and depend on a positional arrangement of racial groups," Blumer (1958:4) argued. The interests of the dominant group include proprietary claims to scarce resources, challenges to which may be viewed as a threat to the prevailing racial order. Dominant group attitudes toward other racial groups are therefore positional: shaped by a sense of superiority over minority groups and a need to defend the dominant group against threats to its interests. The subordinate group, on the other hand, is motivated by a sense of unfair and exclusionary treatment at the hands of the dominant group, and by an interest in securing a greater share of advantages. Indeed, the greater the sense of oppression felt by minority group members, the more likely they are to favor change in the racial status quo (Bobo 1999). Most African Americans, for example, approve of programs that might improve their access to higher education and jobs (Sigelman and Welch 1991).

In a nutshell, racial attitudes reflect not merely individuals' feelings and beliefs but also relations between groups: (1) *perceived threats*: white fears that their racial group is at risk of losing privileges or resources to competing racial groups and (2) *perceived advantages*: minority beliefs that their group interests will be enhanced by challenging the prevailing racial order (Blumer 1958; Quillian 1995; Bobo and Hutchings 1996; Kinder and Sanders 1996; Bobo 1999).

The group-position thesis has been used to explain a particular group's attitudes toward other groups; we extend it to include *groups' relations with social institutions*. If the dominant group believes that it is entitled to valuable resources, it follows that the group should have an affinity with the institutions that serve their interests. One such institution is the criminal justice system. Coercive crime-control practices may, in the aggregate, benefit the dominant group. More specifically, the "power-threat" thesis (Blalock 1967) holds that the amount of control exercised by the authorities is related to the real or perceived threat posed by minority groups to dominant groups. The growth of Hispanic populations in some cities may be seen as a threat by the dominant group, requiring increased control (Kane 2002), but most power-threat research focuses on African Americans. Cities with higher percentages of black residents, for instance, devote greater resources to law enforcement (i.e., expenditures, number of officers), arguably because blacks represent a perceived threat to order, and to perceived white interests, in such places (Jacobs 1979; Jackson 1989). Similarly, arrest rates are higher in cities with larger black populations and lower levels of racial residential segregation, independent of the city's crime rate (Liska, Chamlin, and Reed 1985). High numbers of blacks coupled with low segregation, it is argued, present "threats" to the dominant group, which increases pressure on the police to intensify crime control. A smaller black population or greater residential segregation helps to insulate whites from black crime. In addition to greater police resources and higher arrest rates, police killings of civilians also appear to support the power-threat thesis. Such killings increase as the proportion of minority residents in a city increases, which may reflect perceived threats both to whites and to police officers themselves (Liska and Yu 1992; Jacobs and O'Brien 1998).

The power-threat formulation directs attention away from individuals' attributes and behavior and highlights the ways in which group interests structure both police practices as well as citizen perceptions of the criminal justice system. In other words, policing is not simply a response to individuals or to isolated crimes (the instrumentalist version of conflict theory) but is also responsive in a more subtle and diffuse way to a city's racial order and the interests of dominant groups (the structuralist version of conflict theory). The latter is closely related to the broader structuralist analysis of the state, whose institutions are theorized as "relatively autonomous" of particular elites or elite factions and instead organized to defend the common, shared interests of dominant classes and racial groups (Poulantzas 1973).

Minority-group threat and the interests of racial groups help explain
both the actual practices of criminal justice institutions and, we argue,
group perceptions of those institutions. With regard to dominant
groups, our perspective helps to clarify why their support for the police
is typically so strong. There is abundant evidence that dominant racial
groups see the police as allies in the fight against crime. This is especially apparent in deeply divided societies, such as Northern Ireland
and South Africa, where the police are or were actively and consciously
involved in defending a sectarian sociopolitical system and where the
dominant racial or ethnic group traditionally views the police as an
instrument for suppressing subordinate groups (Enloe 1980; Weitzer
1985, 1990, 1995). This mutual affinity between the police and dominant groups is less pronounced in more democratic and less polar-
ized multiracial societies; yet, we argue that even in these societies,
the general group-position dynamic is important in structuring group
relations with the police.

In the United States, white support for the police has traditionally
been strong and widespread. At the same time, whites tend to associate minority groups with crime and violence (Swigert and Farrell
1976; Hurwitz and Peffley 1997). In the 2000 General Social Survey,
for instance, nearly half of whites expressed the view that blacks
are "violence-prone." Regarding crime, a national poll reported that
blacks were viewed as "more likely to commit crimes" than others in
American society by 37 percent of both whites and blacks, whereas
whites were seen as more likely to commit crimes by only 5 percent of
whites and 12 percent of blacks (Gallup 1993).

It is true that African Americans are disproportionately involved
in violent crime, according to both victimization surveys (where victims identify the offender's race) and self-report surveys (which ask
respondents about their own involvement in crime) (Sampson and
Lauritsen 1997). This does not mean that blacks are "crime-prone,"
but it does mean that they are overrepresented as violent offenders
and that their neighborhoods experience more serious crime than
other neighborhoods (Liska and Bellair 1995; Logan and Stults 1999).
At the same time, many citizens exaggerate the extent of blacks'
involvement in crime. The resulting "racial typification of crime" is
a generalization that colors popular thinking and discourse and leads

people, particularly whites, to overstate the amount of crime among blacks.

Racial typification is documented in some recent studies. Surveys of residents of Baltimore, Chicago, and Seattle reveal that the higher the percentage of young black men in a neighborhood, the greater the perceived severity of neighborhood crime problems, and this relationship held even after controlling for the neighborhood crime rate (Quillian and Pager 2001). In other words, even where crime is not a serious problem, it is *seen* as more serious in neighborhoods with a larger number of blacks, and this perception is strongest among whites. We also know that whites' fear of crime is greater in areas with higher percentages of minorities in the population (Chiricos, Hogan, and Gertz 1997) and that people who associate blacks with crime are inclined to support harsh punishment of offenders (Chiricos, Welch, and Gertz 2004). The latter finding indicates that "social threat may be activated not only by the residential proximity of racial minorities, but by the conflation of race and crime that exists in the minds of many, regardless of where they live" (Chiricos, Welch, and Gertz 2004:380).

For those engaged in the racial typification of crime and who subscribe to the notion of "black criminality," there is a tendency to justify police suspicion, surveillance, and street interrogations of blacks. Disparate treatment is viewed not as invidious but instead as justifiable, rational discrimination. The view of one middle-class white man illustrates this point: "Given who commits most of the crimes, I think it's a legitimate position to take. Police have more fear in dealing with black potential criminals, black citizens, as opposed to whites" (quoted in Weitzer 2000a). Notice how casually this man equates blacks and criminals. And another study found that while whites disliked racial profiling by the police, they generally understood it as "a byproduct of neutral crime fighting activities" (Tyler and Wakslak 2004:275). One white respondent in our 2002 national survey, also a state police officer, offers this view as an article of faith:

> You should try being a cop for a week or two. See how you like being cursed at, spit on, punched, and kicked. Cops are human also, and sometimes they are rude. The streets in some places are similar to a war [zone], and the public has the police fighting this war with Queensbury rules. In reference to racial profiling, it's not

their [police officers'] fault that most crimes are committed by young, black males who live in the inner city. . . . I'm speaking from experience. I've been a state trooper for 15 years.

According to the group-position thesis, these views should be fairly common throughout the white population but also more strongly held by some whites than by others. Indeed, "those in the dominant group who are more oriented toward conflict – for example, those who are more prejudiced against subordinate groups – [are] more likely to want to see the legal system used to control these groups" (Cohn and Barkan 2004:37). The most racially prejudiced whites are more inclined, for instance, to support police use of excessive force against citizens (Barkan and Cohn 1998). The larger point is that, for many whites, controlling crime is roughly equivalent to intensifying law enforcement against minority individuals or in minority neighborhoods.

If whites tend to align themselves with the police and view them as defending a sense of relative group privilege, it follows that, when the police are criticized, whites may perceive their group interests as indirectly threatened (Bayley and Mendelsohn 1969:200–204). Accordingly, our extension of the group-position thesis predicts that whites will tend to be dubious or dismissive of allegations of police misconduct. To accept that minorities are mistreated would lend credence to reforms intended to curb police abuse – reforms that might also dilute crime control or reduce white privilege, thereby threatening whites.

Blacks and Hispanics, by contrast, should be more inclined to view the police as contributing to their subordination, through the use of both legal and improper methods; to believe that misconduct is a serious problem; and to believe that their group interests will be advanced by greater controls on police. This does not mean that blacks and Hispanics will be uniformly critical of or hostile toward the police, but it does increase the chances that they will see the police as a "visible sign of majority domination" (Bayley and Mendelsohn 1969:195) and view police practices as both a serious problem and one that acutely afflicts members of minority groups. Perceptions of unjust treatment by the authorities are thus important indicators of group conflict.

One implication of the group-position thesis is that race and ethnicity play a major role not only in coloring individuals' overall opinions of the police but also their interpretation of specific events, including their own contacts with officers and what they see in the media. In other words, according to the group-position thesis, racial group membership may create expectations that strongly affect citizens' constructions of police actions. Unlike whites, who tend to give police the benefit of the doubt, minority groups may be predisposed to *racialize* policing.[3] For those who enter into encounters expecting negative treatment, an authoritarian or brusque demeanor on the part of officers – a normal part of their occupational persona – can easily be construed as a form of racial bias. That police and civilians enter into encounters with unequal status is another aspect of this racial prism. As Sykes and Clark (1975:590) state, "The asymmetrical status norm, operative in most police-citizen encounters, is difficult [for citizens] to distinguish from the special asymmetrical status norm operative when ethnic subordinates interact with superordinates." A vicious circle can result, where a citizen's stereotypes of officers and expectations of unjust treatment engender a belligerent demeanor or aggressive behavior, which in turn can provoke a harsh police response: "In anticipation of harsh treatment, blacks often behave disrespectfully toward the police, thereby setting in motion a pattern that confirms their expectations" (Black 1971:1109). And the way one interprets an encounter with the police may be influenced by what is seen and heard in the mass media, representations that are often interpreted differently by different groups. Media coverage of disturbing police actions, for instance, resonates more dramatically for blacks and Hispanics than for whites (Tuch and Weitzer 1997; Weitzer 2002).

The group-position thesis stresses perceived (not necessarily real) threats to dominant group interests (Bobo and Hutchings 1996; Kinder and Sanders 1996). In fact, there are issues on which most whites and minorities agree. The desire for greater police crime-control efforts is a case in point. Historically, many blacks complained

[3] Bayley and Mendelsohn make a similar but broader argument that police serve as a lightning rod for discontent with larger societal arrangements, not just race relations. As the most visible and accessible agents of state power, the police may be the most available target of people frustrated with social and political institutions. "Upon [the police] is vented the accumulated frustrations of lifetimes of inequality and subservience," wrote Bayley and Mendelsohn (1969:141). "Minority people project upon them their emotional reactions to deprivation at the hands of the majority."

about inadequate law enforcement in their communities and called for *increased* crime control. As the Kerner Commission (1968:307) concluded four decades ago, "The strength of ghetto feelings about hostile police conduct may even be exceeded by the conviction that ghetto neighborhoods are not given adequate police protection."

This point is no less true today: Polls show that minorities tend to feel that their neighborhoods do not receive sufficient attention from the police. For instance, 74 percent of blacks and 60 percent of Hispanics in Los Angeles, and 55 percent of blacks and 40 percent of Hispanics in Washington, DC, felt that there were not enough police officers on the streets in their neighborhood (*Los Angeles Times* 1988; Police Foundation 2004). Only 1 percent of both groups in Los Angeles and 3 percent in Washington thought that there were "too many" police in their neighborhoods. Nationwide, three-quarters of blacks feel that police protection in black neighborhoods is worse than in white neighborhoods (Gallup 1993), and 46 percent of blacks say they are dissatisfied with police protection in their own neighborhood (*New York Times* 1991). And a recent poll of New Yorkers found considerable support among Hispanics and blacks for the planned installation of 400 surveillance cameras for use in crime fighting: 72 percent of the city's Hispanics, 66 percent of blacks, and 58 percent of whites felt that such cameras are a good idea (Quinnipiac 2005).

In our own national survey, African Americans and Hispanics overwhelmingly supported an increase, in their city, in the number of officers patrolling city streets in police cars (80 percent of both groups) and on foot patrol (80 and 69 percent, respectively) as well as more police surveillance of high-crime areas (88 and 85 percent, respectively).[4] And another study found that blacks' views depend on the issue: They are less likely than whites to endorse police use of force against suspects and harsh sentences for criminals (arguably because they see racial bias in these spheres) but more likely than whites to support greater spending on crime control (Wilson and Dunham 2001).

In other words, there are at least some policing issues on which minority and white interests converge (more crime control, safe

---

[4] White support for these practices was similarly high: 74 percent, 63 percent, and 82 percent, respectively.

neighborhoods), but what is crucial is whether their interests are *perceived* as conflicting. Perceptions are partly a result of claims and counterclaims made about the police in the public arena (Blumer 1958). When leaders within the minority community vociferously criticize the police, which occurs periodically,[5] this may reinforce whites' impressions that minorities are antipolice or intent on hamstringing the police, thus interfering with the pursuit of law and order.

We use the group-position thesis to help account for both white and minority attitudes toward the police and their evaluation of reforms in policing. Although we lack direct measures of group interests and threats, our data do allow us to test key group-position predictions – specifically, that whites will be most reluctant and blacks and Hispanics will be much more inclined to believe that the police often engage in various types of misconduct, routinely discriminate against minorities, and that a whole host of institutional reforms are justified. If whites are skeptical of charges of police misconduct and doubt the need for reforms, this may be partly rooted in their attachment to the law-and-order status quo; blacks' and Hispanics' beliefs about policing and the need for reform, by contrast, may be partly a function of their desire to gain improvements in their treatment by the police.

None of this is to suggest that whites, blacks, and Hispanics live in completely separate perceptual worlds. There may be substantial group differences on *most policing issues* – as predicted by the group-position thesis – but there also may be *some issues* on which the groups converge. We would expect, for instance, greater consensus on general principles (such as fairness, respectful treatment, minimum force, etc.) than on specific problems and remedies, as has been documented in surveys on other kinds of racial issues and policies (Sigelman and Welch 1991; Schuman et al. 1997). In addition to documenting racial

---

5 A recent example is the controversy surrounding the deaths in 2004 of two black men in police custody in Jacksonville, Florida. More than 200 people participated in a rally against police brutality outside the police department, and black leaders denounced the police both in Jacksonville and throughout Florida. Rep. Corrine Brown, the local member of Congress, said, "We have no confidence in the police department or the policies regulating law enforcement in this town," and Florida's NAACP president stated, "The degree to which police brutality occurs in Florida is the worst I've seen in 50 years" (quoted in Black [2005]).

differences, this book also explores issues that register a great deal of consensus between whites, blacks, and Hispanics.

As discussed earlier, it is unclear from previous studies whether Hispanics' relations with the police are more consistent with a minority-group or racial-hierarchy pattern. The conventional wisdom is that Hispanics share with African Americans a roughly similar orientation, simply because they are both subordinate minority groups, and they are often lumped together in both popular discourse and in academic studies. The racial-hierarchy perspective challenges this monolithic picture and points to important differences in the historical and contemporary experiences of each group:

> Among racial minority groups, the level of alienation [from major social institutions] would vary based on differences in the persistence, pervasiveness across domains of life, and extremity of inequality of life chances. This argument implies that members of more recent and voluntarily incorporated minority groups will feel less alienation than members of long-term and involuntarily incorporated minority groups. (Bobo 1999:461)

This proposition can be applied to group relations with the criminal justice system. Just as African Americans have a deeper and more crystallized sense of relative group position vis-à-vis whites than is true for Hispanics, they also have a longer and more fractious history with the police in America. This is one key reason why blacks' opinions of the police might be more negative than Hispanics'. By contrast, in cities where the Hispanic population has grown rapidly in recent years, it is possible that the police (and white population) perceive this group as a growing threat. One study suggested this Hispanic-threat explanation for the association between incidents of police misconduct and neighborhoods with increasing Hispanic population (Kane 2002). Again, we lack a critical mass of studies on black-Hispanic patterns in attitudes and experiences, which is one of the major questions examined in this book.

Factors Shaping Police-Citizen Relations

Most of the research on police relations with citizens is not only atheoretical, as noted earlier, but is also deficient in identifying the specific factors that are most salient in structuring attitudes toward the police. As one recent literature review concluded, "there is no consensus as to which combinations of variables explain the greatest variance in attitudes toward the police" (Brown and Benedict 2002:564). Studies typically link citizens' attitudes toward police to individual-level demographic characteristics, such as age, class, and race (Flanagan and Vaughn 1996). This literature has helped to identify individual-level predictors (e.g., young people are typically more critical than older people), but much less research has focused on nondemographic factors, either at the micro or macro level. For instance, we know little about the role played by "the public's personal experiences with the police, what they learn second-hand from friends and acquaintances, and what they learn from the media" (Gallagher et al. 2001:v). A few studies, discussed below, suggest that citizens' personal interactions with police officers (micro level) may be an important determinant of attitudes. Even less attention has been devoted to macro-level variables such as mass media reporting on the police, neighborhood conditions, or city-level characteristics. This book examines both micro- and macro-level factors in addition to standard demographic factors. We investigate whether and how citizens' perceptions of the police are affected by their personal and vicarious experiences with officers, exposure to media reporting on police abuses, and selected neighborhood conditions.

Personal Experiences with Police Officers. It is reasonable to expect that a citizen's experiences with police officers will have at least some influence on general satisfaction with the police. Unpleasant contacts tend to have a stronger effect than positive contacts. The former lowers opinions of the police, while the latter may, but does not necessarily, engender favorable views (Walker et al. 1972; Smith and Hawkins 1973; Scaglion and Condon 1980; Leiber et al. 1998; Skogan 2005). Moreover, it appears that police treatment of citizens during an encounter (especially whether the person experiences "procedural justice") has a larger effect on views of the police than the positive or negative outcome of the encounter (e.g., problem resolution, a citation, an arrest) (Tyler 1990; Tyler and Huo 2002). In other words, the *process* trumps the outcome. When police treat citizens in a discourteous, brusque, or unfair manner, this experience colors not only their assessments of the immediate encounter but also their overall opinions of the police (Wortley, Hagan, and Macmillan 1997; Reisig and Chandek 2001). When officers treat citizens courteously and fairly, and when they explain to them their rights and the reasons for police actions, citizens are more likely to be satisfied (Wiley and Hudik, 1974; Skogan and Hartnett, 1997:217; Stone and Pettigrew, 2000; Tyler and Huo, 2002). There also appears to be variation by race. Although both whites and blacks are attuned to how they are treated by authority figures, African Americans are more likely than whites to report negative experiences with the police and to feel that they have not received fair or respectful treatment from officers (Bordua and Tifft 1971; Walker et al. 1972; Dean 1980; Tyler and Huo 2002; Davis 2004).

Personal experience is not a necessary condition for evaluating the police, however. Most Americans seldom interact with police officers (Bureau of Justice Statistics 2001, 2005) and some have never had a contact with an officer; yet, this does not prevent them from forming opinions of the police. For example, more people believe that police verbally or physically abuse citizens than the number who have personally experienced these actions. Even for those who have had contacts with officers, such contacts do not necessarily influence their overall attitudes toward the police (Brandl et al. 1994). Some people who have had a positive interaction with an officer still view the police negatively (Jacob 1971), and some who have had a negative encounter continue to express general satisfaction with the police (Frank, Smith, and Novak 2005). The former may dismiss the positive encounter as exceptional, whereas the latter's trust in the police may be so strong that it overshadows specific experiences. For citizens who fall into these categories, views of the police seem to come from sources other than personal contacts (Smith 1991). Although personal experience influences at least some types of attitudes for those who have had contact with police, perceptions are also shaped by other factors. Such factors include a nation's history of police relations with a particular racial group (which may remain firmly rooted in the group's collective memory), a single controversial incident that attracts a great deal of media coverage, and other factors that transcend one's direct experiences.

Vicarious Experiences with Police Officers. One such factor is an individual's knowledge of other persons' experiences. Hearing about another person's experience with an officer, especially when that person is a friend or relative of the listener, can be internalized as a "vicarious experience." And what is learned may then be communicated to yet other friends, family members, acquaintances, and neighbors – amplifying the effect of the initial experience and perhaps influencing beliefs about the police within a whole network of people, including one's neighborhood. Researchers have rarely explored the frequency of such vicarious experience, or its "multiplier effects" within social networks (which are, admittedly, difficult to measure), but there is some evidence that blacks are more likely than whites to know someone who has had a bad interaction with the police (Gallup 1991). A study of Cincinnati found that 66 percent of blacks, compared to only 13 percent of whites, said that they knew someone personally who had been "stopped or watched closely by a police officer, even when they had done nothing wrong" (Browning et al. 1994).

It also appears that some African Americans take pains to instruct their children in proper etiquette when dealing with the police, such as keeping their hands in plain view, avoiding sudden movements, and remaining courteous and respectful toward officers (Kennedy 1997; Harris 2002). As one middle-class African American man stated, "I tell young people, or people I know, 'whenever the police stop you, put your hands up high so they can see them'... because you don't want them to think that you are reaching for something" (quoted in Weitzer 1999:833). Such instructions on proper impression management may help to prevent altercations, but they also "cannot help but pass the attitudes, resentments, and injuries created by profiling on to the next generation" (Harris 2002:113) – a good example of how vicarious experiences may have far-reaching ramifications.

Whites, by contrast, benefit from a *racial halo effect* when they are observed by police officers, a dynamic whereby being a white American, in and of itself, reduces the odds of being viewed with suspicion or being questioned by an officer (Weitzer 1999). Consequently, whites have less need to instruct each other on proper etiquette when dealing with the police. Indeed, whites in America generally do not feel the need to discuss the police with others, unless they have had a bad experience that they wish to share. Policing, for the most part, is simply not on the radar screens of most whites, in stark contrast to how minorities perceive, experience, and talk with one another about the police (Bayley and Mendelsohn 1969). In a sense, we are describing rather different, race-specific subcultural understandings of the police in America, meanings that are reproduced in people's social networks and also influenced by the mass media.

Mass Media Reporting on the Police. It is axiomatic that the media affect public perceptions of social problems, although some people are more receptive than others to media messages (Gerbner et al. 1980; Dahlgren 1988; Weitzer and Kubrin 2004). It is therefore reasonable to expect public opinion of the police to be shaped by media reports on police actions, though this has rarely been studied. Indeed, it is surprising that researchers have given so little attention to how the media affect such perceptions, in light of the abundant research documenting media influences on citizens' views of crime and fear of crime (Surette 1998). Research indicates that watching police "reality" shows, such as *COPS*, increases white viewers' satisfaction with the police, though this is not true for blacks (Eschholz et al. 2002). Such shows typically present the police in a sympathetic light; when officers employ verbal or physical aggression against citizens, it usually is portrayed as justified (Oliver 1996). A few other studies have found that media coverage of incidents of police misconduct lowers public confidence in the police. As discussed earlier, these studies document an increase in negative views of the police during or immediately after news coverage of major brutality incidents or corruption scandals (Lasley 1994; Sigelman et al. 1997; Tuch and Weitzer 1997; Kaminski and Jefferis 1998; Weitzer 2002).

If exposure to media reports on a single incident of police abuse influences public opinion, frequent exposure to media coverage of separate instances of police misconduct (e.g., brutality, racial profiling, corruption) should have a particularly strong impact on citizens' views of the police, as well as on support for reforms in policing. Although most media reporting is episodic and fails to address either the prevalence of or patterns in police misconduct (Lawrence 2000:43–46), it is possible that frequent exposure has a cumulative effect, contributing to a belief that police abuse is rampant. Some support for this prediction can be found in the public's response to unfolding scandals that attract extensive news coverage. A case in point is the Mollen Commission's investigation of police corruption in New York City. A series of commission hearings in 1993 and 1994, covered by the media, aired allegations of serious abuses in certain precincts, including police brutality, drug selling, stealing money and drugs from suspects, and other crimes. At the height of the scandal, a June 1994 *New York Times* poll of New Yorkers reported that 58 percent of blacks and 32 percent of whites thought corruption was "widespread" in the NYPD.

Neighborhood Context. Relations between police and citizens may be shaped by neighborhood conditions. We know that police practices are geographically patterned, varying from one place to another in greater or lesser degree. In other words, police treatment of citizens is attuned not only to citizen characteristics (e.g., demeanor, appearance, age, race) but also to characteristics of the areas in which citizens are encountered. A report by the National Research Council concludes that, although neighborhood effects on policing have not been fully studied and appear to be complex, "disadvantaged and higher crime neighborhoods are more likely to receive punitive or enforcement-oriented policing" (National Research Council 2004:192, 189). For instance, one study, based on systematic observations of a large number of police-citizen contacts in three cities, concluded that "offenders encountered in lower-status neighborhoods have a higher categorical risk of being arrested independent of factors such as type of crime, race of offender, offender demeanor, and victim preferences for arrest" (Smith 1986:338). If police practices vary across different types of neighborhoods, it is reasonable to expect residents' attitudes toward the police to reflect this.

One variable that seems important is a neighborhood's socioeconomic status. Inner-city neighborhoods are often the sites of multiple, compound problems – including high rates of poverty, unemployment, single-parent households, physical dilapidation, transience – and the concentration of such conditions in particular areas causes severe community disorganization (Wilson 1987). A few studies have suggested that this "concentrated disadvantage" may also contribute to strained police-community relations (Smith, Visher, and Davidson 1984; Sampson and Bartusch 1998; Velez 2001; Terrill and Reisig 2003). The largest study in this genre, of 343 neighborhoods in Chicago, found that neighborhood socioeconomic disadvantage was an especially robust predictor (Sampson and Bartusch 1998). Indeed, it was a neighborhood's class status, not an individual's class or race, that most strongly shaped attitudes toward the police. Similarly, a study of Washington, DC, found that relations with the police were positive in two middle-class neighborhoods (one white, one black), whereas a disadvantaged black neighborhood had decidedly worse relations with the police (Weitzer 1999, 2000a). Some other studies also find that once neighborhood context is factored into the equation, the effects of the individual-level, demographic factors are either reduced or eliminated (Smith et al. 1991; Cao, Frank, and Cullen 1996; Reisig and Parks 2000; Schafer, Huebner, and Bynum 2003).

The magnitude of socioeconomic disadvantage in a locale may influence not only citizens' views of the police but also police behavior itself. A recent study of New York City, based on police department records of officers who were fired or resigned for misconduct, found that neighborhoods marked by concentrated disadvantage had higher rates of police abuse (Kane 2002). An observational study of police-citizen interactions found that police were more likely to be disrespectful (e.g., cursing, using slurs, belittling, name-calling) toward residents of neighborhoods with high levels of concentrated disadvantage (Mastrofski, Reisig, and McCluskey 2002). Other studies similarly find police misconduct to be more prevalent in disadvantaged minority communities (Smith 1986; Mollen Commission 1994; Fagan and Davies 2000).

There are two reasons for this. First, police behavior can be linked to the *opportunity structure* of a community: Opportunities for misconduct are simply greater in disadvantaged communities than elsewhere. Because of street crime and disorder, the sheer number of officers patrolling these neighborhoods is typically greater, increasing the number of police-citizen contacts and the potential for obtrusive or disputatious contacts. Routine police work in these areas thus inevitably amplifies friction between officers and residents.

Moreover, these communities offer greater opportunities for officers to engage in corrupt activities, such as robbing drug dealers or planting evidence on suspects.

Second, such neighborhoods *lack constraints* on police misconduct. According to both conflict theory and social disorganization theory, socioeconomic conditions are important determinants of citizens' social capital and access to elites. Residents of poor neighborhoods are typically powerless in the face of abusive police practices (Weitzer 2000a; Kane 2002; Kubrin and Weitzer 2003), whereas residents of more affluent communities have greater resources and connections to elites, which can be mobilized to hold police accountable. Residents of two affluent neighborhoods in Washington, DC, for instance, stated that if police mistreated people in the neighborhood, the "well off and powerful" residents "would be up in arms" complaining at the local police station and that the officers "wouldn't get away with it," whereas in a poor black neighborhood, "We don't have that power. They know who they can push around and who they can't" (quoted in Weitzer 1999:841–842). In a nutshell, police misconduct is higher in disadvantaged neighborhoods because of a combination of greater opportunities and fewer constraints than in middle-class and affluent neighborhoods.

The preceding paragraphs hinted at the importance of neighborhood crime. Crime is the second neighborhood condition that appears to shape police-community relations. Neighborhood crime rates strongly correlate with disadvantage and disorganization. Poor neighborhoods (of any race) typically have more crime than middle-class neighborhoods (Krivo and Peterson 1996), thus generating more frequent police-citizen encounters and increasing the chances that the encounter will go awry and result in conflict – which is likely to have a cumulative, adverse effect on residents' opinions of the police. High levels of neighborhood crime might be expected to affect views of the police in another way as well: The police may be blamed for failing to prevent crime, for inadequate responsiveness to citizen calls, or for solving too few of the crimes that have occurred.

The amount of crime in a neighborhood is difficult to measure precisely, but it can be gauged with the help of several proxies: crime as perceived by residents, officially recorded crime rates, personal

victimization, and residents' fear of crime. Some research has found
that residents' assessments of crime influence their views of the police
(Murty, Roebuck, and Smith 1990; Reisig and Parks 2000; Brown and
Benedict 2002). For instance, people who believe that their neighborhood is afflicted by drug dealing and gangs are more likely than
residents of other areas to be critical of the police (Jesilow, Meyer,
and Namazzi 1995), and the same is true for people who believe that
crime is a serious problem in their neighborhood (see Chapter 2) and
who report that their neighborhood was the site of a violent crime
in the past year (Weitzer and Tuch 2002). Officially recorded crime
shows the same pattern as perceived crime: High violent crime rates
lower residents' approval of the police (Murty, Roebuck, and Smith
1990; Sampson and Bartusch 1998; Reisig and Parks 2000; Schafer,
Huebner, and Bynum 2003). Regarding fear of crime (a rough proxy
for local crime), a 12-city study found that fear of neighborhood crime
increased residents' dissatisfaction with the police (Bureau of Justice
Statistics 1999:26), but overall, studies report mixed results on the association between fear of crime and opinions of the police (Brown and
Benedict 2002). The same is true for personal victimization: Some
studies find that being a crime victim affects one's attitudes toward
the police, whereas others find no effect (Brown and Benedict 2002).
Although the literature is inconclusive regarding the impact of certain
neighborhood crime conditions or proxies for crime, there appears
to be a slight preponderance of evidence that such conditions have
some influence on attitudes toward the police.

We want to know whether neighborhood crime levels influence
(1) overall satisfaction with one's local police department, (2) opinions of police performance in fighting crime, and (3) beliefs about
police misconduct. Of these three, the association between neighborhood crime and perceived police misconduct may seem the least
obvious. Our reasoning in predicting such a relationship is grounded
in social disorganization theory: The same conditions that foster
crime in a neighborhood may also increase the chances for police
deviance. Neighborhood disorganization is associated both with residents' inability to organize against crime and disorder and their inability to resist abusive police practices (Weitzer 1999; Kane 2002; Kubrin
and Weitzer 2003). In addition to the lack of neighborhood constraints
on misconduct, there are also greater incentives in these communities

for the police to mistreat people. In their efforts to fight crime in these communities, police tend to typify residents as troublemakers (Smith 1986) and act indiscriminately and aggressively toward them. The result is that verbal and physical abuse, unjustified stops of people on the street, and corrupt activities are much more likely to occur in high-crime than in low-crime areas (Smith 1986; Mollen Commission 1994; Fagan and Davies 2000; Mastrofski, Reisig, and McCluskey 2002).[6]

Based on the literature reviewed here, we expect that citizen attitudes toward and assessments of the police will be affected by a combination of factors: citizens' race and ethnicity, their personal and vicarious experiences with police officers, media reports on police misconduct, and selected neighborhood conditions.

KEY POLICING ISSUES

Police Misconduct

Police misconduct is a serious problem in America, although it is impossible to know its precise magnitude. The hidden nature of much police work means that a great deal of misconduct is never observed or reported. What comes to light may be just the tip of the iceberg.

Every measure of the incidence of police misconduct is fraught with problems. One such measure is the number of formal complaints made by citizens – complaints filed with a police department or with a civilian complaint board. Complaints of this nature consistently underreport misconduct: They are but a fraction of the events that could justifiably result in a formal complaint. Many people are unaware of the procedures for filing a complaint, and others decline to do so because they see it as a waste of time or fear retribution from the accused officer. Overreporting is yet another problem, with some unknown number of people making false complaints out of malice or in the

---

[6] It is possible that even larger-scale macro-level variables shape police-citizen relations, including region of the country and urban versus suburban residence. Although region does not seem to be a strong predictor (Weitzer and Tuch 2002), there is some evidence that urban residence makes a difference. Hagan and Albonetti (1982), for instance, found that people living in central cities were more likely than others to believe that the police and the courts treated the poor and minorities in an unjust manner. Region and urban-suburban residence are treated as control variables in our analyses.

hope of receiving financial compensation. In short, the number of formal complaints made in any jurisdisction tells us fairly little about the amount or distribution of police misconduct (Goldsmith and Lewis 2000).

Another way of studying police misconduct is observational. Researchers accompany officers on their routine patrols and take detailed fieldnotes on their observations of police interactions with civilians. The advantage of this method is that it allows researchers to observe officer behavior directly in the context of citizen behavior and other situational factors. Observers use standard criteria to determine whether an officer acted improperly. Again, this is far from a perfect measure of police behavior, because at least some of the latter may be influenced by the very presence of observers. In other words, some officers may alter their behavior simply because it is being observed and recorded. When recording takes the form of videotaping, such as on the show *COPS*, there is a strong incentive for officers to be on their best behavior.

This book occasionally draws on studies that use formal complaints and systematic observations as sources of information on misconduct, but most of the book uses data from public opinion surveys, including our own national survey.

Police misconduct takes many forms, and in this book we examine four major types: unwarranted stops, verbal abuse, excessive force, and corruption.

Unwarranted Street Stops. Police stops of citizens have long been controversial, especially in minority communities. The traditional legal standard for lawful stops was whether an officer had "probable cause" to believe that a person had committed or was about to commit a crime. In a 1968 Supreme Court case, *Terry v. Ohio*, the lower threshold of "reasonable suspicion" became the norm. Stops are unlawful when there is no indication of illegal conduct or when based solely on an officer's vague suspicion regarding a citizen; police must be able to articulate specific reasons for stopping and questioning a person. However, evidence of even a minor offense, such as a traffic violation, may be used as a pretext for a stop whose real motive is to discover evidence of a crime unrelated to the minor offense. Stopping a car with a defective tail light when the officer is really looking for drugs is one example. In its controversial 1996 decision, *Whren v. United States*, the Supreme Court declared that such pretextual stops were not unconstitutional. The decision is widely regarded as undermining, at least to some extent, the previous standards of probable cause and reasonable suspicion (Harris 1997).

It is unknown what proportion of stops are legitimate and what proportion are unlawful or otherwise unwarranted. We do know that a significant number of people are stopped every year. A huge survey of 76,910 Americans in 2002, for example, found that 9 percent of drivers reported that they had been stopped by police in the past year (Bureau of Justice Statistics 2005). Although there was no difference in the rates of white, black, and Hispanic drivers stopped (9 percent of each group), blacks and Hispanics were more likely than whites to report that they had been ticketed, handcuffed, arrested, or searched and that excessive force had been used against them. Among those stopped, twice as many blacks (27 percent) as whites (14 percent) felt that the stop was not justified, a view held by 18 percent of Hispanics. In general, however, little is known about how about how citizens perceive police stops.

Verbal Abuse. Use of foul or offensive language is discouraged by most police departments. Nevertheless, derogatory language is part of police officers' everyday discourse and serves various functions – such as getting citizens' attention, keeping them at bay, and extracting compliance with officer commands – even if it sometimes backfires and causes serious altercations (White, Cox, and Basehart 1991). Verbal abuse by officers comprises a substantial proportion of citizen complaints against the police. A significant number of Americans (about one-quarter) claim to have personally experienced verbal mistreatment by the police (*New York Times* 1991; CBS 1995), and it appears that minorities experience this more often than whites. Of course, verbal abuse can go both ways. Observational studies have found that blacks are more likely than whites to show unilateral disrespect toward police officers or to engage in mutual insults with officers (Black and Reiss 1967; Sykes and Clark 1975). But officers also appear more likely to engage in unilateral verbal abuse of minority individuals.

Excessive Force. Excessive force refers to more force than is necessary, under the circumstances, to accomplish a lawful objective. What is excessive in one situation may not be excessive in another; it depends on the particular circumstances of an encounter. The Supreme Court has ruled that the use of force must be "objectively reasonable" taking into account the "facts and circumstances of each particular case, including the severity of the crime at issue, whether the suspect poses an immediate threat to the safety of the officers or others, and whether he is actively resisting arrest" (*Graham v. Connor*, 1989). At the same time, the Court recognized that "reasonableness" should take into account the fact that officers often make split-second judgments, in tense and fractious situations, about the amount of force to use. Police departments have helped to clarify matters by training officers in the use-of-force continuum, which stipulates the amount of force that can be used in situations of varying seriousness. However, this continuum is not necessarily followed in practice, especially in split-second decisions by officers, and on the ground there is sometimes a gray area between reasonable and excessive force (Alpert and Smith 1994). Nevertheless, the prevailing legal standard is that of situationally appropriate force.

How often do police use excessive force against citizens? It is estimated that only 1 percent of all encounters (about 500,000 per year) involve any use of force (Bureau of Justice Statistics 2001) and one-third of those involve excessive force, according to two observational studies (Friedrich 1980; Worden 1996). Using these figures, Walker (1999) estimates 456 incidents of excessive force occur each day somewhere in the country. Assuming that most of these incidents occur in cities, he concludes that "the result is a large number of annual incidents in every city" and more than 166,000 per year nationwide (Walker 1999:225). If this is true, then police use of excessive force does not appear to be a rare occurrence.

However often it occurs, excessive force is certainly *perceived* as a serious and widespread problem by many Americans, and a sizeable number of people report that they or someone they know has *experienced* it at some time in their lives. In 1991, 26 percent of blacks and 10 percent of whites said they or someone they knew had been "roughed up unnecessarily" by cops in their neighborhood (*New York Times* 1991). In another poll, 18 percent of blacks and 7 percent of whites reported that someone in their household had been physically mistreated by police at some time in their lives (Gallup 1991:79). A larger number of people believe that excessive force is a problem where they live. Asked in 2002 how often "police brutality against blacks and Hispanics in your community happens," 32 percent of blacks, 24 percent of Hispanics, and 6 percent of whites thought it occurred frequently (Harris 2002).

Corruption. Corruption involves profiting from the abuse of power – that is, accepting or demanding money or goods for doing something improper or for doing something that the official is obligated to do anyway (Punch 1985). Insofar as corruption involves "mutual gain" for both officers and citizens, the citizens involved are unlikely to report it to the authorities – making this type of misconduct particularly difficult to measure (Ivkovic 2003). Examples of corruption include bribery (accepting money in return for not making an arrest); extortion (e.g., demanding sex from a motorist or payment from a merchant); stealing money, drugs, or other items from suspects ("shakedowns"); and resale of seized items (e.g., paying informants with illegally obtained money or drugs).

Police corruption was rampant in nineteenth-century America, when police demanded payoffs for their services and for not enforcing laws against vice. Reforms in the twentieth century greatly reduced corruption, although it remains a serious problem today. Most of what we know about corruption comes from commissions of inquiry formed in the wake of major scandals. In 1931, the Wickersham Commission concluded that corruption was so rampant in Chicago's police department that eliminating it would require replacing all serving officers. Four decades later, the Knapp Commission in New York City found that corruption was "extensive" throughout the police department, engaged in by a "substantial majority" of officers (Knapp Commission 1973:61), and two decades later the Mollen Commission (1994) found that although corruption was less widespread throughout the NYPD, it was rife in high-crime precincts, especially where drug crimes were common. Corruption in New York also had taken more serious forms in the period between the Knapp and Mollen commission reports, with officers increasingly involved not just in taking payoffs but in actively promoting and planning drug-related crimes in partnerships with street criminals (Mollen Commission 1994:15–18). Criminals "paid cops to work hand-in-hand with them to actively facilitate their criminal activities. And many cops went so far to assist criminals that they used their police powers to become criminals themselves" (Mollen Commission 1994:17). In both time periods – the 1970s and 1990s – corruption was not confined to a few "rotten apples" but was much more pervasive, at least in certain precincts in New York. Corruption scandals have recently tainted police departments in some other cities, one of which engulfed the entire Rampart Division in Los Angeles in 1999–2000. We do not know how pervasive corruption is in other cities, because it is fairly hidden from public view.

Almost no polls have included questions on police corruption, so we do not know whether people perceive it as an aberration or as widespread. Gallup periodically asks people to rate the "honesty and ethical standards" of officers, but this general integrity question does not measure corruption per se. Police typically receive fairly high ratings on honesty/ethical standards, although blacks are more likely than whites to rate them low (Tuch and Weitzer 1997). One survey asked about crimes committed by officers, which may overlap with corruption. Fully one-quarter of blacks and one-tenth of whites thought that police were more likely to commit crimes than other groups in American society (Gallup 1993). Some polls are taken during an ongoing corruption scandal. In the midst of such a scandal in New York City in 1994, a majority of blacks and a third of whites thought corruption was "widespread" in the NYPD (*New York Times* poll, June 1994), but these numbers were likely influenced by extensive media coverage of the scandal.

All four types of police misconduct are examined in Chapter 2.

Racialized Policing
In addition to the types of police misconduct described above, another enduring problem in American policing has been racial bias and discrimination. The book investigates several aspects of racial bias, or what we call *racialized policing*: (1) disparities in treatment of

individuals of different races, (2) unequal treatment of neighborhoods populated by different racial groups, (3) officers' racial prejudice, (4) racial profiling in the context of stops of citizens, and (5) behavioral differences between officers of different racial backgrounds.

Americans are overwhelmingly opposed *in principle* to racially biased law enforcement. When asked in one poll whether it is the responsibility of the federal government to ensure that minorities and whites receive equal treatment from the police and the courts, large majorities (74–89 percent) of whites, blacks, Hispanics, and Asians answered affirmatively (Kaiser 1995). But support for the principle of equal justice does not necessarily mean that a person believes the system is unjust. Some people are convinced that police treat all citizens impartially, and the group-position thesis would predict that this is especially true for whites. Many whites are skeptical of the existence of racial discrimination in American society generally – whether in housing, employment, education, or other arenas (Hochschild 1995; Schuman et al. 1997). In one poll, for instance, only one-sixth of whites – compared to nearly half of blacks – thought that blacks are discriminated against "a lot" in America (*Washington Post* 1997).[7] The same skepticism exists regarding racially biased policing, with most whites believing that this, like other forms of racial discrimination, is a thing of the past. A 1977 poll reported that 7 out of 10 blacks felt that police "discriminate against blacks," whereas only 28 percent of whites agreed (Harris 1977). Have views changed in the past three decades? Our research examines current perceptions.

Police may discriminate not only against individuals but also against neighborhoods. As mentioned earlier, officers draw distinctions between communities in terms of their crime problems and their racial and class makeup, and such typifications influence, at least to some degree, how police treat residents in different locales (Smith, Visher, and Davidson 1984). Living in a high-crime, disadvantaged neighborhood is a liability for those residents who are law-abiding, insofar as police officers see the entire neighborhood as troublesome

---

7 Whites are more likely to believe in reverse discrimination: Three-fourths of white respondents in the 2002 General Social Survey thought that it is very or somewhat likely that whites "won't get a job or promotion while an equally or less qualified black person gets one instead."

or crime-prone and thus treat all residents indiscriminately; this is known as "ecological contamination" (Werthman and Piliavin 1967). Over time, officers tend to lose sight of the fact that a segment of the neighborhood is positively disposed toward the police. Cops tend to be both less responsive to the needs of residents of poor and high-crime communities (Klinger 1997) and harsher in their treatment of people in such areas (Smith 1986; National Research Council 2004:189) – a combination of underpolicing and aggressive policing. If police practices differ across neighborhoods, we should expect parallel differences in residents' views of the police.

To what extent are American police officers prejudiced toward minority racial and ethnic groups? The existence of police prejudice has been documented in studies going back several decades (Skolnick 1966; Bayley and Mendelsohn 1969; Westley 1970). A classic observational study of three cities found that four-fifths of white officers and about a third of black officers working in black neighborhoods expressed racial prejudice in the company of researchers (Black and Reiss 1967). A subsequent analysis of these data found that the most prejudiced officers were more likely than nonprejudiced officers to arrest black suspects, even after controlling for other factors (Friedrich 1979). More recently, the Christopher Commission (1991) discovered transcripts of police communications with dispatchers that contained a great deal of racist discourse about minority citizens. Some officers referred to minorities as "natives," "rabbits," and "monkeys." A survey of 650 LAPD officers found that one-quarter of them agreed that "racial bias on the part of officers toward minority citizens currently exists and contributes to a negative interaction between police and the community" (Christopher Commission 1991). Summarizing the research literature, Jefferson (1988:522) concludes that, "All the major British and North American studies, from the early post-war period on, agree that negative, stereotypical, prejudiced, and hostile attitudes to blacks are rife amongst police officers." Even if this indictment is somewhat exaggerated, the existence of police prejudice is undeniably real.

That police prejudice toward minorities exists in America should not be surprising. Police live in a society with a long history of racism, and they frequently come into contact with minority citizens. Whether they act on their prejudice, or whether prejudiced officers treat minorities worse than nonprejudiced officers, is a question that has rarely been investigated, with the exception of Friedrich's (1979) finding that prejudice does affect officer behavior. Our study was not designed to answer this question – which would require careful comparisons of officer words and deeds – but we do examine popular perceptions of police prejudice. How widespread is officer prejudice thought to be in the nation and in one's own city and neighborhood? This question is examined in Chapter 3.

Also addressed in Chapter 3 is the issue of racial profiling. Police have been accused of profiling and stopping African American drivers – known colloquially as "driving while black." It is commonly believed that blacks are more likely than whites to be stopped by the police, and the data available on such stops corroborate this disparity. A study of Cincinnati residents found that five times as many blacks as whites (47 vs. 10 percent) said that they had been "stopped or watched closely by a police officer, even when you had done nothing wrong" (Browning et al. 1994). In a 1999 nationwide poll, 40 percent of blacks (and 5 percent of whites) said that they had been stopped "just because of their race" (Weitzer and Tuch 2002). Moreover, many blacks have been stopped *repeatedly* (Bureau of Justice Statistics 2001). These sour experiences accumulate over one's lifetime. In other words, there is an important, although often overlooked, *cumulative* dimension to the minority experience of police practices.

Survey findings are bolstered by evidence from studies based either on systematic observations or on video or written records of stops. A few studies have found no significant difference in police stops of whites and blacks but also that, once stopped, blacks are more likely to be searched than whites. Most profiling research, however, finds significant or huge disparities in both the stop rates and search rates for whites, blacks, and Hispanics. A major investigation of 175,000 street stops in New York City (based on forms completed by officers during each stop) found that blacks and Hispanics were more likely to be stopped by police, even after controlling for the racial composition and crime rate of the area in which the stop occurred (Fagan and Davies 2000). In eight of the city's precincts, about 4 in 10 stops failed to satisfy the legal requirement of reasonable suspicion.

It appears that minorities are especially susceptible to being treated with suspicion when they are observed outside minority neighborhoods – that is, when they are deemed to be "out of place." Studies have found that, for blacks, the likelihood of being stopped increases outside their neighborhoods (Smith 1986; Weitzer 1999; Fagan and Davies 2000). African Americans are also more likely to be deemed suspicious when they are observed driving in predominantly white areas. Meehan and Ponder (2002) found that police conducted computer checks on black motorists at a higher rate as the distance from predominantly African American sections of town increased. Both race and place matter.

Other studies focus on the practices of the state police on highways outside cities. Recent studies show that blacks are stopped out of all proportion to their numbers as motorists on the nation's highways (Harris 2002). A particularly disquieting pattern was documented in Volusia County, Florida, in 1992, in an analysis of 148 hours of police car videotape by the *Orlando Sentinel*. Blacks and Hispanics comprised only 5 percent of the drivers on the county's stretch of I-95, but they accounted for a stunning 70 percent of all drivers stopped by state police (Harris 1997). Blacks and Hispanics were also detained longer than whites (an average of 12 and 5 minutes, respectively), and 80 percent of all searches were of cars driven by blacks and Hispanics. Although police claimed they had stopped the cars for traffic violations, only 9 of the drivers received traffic tickets and only 31 drug arrests were made – out of a total of 1,100 stops!

The reported racial disparities in traffic stops are sometimes so large as to constitute prima facie evidence of racial bias, suggesting that police use race as a proxy for criminal propensity (Kennedy 1997). This is only underscored when we take into account the success rates of these stops, that is, whether they result in the discovery of contraband (drugs, guns, stolen items, an open container of alcohol) or other evidence of crime. Several studies have found that the "hit rates" for Hispanics and African Americans who have been stopped by police is either similar to or lower than for whites. In Maryland, although many more blacks were searched than whites, the hit rates for drugs were similar for the two groups (Harris 1999). The North Carolina Highway Patrol found contraband on whites 33 percent of the time and on blacks 26 percent of the time; New Jersey state troopers found evidence of crime 25 percent of the time for whites, 13 percent of the time for blacks, and 5 percent of the time for Hispanics (Harris 2002:80–81). In San Diego, Hispanics stopped by the police in 2001 were much more likely than whites to have their persons or vehicles searched (50 percent vs. 29 percent), yet the contraband hit rates for Hispanics were much lower than for whites (5 percent vs. 12 percent) (Cordner, Williams, and Velasco 2002). The findings from these studies are consistent with self-reports from a national survey of citizens who had been stopped by police, which found that searches of whites yielded the highest hit rates. Criminal evidence was found on the person or in the car of 15 percent of whites, compared to only 3 percent of blacks (Bureau of Justice Statistics 2005:14). Apparently, if police want to increase their hit rates, they should stop more white motorists!

Further evidence of racial profiling comes from a unique study of 158 off-duty black police officers in Milwaukee. Police officers arguably have the best grasp of whether a stop is justified and should be less likely than citizens to construe a stop as racially motivated when it is not. In the Milwaukee study, 7 out of 10 black officers stated that, in their professional opinion, they had been stopped "as a result of racial profiling."[8] When they were stopped, most identified themselves as police officers, which had a dramatic effect: "At this point, in many of the encounters . . . the police officer initiating the contact quickly backed off and released the respondent . . . [and] quickly left the scene" (Barlow and Barlow 2002:350). Such swift disengagement suggests that the officer lacked grounds for the stop and was concerned that the incident would be reported to superior officers.

The final racial dimension of policing concerns the race of police officers. Little is known about whether the race of individual officers affects citizen attitudes toward the police. Traditionally, the racial complexion of police departments mattered greatly to African Americans, and the presence of white police in black neighborhoods was a major source of friction (Myrdal 1944). Since the 1960s, a body of literature has singled out racial differences between police and

---

[8] Respondents who described themselves as dark-skinned were more likely to be stopped than those who described themselves as light-skinned.

minorities as a key source of tensions (Levy 1968; Fogelson 1968; Sherman 1983; Cashmore and McLaughlin 1991). Police have been portrayed as agents of the local white power structure acting as an "occupation force" in black neighborhoods, oppressing and routinely mistreating residents. Both the 1967 President's Commission on Law Enforcement and the 1968 Kerner Commission on Civil Disorders advocated greater recruitment of black officers in order to defuse tensions with residents, foster more impartial law enforcement, and bolster the image of the police in minority communities. The importance of police racial diversification is now an article of faith in official circles, both in America and in some other nations. Diversification is expected to result in improvements in police treatment of minorities and in building minority trust in a police department. The U.S. Department of Justice (2001) holds that, "A diverse law enforcement agency can better develop relationships with the community it serves, promote trust in the fairness of law enforcement, and facilitate effective policing by encouraging citizen support and cooperation. Law enforcement agencies should seek to hire a diverse workforce." While there has been progress over the past two decades, most police departments remain unrepresentative of their city's minority populations.

Do citizens care about the race of officers working in their community, as the conventional wisdom holds and, if so, why? Do they believe black, white, and Hispanic officers behave differently while on the job? Does an officer's race make a difference in popular perceptions of individual officers and police departments? Do citizens view officers primarily in racial terms, or are they seen first and foremost as police officers, with their race secondary or irrelevant? Answers to these questions have obvious policy implications. If citizens believe that officers of different races behave differently toward citizens, or if citizens prefer to interact with officers of the same race as themselves, this information may be valuable to those who make hiring and deployment decisions – and has the potential to increase trust and confidence in the police more broadly.

Much more remains to be known about citizens' views of officers of different races. Some single-city studies have examined citizens' perceptions of officers of different races (Dresner et al. 1981; Weitzer

2000b), but nationally representative studies are lacking. We investigate this issue using our national sample of respondents.

Reforms

History teaches us to be skeptical of the potential for progressive reform of police practices and the police institution itself. Even after major scandals and investigations by blue-ribbon commissions, it is rare that a police department undergoes major, lasting reform. Radical overhaul of an entire police force has been attempted in societies where the police were a central pillar of state repression – for example, Haiti, South Africa, Northern Ireland, several Eastern European nations – and some American police departments have undergone significant changes, either as a result of a scandal or under the leadership of an enlightened chief of police (Sherman 1978; Skolnick and Fyfe 1993; Goldsmith 2005; Weitzer 2005).

We might expect to find broad support in the United States for principles of good policing (e.g., use of minimum force, impartial law enforcement, accountability) because it is easy to endorse police integrity and professionalism in the abstract. But how are these ideals to be institutionalized, and how are departures from them to be remedied? Surprisingly little is known about the level of popular support for specific kinds of reform. The public may be enthusiastic about some types of reforms, lukewarm on others, and opposed to still others; the latter – opposition – may be based on a belief that the change would interfere with police work or is politically motivated.

There are several reasons why it is important to study citizens' preferences regarding police reform. First, their preferences may be useful in informing public policy. Where popular support for a specific change is widespread, this may highlight a problem in need of fixing. If implemented, reforms may help to improve police practices, including how officers treat citizens. Second, certain kinds of reforms may have a significant impact on public trust in the police. Regardless of whether a change (e.g., hiring more minority officers) alters police practices on the ground, it may be symbolically important to citizens and thus contribute to the legitimacy of the police. Third, reforms that directly affect police-citizen encounters (e.g., explaining the reason for a stop, increasing sensitivity to minority citizens, reducing verbal abuse) may increase citizens' willingness to cooperate with the police. Research indicates that when officers communicate well and treat citizens with respect, citizens respond in kind and are more willing to comply with the officers (Wiley and Hudik 1974; Skogan and Hartnett 1997; Stone and Pettigrew 2000).

In this book, we examine public support for several kinds of reform and the key determinants of citizens' preferences for each. Included here are changes that would increase the sensitivity of the police to the public and reduce officer abuses, on the one hand, and changes that would serve to expand police powers or bolster their crime-control efforts, on the other:

- racial diversification of police departments,
- procedural justice in police-citizen encounters,
- mechanisms of accountability,
- community policing, and
- intensification or expansion of police crime-control activities.

Popular support for specific reforms, and the factors that shape this support, are issues that have been ignored in previous studies. We address each of these dimensions in Chapter 4.

OVERVIEW OF THE BOOK

Much of the book is based on the authors' nationally representative survey of Americans. The Appendix describes our data collection and sampling procedures and provides full details on our measures and data analysis techniques. Chapter 2 examines two issues: the public's overall satisfaction with their local police and the issue of police misconduct. Following chapters focus on racially biased policing (Chapter 3) and reform and related policy issues (Chapter 4). The Conclusion (Chapter 5) summarizes key findings and discusses their implications.

CHAPTER TWO

Police Misconduct

Before turning to the issue of police misconduct, it will be helpful to first profile Americans' *overall satisfaction* with the police who serve their cities and neighborhoods. It is important to document such general opinions because they are indicators of the level of popular trust in and legitimacy of the police as well as the amount of basic confidence citizens have in their local police department. It also provides a baseline for our examination of more specific attitudes later in this and following chapters.

OVERALL SATISFACTION WITH THE POLICE

Opinion polls and our own survey show that the vast majority of Americans rate the police favorably in general terms. Most Americans say that they "trust," have "confidence" in, and "approve" of the police. However, the factors that shape such overall satisfaction are not fully understood. To what degree and in what ways is satisfaction influenced by race and ethnicity, by the conditions in one's neighborhood, by personal encounters with police officers, by people's general beliefs about police misconduct, or by media reporting on the police? As noted in Chapter 1, consensus is lacking on the impact of these factors on citizens' perceptions of the police; instead, the research literature contains a hodgepodge of diverse findings (Brown and Benedict 2002). Nor have previous studies examined all of these factors simultaneously, as we do here. In addition to standard demographics, we include the following independent variables in our analysis of overall satisfaction with the police.[1]

Neighborhood crime and socioeconomic status: Crime is indicated by respondents' feelings of personal safety as well as their assessments of the extent of crime in their neighborhoods. Using 2000 Census tract data, the socioeconomic status of the respondent's neighborhood is examined to determine if people who live in highly disadvantaged neighborhoods express less satisfaction with the police than those living in other types of communities. In Chapter 1 we noted that there is some reason to expect that a neighborhood's socioeconomic status will have at least some effect on residents' relations with the police, although the studies in this genre are few in number.

Police effectiveness at crime control: Because citizens regard crime control as the principal function of the police, we examine police performance in fighting crime as a possible predictor of overall satisfaction. If a city's police department is viewed as doing a poor job of dealing with crime, this assessment may erode basic trust and confidence in the department, and vice versa for those who believe the police are doing a good job at crime control.

Police misconduct: Do people who believe that police misconduct (corruption, verbal and physical abuse, unwarranted street stops) is widespread in their city express less overall satisfaction with police? It seems reasonable to expect that misconduct would indeed lower approval ratings, but this may not be true for all racial groups.

Citizen experiences with officers: Contacts with police officers might have at least some influence on larger evaluations of the police, as explained in Chapter 1. We expect that bad experiences, either personal or vicarious, will decrease overall satisfaction with the police.

Community policing: In theory, community policing brings residents and officers together to identify problems and devise solutions to crime, a "partnership" that should also improve overall police-community relations. Whether residents of such neighborhoods really have a better relationship with the police than in areas where

---

[1]   Throughout the book, we provide question wording for our dependent variables in the text; unless otherwise noted, question wording for all other variables are provided in the Appendix.

TABLE 2.1. *Satisfaction with local police*

	Satisfaction with the police department in respondents' city[a]			Satisfaction with the police officers who serve respondents' neighborhood[b]		
	Whites	Blacks	Hispanics	Whites	Blacks	Hispanics
Very satisfied	46%	22%	36%	48%	26%	36%
Somewhat satisfied	40	51	44	39	51	43
Somewhat dissatisfied	11	19	13	9	15	13
Very dissatisfied	3	8	7	4	8	8
N (unweighted)	615	561	605	613	556	598

[a] chi-square = 69.16, $p < .001$
[b] chi-square = 55.32, $p < .001$

traditional policing (reacting to incidents after the fact) predominates is a question that only a few studies examine, with mixed results. We examine whether community policing makes a difference in overall satisfaction with the police.

Media reporting: It is reasonable to expect that news media reports on police actions influence citizen's generic perceptions of the police, for the reasons sketched in Chapter 1. Cumulative exposure to media coverage of separate instances of police misconduct might well dampen public confidence in the police. We examine this proposition.

Overall satisfaction was measured by two items: (1) "In general, how satisfied or dissatisfied are you with the police department in your city?" (2) "In general, how satisfied or dissatisfied are you with the police officers who serve your neighborhood?" Respondents were asked whether they were very satisfied, somewhat satisfied, somewhat dissatisfied, or very dissatisfied (high scores indicate more satisfaction).

What Shapes Overall Satisfaction?
Our research shows that satisfaction with the police varies by race (see Table 2.1). Nearly half of whites are "very satisfied" with the police in their cities, compared to just 22 percent of blacks and 36 percent of Hispanics. Twice as many blacks as whites (27 vs. 14 percent) are dissatisfied with their city's police department, and dissatisfied Hispanics rank midway (20 percent) between the other groups.

A similar pattern exists when the context is the respondent's neighborhood. Nearly half of whites express the highest level of satisfaction with the police who serve their neighborhoods, but only about a quarter of blacks, and slightly more than a third of Hispanics, are very satisfied. At the other end of the continuum, over one-fifth of blacks and Hispanics, but only 13 percent of whites, are somewhat or very dissatisfied with officers working in their community.

Do these racial differences persist after taking account of other variables? What factors, if any, besides race shape satisfaction? And – of primary concern to us – do the ingredients resulting in satisfaction differ for whites, blacks, and Hispanics? By presenting regression models both for the total sample and for each racial group separately, Table 2.2 allows us to answer each of these questions.[2]

In each chapter in the book, we begin our multivariate analysis by examining a baseline model for the total sample that contains race as the only explanatory factor. Next, we compare this baseline model to a comprehensive model that includes all of our explanatory factors (the coefficients for which are displayed in the total sample columns in the regression tables) in order to gauge whether race differences persist after incorporating other variables. Finally, we examine the comprehensive model separately for each racial group; we refer to these as "race-specific" models. Because our ultimate purpose is to examine how race impacts views of policing, we focus the bulk of our discussion on the race-specific models.

To streamline our presentation, the coefficients from the baseline race-only model are not shown in Table 2.2 (nor in the regression tables in subsequent chapters), but we discuss them in the text. In the baseline model in Table 2.2, both blacks and Hispanics were significantly less satisfied than whites with the police, and Hispanics were significantly more satisfied than blacks. These results tell a story that is consistent with the findings in Table 2.1 as well as with other studies: At the most general level, blacks and Hispanics are significantly more dissatisfied with the police than are whites.

---

[2] In the multivariate analysis, we combined responses to the two satisfaction items and then standardized them to form a single, overall satisfaction index. The alpha reliability coefficient for the index is .92, indicating a high level of consistency.

TABLE 2.2. *Satisfaction with police*

	Total sample		Whites		Blacks		Hispanics	
	b	beta	b	beta	b	beta	b	beta
Black	-.054	-.018	—	—	—	—	—	—
	(.057)		—		—		—	
Hispanic	.015	.005	—	—	—	—	—	—
	(.049)		—		—		—	
Neighborhood crime	.077**	.058	.075	.053	-.072	-.061	.029	.025
	(.026)		(.045)		(.044)		(.042)	
Safety (day)	.124***	.071	.186*	.088	-.046	-.031	.026	.020
	(.039)		(.075)		(.065)		(.059)	
Safety (night)	.064*	.049	-.011	-.007	.246***	.204	.070	.065
	(.030)		(.053)		(.053)		(.050)	
Concentrated disadvantage	.010	.010	-.023	-.023	.006	.006	.092**	.092
	(.021)		(.031)		(.033)		(.035)	
Perceived misconduct	-.186***	-.186	-.164***	-.164	-.084*	-.084	-.225***	-.225
	(.023)		(.036)		(.038)		(.039)	
Personal experience with misconduct (1 = yes)	-.066	-.029	-.163*	-.067	-.096	-.048	.057	.028
	(.044)		(.079)		(.072)		(.072)	
Vicarious experience with misconduct (1 = yes)	-.155***	-.064	-.187*	-.069	-.173*	-.084	-.092	-.044
	(.043)		(.079)		(.069)		(.073)	
Police effectiveness	.567***	.567	.580***	.580	.518***	.518	.595***	.595
	(.019)		(.032)		(.038)		(.039)	
Community policing (1 = yes)	.183***	.091	.206***	.102	.162*	.080	.109	.054
	(.035)		(.059)		(.067)		(.064)	
Media exposure	-.005	-.004	-.003	-.002	-.109**	-.089	.037	.029
	(.024)		(.042)		(.040)		(.039)	
N of cases (unweighted)	1,468		539		427		502	
Constant	-1.030		-.952		-.342		-.763	
R² (adjusted)	.593		.578		.627		.622	

Note: Standard errors in parentheses; estimates are net of controls for education, household income, gender, age, city size, city-suburban residence, and region; * $p < .05$; ** $p < .01$; *** $p < .001$.

What happens to these racial differences when the other variables are introduced? If the differences between whites, blacks, and Hispanics in the baseline model are reduced or disappear when other factors are taken into account, we conclude that these factors "mediate" the impact of race on satisfaction – that is to say, the race differences in the baseline model can be attributed, in whole or in part, to differences between the groups on these additional factors. The total sample columns in Table 2.2 show that race is no longer significant once these additional variables are taken account of. Specifically, among all respondents, satisfaction is higher among those who feel safe in their neighborhoods, who credit the police with being effective in fighting crime, and whose areas receive community policing; those who live in low-crime neigborhoods, who believe that police misconduct is common in their locale, or have had vicarious experience with police misconduct are less satisfied. No significant differences were found between the different Hispanic nationality groups: People of Mexican, Puerto Rican, Cuban, and other Hispanic ancestry do not differ in their level of general satisfaction with the police.

As mentioned, we are primarily interested in whether the nonracial factors operate for whites, blacks, and Hispanics alike. In other words, do the variables shape satisfaction uniformly across the racial groups?[3] The remaining columns in Table 2.2 show the following:

- Whites, blacks, and Hispanics alike who believe that police misconduct occurs frequently in their city or neighborhood are more likely to be dissatisfied with their local police.

---

[3] In statistical parlance, this is the question of whether race interacts with any of the other independent variables in the model as it impacts the dependent variable. If no such interactions exist, the effect of each regressor is uniform across racial groups and the coefficient for the combined sample adequately describes its effect. In all models examined in this book, we fit interaction terms between race and every other predictor, and in each case at least some of these interactions were statistically significant – an indication that the predictors did not always affect whites, blacks, and Hispanics uniformly. Rather than reporting results from models with so many interaction terms, however, we opted for the statistically equivalent and more streamlined procedure of reporting regression coefficients separately for each racial group. Because we are primarily interested in whether coefficients are significant or not in each group – not whether they differ significantly from each other – we do not perform tests of significance on the differences in slopes.

- The view that local police are effective in controlling crime increases confidence in the police among all groups.
- At the neighborhood level, personal safety has some influence on white and black residents' approval of the police: Feeling safe during the day increases satisfaction for whites and feeling safe at night does so for blacks. Concentrated disadvantage unexpectedly increases overall satisfaction among Hispanics but has no effect among whites or blacks.
- Citizen contacts with police officers have some effect. Personal experience with some kind of police misconduct lowers satisfaction among whites and vicarious experience decreases it among whites and blacks.
- Whites and blacks who believe that community policing is practiced in their neighborhoods are more likely to express favorable opinions of the police. It seems logical that positive police practices, such as community policing, would bolster overall satisfaction, whereas negative practices, such as our four types of misconduct, would lower approval of the police – and this is precisely what the findings show.
- Exposure to incidents of police misconduct via the media decreases satisfaction among those African Americans who report frequently hearing or reading accounts of police misbehavior. The fact that many of the incidents reported in the media involve black recipients of abuse undoubtedly helps to explain this finding (Lawrence 2000).

Overall, more of the explanatory factors shape general satisfaction with police for whites and blacks than for Hispanics, despite roughly equivalent R^2 coefficients. For Hispanics, perceived misconduct and effective crime fighting tell most of the story, whereas for whites and blacks concerns about neighborhood safety, their experience with police misconduct, community policing in their neighborhood, and/or media exposure are also implicated. We turn now to the issue of police misconduct.

POLICE MISCONDUCT

Police misconduct can greatly affect public opinion of the police as well as citizens' willingness to contact and cooperate with officers. When it attracts media coverage, an incident of misconduct can severely

damage the reputation of a police department, but even when not
widely publicized, it may significantly sour opinions of the police if people learn about it from others in the community. Separate abuses that
occur in a neighborhood may have a cumulative effect on residents'
trust in the police, over time becoming ingrained in the neighborhood
culture.

Some amount of misconduct is inevitable in any organization, but
it is more prevalent in police departments than in most other organizations by virtue of the demands placed on officers and the kinds of
contacts officers routinely have with citizens. Police officers frequently
encounter aggressive, belligerent, and angry citizens (offenders, victims, bystanders), and the very mission of the police, as forces of order
and social control, necessarily generates at least some friction with a
segment of the populace:

> Police often identify themselves as a moral force, protecting inno-
> cent and productive members of the public against those who would
> brutalize and victimize ordinary decent citizens. . . . Oddly enough, it
> may be precisely this sense of mission, this sense of being a "thin blue
> line" pitted against forces of anarchy and disorder, against an unruly
> and dangerous underclass, that can account for the most shocking
> abuses of police power. (Skolnick and Fyfe 1993:92, 93)

The amount of police misconduct that occurs in any jurisdiction is
unknown. What comes to light may be only the tip of the iceberg. A
leading criminologist concluded that, every year, "a substantial minority of all police officers violate the criminal law, a majority misbehave
toward citizens in an encounter, and most engage in serious violations of the rules and regulations of the department" (Reiss 1971:169).
Although this assessment does not tell us how frequently abuse happens, it does suggest that it is not limited to a handful of "rotten apples,"
as police chiefs typically claim.

We also know that police misconduct varies over time and place.
Much more serious and widespread in the past, abuses have declined
considerably in recent decades (Skolnick and Fyfe 1993; Johnson
2003). The unchecked power of officers that was the norm many
decades ago (Wickersham Commission 1931) has been curbed as
policing has become more professional and more accountable. Not

only have police practices changed over time, but they also vary from place to place. Some cities are known for having high rates of officer misconduct, whereas others have much better records. The rate of corruption, for instance, varies from one jurisdiction to another, which depends in part on how diligent superior officers are in combating it (Sherman 1978). And cities that have instituted strict guidelines on the circumstances in which officers can fire their guns have seen a significant drop in the number of police shootings of civilians (Blumberg 1989).

One source of information on police misconduct comes from citizen complaints filed with a police department or with a civilian review board. Most civilian review boards issue annual reports on the number of complaints filed, investigated, and substantiated. In Washington, DC, for instance, between 2001 and 2003, 276 complaints of excessive force, 499 complaints of offensive language, and 370 complaints of harassment were filed with the Office of Citizen Complaint Review, according to the agency's website. A study of 731 police departments in the United States found that blacks were overrepresented among complainants, accounting for twice as many complaints as their proportion in the population in the cities studied (Pate and Fridell 1993). Whites, by contrast, were less likely to file a complaint, relative to their proportion in the population. Although these racial differences are significant and suggestive of larger patterns, official complaints are not reliable indicators of differential group experiences of misconduct. Moreover, as indicated in Chapter 1, formal complaints are bedeviled by the twin problems of gross underreporting and misreporting by citizens, seriously undermining their utility as measures of misconduct.

An alternative method is a survey of a representative sample of the population. The remainder of this chapter draws on our survey questions on perceptions, observations, and personal experiences with several types of misconduct. Four issues are addressed: (1) the perceived magnitude of misconduct, (2) patterns of personal and vicarious experiences of abuse, (3) the factors that influence public perceptions, and (4) what police misconduct means to people. The group-position thesis would predict, and some previous research has found, clear racial differences on this aspect of policing. Thus, we expected that, compared to whites, blacks and Hispanics in our study would report much more personal experience with police mistreatment and also would be inclined to believe that it is a serious and widespread problem.

Misconduct takes many forms. Some are largely the concern of the police department (e.g., absenteeism, sleeping on duty, not coming to the aid of a fellow officer, etc.). Others directly or indirectly affect citizens, which is our interest. Four types of wrongdoing are examined: unwarranted street stops, verbal abuse, excessive force, and corruption.

Unwarranted stops are those lacking any indication of illegal conduct or those based solely on an officer's vague intuition or hunch regarding a citizen. We know that police stop a significant number of people every year. In 2002, 9 percent of Americans reported that they had been stopped in the previous year (Bureau of Justice Statistics 2005). But there is no way of knowing what proportion of stops are proper and what proportion unlawful or otherwise unjustified, because, as noted in Chapter 1, so many stops occur without being documented by patrol officers or monitored by police departments. Policing is "low visibility" work, largely hidden from most citizens and other officers.

Research indicates that citizens hold varying definitions of whether a stop is justified, both in the abstract and regarding their own experiences (Weitzer 1999). For example, in one study, a young black man reported that he was "harassed" by an officer who followed his car for two miles and then stopped him. When asked to justify the stop, the officer replied, "You look suspicious. You were making too many turns." The citizen was incensed that "too many turns" could be seen as suspicious (see Weitzer 1999:833). Yet, from the officer's perspective, the driver's behavior may have suggested that he was casing the neighborhood or otherwise engaged in some deviant pursuit. Although citizens vary in their evaluations of whether or not a stop is justified, and while their views may be out of sync with officers' decisions to make a stop, what matters for our analysis in this chapter is the citizens' point of view. We are interested in whether citizens believe they have been stopped without due cause, whether these perceptions vary by racial group, and whether those who have had such experiences are inclined to believe that police misconduct is a widespread problem.

Most police departments prohibit officer use of offensive speech toward citizens; yet, insulting language occurs nonetheless (White, Cox, and Basehart 1991). Harsh language may help an officer gain control over an unruly citizen, keep bystanders at bay, or may be entirely gratuitous and counterproductive. It appears that verbal abuse is not a rare or isolated event. As a former police chief in Washington, DC, stated, "We're hearing from citizens that a lot of officers are disrespectful, verbally abusive, [or] insensitive to folk of different cultures" (quoted in Harriston 1993). Our research allows us to document how frequently verbal abuse occurs according to citizens' self-reports, and whether any particular racial group is especially vulnerable to this kind of treatment.

As discussed in Chapter 1, excessive force is defined as more force than is necessary, under the circumstances, to accomplish a lawful objective. What is excessive, therefore, depends on the specific circumstances of an encounter (*Graham v. Connor*, 1989). Studies cited in Chapter 1 indicate that, when officers use force, it is excessive about one-third of the time. Using this figure, it is estimated that about 450 incidents of excessive force occur each day somewhere in the country, totaling more than 166,000 annually nationwide (Walker 1999:225).

Whether this is frequent or not is a judgment call, but these figures do provide a backdrop to our investigation of how citizens perceive its frequency and how many believe that excessive force has been used against them. Although some individuals are prone to define any use of force as excessive, others are more generous toward officers even when they are the recipients of force. A case in point is the following account of a middle-aged black man:

> He grabbed me, threw me up on the car, and put the cuffs on real tight. . . . When I look back on it, it wasn't no more [force] than what I brought on myself by running my mouth. If I had shut up, I'd have come out better. (quoted in Weitzer 1999:838)

The final type of misconduct covered in the chapter is corruption. Corruption involves the abuse of power for personal profit, which includes accepting something of value in return for improper behavior (Punch 1985). Examples are bribery, extortion, stealing from suspects, resale of seized items, and so forth. Surprisingly, almost no polls have asked about police corruption, so we do not know whether Americans perceive it as serious or widespread in their city or nationwide. Realizing that most citizens have no direct knowledge of police corruption (National Research Council 2004:269), we nevertheless wanted to find out whether people consider it widespread and whether they have ever observed an instance of it.

PERCEPTIONS AND EXPERIENCES OF MISCONDUCT

How do whites, blacks, and Hispanics compare in their beliefs about police misconduct? Respondents were asked how often they thought police officers stop people on the street without good reason, verbally or physically abuse people, and engage in corruption.[4]

Figure 2.1 displays evaluations of these behaviors. Group differences stand out: Blacks are the most likely to believe that each type of misconduct occurs frequently in their city, whites are the least likely, and Hispanics fall between the two groups. More than half of blacks (54 percent) and more than a third of Hispanics (38 percent), but only 16 percent of whites, believe that cops stop people on their city's streets without good reason very or fairly often. Similar racial disparities are found for verbal and physical abuse: Officers in the respondent's city frequently use insulting language according to over a third of blacks and a fifth of Hispanics (but fewer than 1 in 10 whites), and excessive force according to 48 percent of blacks, 29 percent of Hispanics, and 13 percent of whites. The figures are lower when the context is the respondent's neighborhood (not shown in a graph), but racial differences are no less evident: Unwarranted stops occur frequently in the neighborhood in the view of 36 percent of blacks and 27 percent of

---

4 Questions were worded as follows: (1) "How often do you think police officers stop people on the streets of [your neighborhood/your city] without good reason?" (2) "How often do you think police officers, when talking to people in [your neighborhood/your city] use insulting language against them?" (3) "When police officers use force against people, how often do you think they use excessive force (in other words, more force than is necessary under the circumstances) against people in [your neighborhood/your city]?" (Response options for these three questions are: never, on occasion, fairly often, or very often.) (4) "How common do you think corruption (such as taking bribes, involvement in the drug trade) is in your city's police department − not at all common, not very common, fairly common, or very common?"

Figure 2.1. Police misconduct in city

Percent

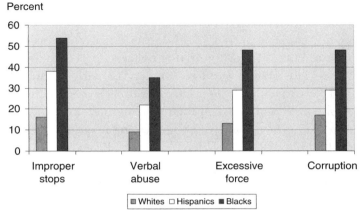

| | Whites | Hispanics | Blacks |

Note: Percentages of respondents who believe that each practice happens very often or fairly often in their city.

Hispanics, and neighborhood cops often use excessive force according to nearly a third of blacks and a quarter of Hispanics.[5] This compares to only 7 percent of whites on both questions. The fourth item in Figure 2.1 is that of corruption in one's local police department. Again, the racial gap is substantial. Only a sixth of whites think corruption is common, compared to 48 percent of blacks and 29 percent of Hispanics. This is consistent with some other evidence on the distribution of police corruption, such as the Mollen Commission's (1994) finding that corruption was most common in New York's high-crime, minority neighborhoods. There is also a sense that more accountability is needed, as one of our respondents stated: "Corruption has to be addressed. Police are benefiting from crack-dealing. But the 'brotherhood' is strong and so is temptation. There ought to be some incentive for officers to report corruption without being labeled snitches" (MC black female, 31).[6]

---

[5] An earlier poll reported that 43 percent of blacks and 14 percent of whites had very little or no confidence in the police in their community with respect to "not using excessive force on suspects" (NBC 1995).

[6] In the interview statements quoted in this and subsequent chapters, we use the following abbreviations to refer to respondents' social class position: LC = lower class, LMC = lower middle class, MC = middle class, UMC = upper middle class. See the Appendix for a discussion of the measurement details.

Turning to the Hispanic nationality groups, Puerto Ricans perceive significantly higher levels of misconduct on all four items than people whose ancestry is Mexican, Cuban, other Caribbean, Central American, or South American (results not shown in a figure). A majority (58 percent) of Puerto Ricans think that police stop people on the streets of their city without good reason very or fairly often, and 38 percent believe that such stops occur often in their neighborhood. Similarly, 4 in 10 say that police in their city often use insulting language; more than 3 in 10 believe the same thing about the officers in their neighborhood. Roughly half of our Puerto Rican interviewees believe that police use excessive force often in their city (54 percent) and neighborhood (49 percent) and think that corruption among their city police is common (54 percent). When asked in another national poll whether they had a favorable or unfavorable opinion of the police in their community, Puerto Ricans were again more dissatisfied than other Hispanic groups, with one-third expressing a negative view (Kaiser 2000).[7]

Census data indicate that Puerto Ricans have lower incomes and a higher incidence of poverty than any other Hispanic group besides Dominicans. This level of disadvantage likely contributes to their more negative assessments of the scope of police misconduct. It would be premature, however, to conclude that Puerto Ricans are uniformly more critical of all aspects of policing. Our study did not find this to be the case with regard to overall satisfaction, views of racially biased policing, or support for various reforms in policing (discussed later in this book), but more research is clearly needed for a comprehensive understanding of Puerto Rican and other Hispanic groups' relations with the police.

The number of blacks who say that police misconduct occurs *very often* is noteworthy. Depending on the question, three to five times more blacks than whites believe that misconduct occurs very often in their city or neighborhood. The Hispanic-white gap is also wide. One way of interpreting these results is in terms of the "rotten apple" versus "rotten barrel" concepts in the scholarly literature. People who

---

[7] This compares to 13 percent of Cubans, 18 percent of Mexicans, and 20 percent of Central/South Americans (Kaiser 2000).

Figure 2.2. Personal experience in city

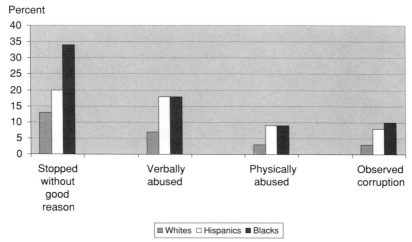

Note: Percentage of respondents saying that they have personally experienced an unjustified stop, insulting language, or excessive force, or have seen an officer engage in a corrupt act in their city.

believe that misconduct is a rare event may feel that it is limited to a few "rotten apples" in the police department, whereas people who see misconduct as widespread may view it as an institutionalized, "rotten barrel" phenomenon. Police chiefs typically take the rotten apple approach when confronted with allegations of misconduct, whereas African Americans and Hispanics are more likely to believe that the barrel is rotten.

One reason why sizeable segments of minority populations may see their police department as rotten is their greater chance, compared to whites, of *experiencing* abuse. Reported experiences with police misconduct are displayed in Figure 2.2. As expected, the two minority groups report more of each type of mistreatment. On three types, Hispanics are aligned with blacks: Roughly the same percentages say they have been subjected to insulting language or excessive force or have observed police corruption. Blacks stand out, however, in their experience of being stopped by police without good reason in their city (34 percent of blacks versus 20 percent of Hispanics).

When the sample is broken down into different age categories, it becomes clear that police misconduct is something that acutely affects

Figure 2.3. Personal experience in city, young males

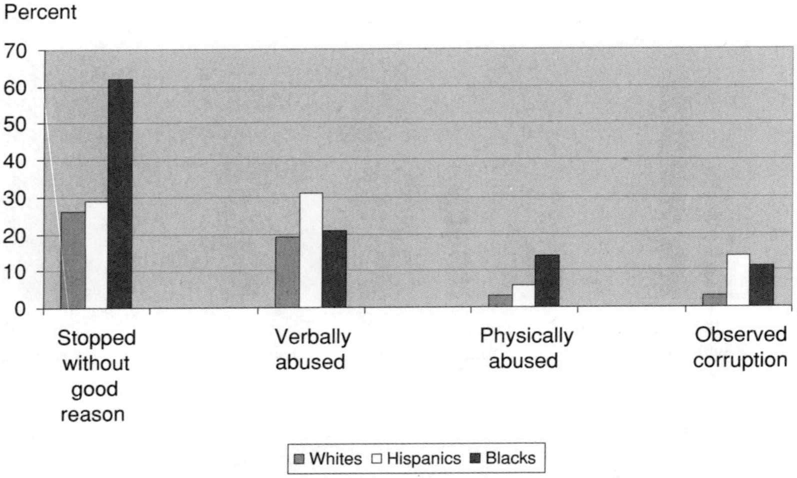

Percent

Note: Percentage of male respondents, ages 18–29, saying that they have personally experienced an unjustified stop, insulting language, or excessive force, or have seen an officer engage in a corrupt act in their city.

young minority males (and especially black males), based on self-reports. Black men between the ages of 18 and 29 are the group most likely to report that they have been the victims of unwarranted stops and physical abuse at the hands of the police, whereas young Hispanic men are the most likely to report being verbally abused (Figure 2.3). The most troubling statistic is the 62 percent of young black males who report being unjustifiably stopped by police in their own city. Judging from our self-report data as well as some other studies, young black men are more susceptible to police mistreatment than older black males and at much greater risk than young black women (data not shown in figure). At least twice as many young black men as women say they have personally experienced each type of misconduct. Figure 2.4 pertains to vicarious experience – that is, abuse that has happened to someone else in the respondent's household. This experience is not a rare occurrence, according to Hispanics and African Americans.

In light of both vicarious and personal experiences, it is not surprising that minorities are apprehensive about the police. A recent Harris (2002) poll, for example, revealed that a substantial number of blacks and Hispanics were "sometimes afraid that

Figure 2.4. Vicarious experience in city

Percent

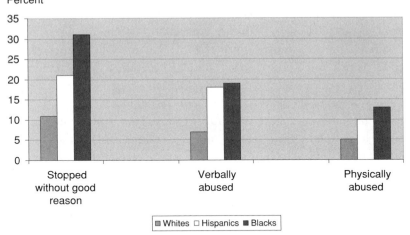

Note: Percentage of respondents saying that someone else in their household has experienced an unjustified stop, insulting language, or excessive force in their city.

the police will stop and arrest you when you are completely innocent":
39 percent of Hispanics, 42 percent of blacks, and 16 percent of whites expressed this fear.

Figures 2.1 through 2.4 portray city-level perceptions and experiences. Fewer people are critical of police behavior in their neighborhood – consistent with other polls that find that assessments grow more negative along a continuum from neighborhood to city to nation. People view policing most favorably in their own residential neighborhood and most negatively in other parts of the nation. Yet the same racial hierarchy characterizes each level: Blacks perceive more police abuse in each context than do Hispanics, and Hispanics more so than whites. The difference is especially striking at the neighborhood level (not reported in a figure). Misconduct is simply not a salient issue in white neighborhoods. Only 7 percent of whites say that verbal abuse, excessive force, and unjustified stops occur often in their neighborhoods, compared to 25 to 36 percent of blacks, depending on the type of misconduct. Similarly, while only 2 to 7 percent of whites say that they have personally or vicariously experienced these three types of misconduct in their neighborhood, 7 to 20 percent of blacks have. These racial disparities are *not simply a matter of opinion*. Contrasting perceptions of police misconduct reflect, at least to some extent, real differences in police practices across different kinds of neighborhoods, judging from research based on police records and on systematic observations of officers on the streets (Smith 1986; Fagan and Davies 2000; Kane 2002; Terrill and Reisig 2003).[8] Both these studies and our respondents' self-reports indicate that *at the neighborhood level, police misconduct is largely confined to disadvantaged minority communities*.

At the same time, the two minority groups view misconduct as particularly prevalent elsewhere in their city (Figure 2.1). In areas outside one's residential neighborhood, police may regard Hispanics and blacks as being "out of place" and more "suspicious" than when they are observed inside their residential neighborhoods. This may explain why one-third of blacks and one-fifth of Hispanics report being stopped without good reason in areas of their city outside their own neighborhood. Some other studies have documented a similar pattern (Weitzer 1999; Fagan and Davies 2000).

In addition to the question of whether one has *ever experienced* some type of police misconduct, it is important to consider *repeated* abuse. Respondents were asked how many times they had experienced each type of abuse. This is not a problem for whites – less than 1 percent of whom say that a police officer has used excessive force against them three or more times in their city, and only 3 percent say they have been verbally abused by the police three or more times. Blacks and Hispanics are somewhat more likely to report repeated experience with these two types of abuse, and the white-minority differences are even more pronounced for street stops: 16 percent of blacks and 12 percent of Hispanics report that they have been unjustifiably stopped by police three or more times in their own city, compared to just 4 percent of whites.

These findings are remarkably consistent with those of other studies. Another national survey found that blacks were disproportionately subjected to repeated police stops (Bureau of Justice Statistics

---

[8] Additional studies are needed to corroborate these findings. To date, patterns of actual police behavior across different kinds of neighborhoods have been investigated systematically in only a few studies.

2001); a study of residents of Washington, DC, found that 17 percent of blacks (but only 4 percent of whites) reported that they had been stopped three or more times in the past year (Police Foundation 2004); and, in Britain, 14 percent of blacks and 4 percent of whites said they had been stopped in a car five or more times in the past year (Home Office 2001:60). Recurring personal experiences of this nature can have adverse, cumulative effects on the individual recipients and, if others are told about these experiences, on the latter's vicarious experiences.

Of course, police mistreatment of citizens is not directed *only* at minority group members. A number of whites also experience such abuse (see Figures 2.2 through 2.4). To give just one example, a young white man recounted his experience of verbal abuse and harassment:

> When my brother's car got broken into, the cop told me and my brother that it was our fault for having a "low rider." He refused to fill out a police report, and the whole time he was trying to intimidate me and my brother. I don't know why. It seems like all cops are just ex-bullies trying to beat up on someone to vent their frustration. He kept telling me not to use that tone of voice with him; that bitch was just mad because I used his same tone back at him. . . . He pulled out his nightstick and held it like he was about to hit me with it, and he kept reminding me that he had a badge and a gun by unfastening it. He was about to attack me because he didn't like my tone which was the same as his. His way of thinking was probably: you listen to rap [music] and drive a "low rider," so you are a criminal. I can see that cop killing someone someday because of his temper and prejudice. I know all cops aren't bad but one experience like that would piss off anyone. A cop like that deserves death because that is what was being threatened to me. He had a gun; I didn't. (MC white male, 25)

The encounter involved mutual insults between the young man and the officer, rather than a clear-cut case of police misconduct. Still, it demonstrates how an authoritarian police demeanor, including saber rattling, can be construed as offensive, spark an altercation, and destroy trust in the police. This man now believes that "all cops" are "ex-bullies" looking for opportunities to mistreat citizens.

WHAT SHAPES VIEWS OF MISCONDUCT?

The preceding section documented racial differences on the issue of police misconduct and each group's risk of experiencing abuse. But, as with overall satisfaction, we are also interested in what happens to these group differences when other variables are introduced – and, especially, whether these additional factors impact views of misconduct among whites, blacks, and Hispanics alike. We examine each group's profile on the following issues:

- Insofar as officers are more active in high-crime areas, this heightened presence affords them greater opportunities to engage in misconduct. Does the amount of perceived neighborhood crime increase residents' beliefs that misconduct is widespread?
- Concentrated disadvantage at the neighborhood level has little effect on residents' overall satisfaction with the police, but it may be more salient in shaping views regarding misconduct. Are residents of areas with high levels of socioeconomic deprivation more likely than others to believe that police misconduct is a problem?
- Insofar as people use their own experiences to form larger attitudes about the police, it is expected that personal and vicarious experience with officer misconduct will increase the odds of believing that misconduct occurs frequently.[9] Is this the case?
- We have already established that community policing bolsters residents' general confidence in the police. Insofar as community policing is associated with positive and cooperative relationships between cops and residents, it is also reasonable to expect it to diminish both real and perceived police misconduct. Does community policing reduce residents' beliefs that officer misconduct is a problem?
- Insofar as people generalize from media representations to the real world, exposure to media reports on police misconduct should amplify the opinion that such conduct is common. Does exposure to media reports of police wrongdoing increase the chances of perceiving misconduct as widespread?

---

[9] For the sake of parsimony in the regression analyses presented below, we combined responses to the city and neighborhood experience questions.

Answers to these questions are provided in Table 2.3, which displays models corresponding to each type of misconduct: unwarranted stops (model 1), verbal abuse (model 2), excessive force (model 3), and corruption (model 4). For the first three, the questionnaire included separate queries about the context in which the misconduct occurs – in one's neighborhood and elsewhere in one's city (see footnote 4) – which we combine here to simplify our analysis.[10] With the exception of corruption (which was asked in the city context only), we created two-item standardized indices of respondents' views of the prevalence of each type of misconduct.[11]

We first describe the results from including only race in each model (coefficients not reported in the table). These baseline models revealed that both blacks and Hispanics are significantly more inclined than whites to believe that police engage in all four types of wrongdoing and that Hispanics are significantly less likely than blacks to hold this belief. These results are consistent with a racial hierarchy pattern.

When we turn from the race-only to the full model (represented by the combined sample columns in Table 2.3), we see that, compared to whites, blacks continue to perceive more of each type of police misconduct but that, with the exception of unwarranted stops, Hispanics no longer differ from whites. For all respondents, living in neighborhoods where crime is seen as low and where community policing is practiced tends to decrease perceptions of police misbehavior; concentrated disadvantage, exposure to media reports of misconduct, and personal and vicarious experiences of abuse, on the other hand, tend to increase the belief that police misconduct is common.

[10] In a separate analysis (Weitzer and Tuch 2004a), we analyzed neighborhood and city contexts separately and found that people perceive much more misconduct in their cities than in their own neighborhoods and that blacks and Hispanics were more likely than whites to believe that police abuses were common in both their neighborhoods and elsewhere in their city.

[11] Alphas for the three indices are .83, .89, and .86, respectively. Responses to the corruption question were dichotomized into the categories "not at all common/not very common" (coded 0) and "fairly common/very common" (coded 1). Because the presence of a dichotomous dependent variable violates assumptions of OLS regression models, we use a binary logistic regression model for analysis of the corruption variable.

TABLE 2.3. *Perceptions of police misconduct*

	Total sample		Whites		Blacks		Hispanics	
	b	beta	b	beta	b	beta	b	beta
Model 1. Unwarranted stops								
Black	.423***	.144	—	—	—	—	—	—
	(.074)							
Hispanic	.257***	.093	—	—	—	—	—	—
	(.064)							
Neighborhood crime	.149***	.112	.071	.050	.268***	.226	.163**	.141
	(.033)		(.062)		(.059)		(.056)	
Safety (day)	.036	.021	.043	.020	.099	.067	-.030	-.022
	(.051)		(.105)		(.089)		(.083)	
Safety (night)	-.070	-.055	-.103	-.072	-.005	-.004	-.037	.034
	(.039)		(.074)		(.073)		(.071)	
Concentrated disadvantage	.064*	.064	.066	.066	.143**	.143	-.104*	-.104
	(.027)		(.044)		(.046)		(.049)	
Personal experience with misconduct (1 = yes)	.438***	.194	.505***	.208	.257**	.127	.488***	.238
	(.054)		(.101)		(.098)		(.098)	
Vicarious experience with misconduct (1 = yes)	.376***	.156	.335**	.123	.423***	.205	.335***	.159
	(.055)		(.109)		(.094)		(.098)	
Community policing (1 = yes)	-.004	-.002	.036	.018	-.127	-.063	.045	.023
	(.043)		(.079)		(.088)		(.085)	
Media exposure	.116***	.084	.083	.056	.181***	.146	.167**	.133
	(.030)		(.059)		(.052)		(.053)	
N of cases (unweighted)	1,483		545		433		505	
Constant	-.600		.025		-1.817		-.556	
R^2 (adjusted)	.289		.156		.263		.222	

TABLE 2.3. *Perceptions of police misconduct (continued)*

	Total sample		Whites		Blacks		Hispanics	
	b	beta	b	beta	b	beta	b	beta
Model 2. Verbal abuse								
Black	.193**	.066	—	—	—	—	—	—
	(.072)		—		—		—	
Hispanic	−.010	−.004	—	—	—	—	—	—
	(.062)		—		—		—	
Neighborhood crime	.160***	.121	.201***	.141	.088	.074	.198***	.171
	(.032)		(.058)		(.059)		(.053)	
Safety (day)	−.020	−.012	−.108	−.051	.200*	.135	−.089	−.068
	(.050)		(.098)		(.089)		(.078)	
Safety (night)	−.041	−.032	.071	.050	−.235***	−.195	.049	.045
	(.038)		(.069)		(.073)		(.066)	
Concentrated disadvantage	.076**	.076	.112**	.112	.025	.025	.059	.059
	(.027)		(.041)		(.046)		(.046)	
Personal experience with misconduct (1 = yes)	.573***	.253	.634***	.261	.483***	.239	.519***	.253
	(.053)		(.094)		(.098)		(.092)	
Vicarious experience with misconduct (1 = yes)	.430***	.179	.418***	.154	.362***	.176	.486***	.230
	(.054)		(.102)		(.094)		(.092)	
Community policing (1 = yes)	−.179***	−.089	−.229**	−.114	−.237**	−.118	−.105	−.053
	(.042)		(.073)		(.088)		(.079)	
Media exposure	.199***	.143	.159**	.107	.212***	.172	.217***	.172
	(.030)		(.055)		(.052)		(.049)	
N of cases (unweighted)	1,483		545		433		505	
Constant	−.967		−.686		−1.340		−1.232	
R2 (adjusted)	.322		.268		.263		.318	

(*continued*)

61

TABLE 2.3 *Perceptions of police misconduct* (*continued*)

	Total sample		Whites		Blacks		Hispanics	
	b	beta	b	beta	b	beta	b	beta
Model 3. Excessive force								
Black	.288***	.098	—	—	—	—	—	—
	(.069)							
Hispanic	.097	.035	—	—	—	—	—	—
	(.060)							
Neighborhood crime	.173***	.131	.169**	.119	.158**	.134	.331***	.285
	(.031)		(.055)		(.056)		(.051)	
Safety (day)	-.091	-.052	-.231*	-.109	.078	.053	.045	.034
	(.048)		(.094)		(.083)		(.076)	
Safety (night)	-.035	-.027	.035	.024	-.178**	-.148	.014	.013
	(.037)		(.066)		(.069)		(.065)	
Concentrated disadvantage	.079**	.079	.090*	.090	-.001	-.001	.098*	.098
	(.026)		(.039)		(.043)		(.045)	
Personal experience with misconduct (1 = yes)	.601***	.266	.839***	.346	.395***	.196	.362***	.175
	(.051)		(.091)		(.092)		(.089)	
Vicarious experience with misconduct (1 = yes)	.392***	.163	.404***	.149	.333***	.162	.557***	.263
	(.052)		(.097)		(.088)		(.089)	
Community policing (1 = yes)	-.156***	-.077	-.195**	-.097	-.171*	-.085	-.026	-.013
	(.040)		(.070)		(.083)		(.077)	
Media exposure	.229***	.166	.161**	.109	.387***	.315	.212***	.168
	(.028)		(.052)		(.049)		(.048)	
N of cases (unweighted)	1,483		545		433		505	
Constant	-.832		-.073		-1.917		-2.030	
R² (adjusted)	.378		.325		.348		.360	

TABLE 2.3 *Perceptions of police misconduct (continued)*

	Total sample		Whites		Blacks		Hispanics	
	B	OR	B	OR	B	OR	B	OR
Model 4. Corruption								
Black	.648**	1.911	—	—	—	—	—	—
	(.215)		—		—		—	
Hispanic	−.132	.876	—	—	—	—	—	—
	(.205)		—		—		—	
Neighborhood crime	.394***	1.482	.447*	1.564	.180	1.198	.409**	1.505
	(.107)		(.204)		(.153)		(.157)	
Safety (day)	−.264	.768	−.287	.750	−.047	.954	−.305	.737
	(.156)		(.312)		(.232)		(.226)	
Safety (night)	−.231	.794	−.149	.862	−.565**	.569	.008	1.008
	(.126)		(.245)		(.199)		(.195)	
Concentrated disadvantage	.003	1.003	.060	1.061	.066	1.069	.087	1.091
	(.083)		(.139)		(.118)		(.135)	
Personal experience with misconduct (1 = yes)	1.137***	3.116	1.381***	3.980	.854***	2.349	.574*	1.775
	(.160)		(.292)		(.246)		(.265)	
Vicarious experience with misconduct (1 = yes)	.396*	1.487	.539	1.714	.067	1.070	.657*	1.929
	(.164)		(.313)		(.239)		(.263)	
Community policing (1 = yes)	−.472***	.624	−.601*	.548	−.115	.891	−.183	.832
	(.145)		(.277)		(.225)		(.239)	
Media exposure	.756***	2.130	.568**	1.765	.586***	1.796	.911***	2.487
	(.108)		(.212)		(.140)		(.166)	
N of cases (unweighted)	1,483		545		433		505	
Constant	−1.685		−1.227		.250		−3.586	
R² (Nagelkerke)	.373		.344		.257		.304	
Model chi-square	455.32***		131.45***		98.57***		117.80***	

Note: Standard errors in parentheses; estimates are net of controls for education, household income, gender, age, city-suburban residence, and region;
* $p < .05$; ** $p < .01$; *** $p < .001$; OR = odds ratio.

How do these factors shape attitudes within each racial group? Regarding unwarranted stops (model 1), only experience with misconduct influences whites' views, heightening their belief that such stops occur frequently. Among blacks and Hispanics, in addition to experience, we find that neighborhood crime and media exposure also increase the chances of viewing this type of misconduct as common. Among blacks, residing in areas of concentrated disadvantage increases these chances as well, though, interestingly, the opposite is true for Hispanics. Thus, for whites, perceptions of unwarranted police stops are largely a consequence of their own experiences with police misconduct, but for minorities these perceptions are influenced by neighborhood and media factors as well.

Model 2 summarizes findings for police verbal abuse. Among all three groups, personal and vicarious experiences with misconduct and media exposure increase the chances of viewing verbal abuse as common. As indicated by the standardized coefficients (the betas), each of these variables is a robust predictor, among the strongest in the models. The more often one is exposed to personal or vicarious experiences with police abuse and to negative media coverage of the police, the more widespread this type of misconduct is perceived to be. In addition, community policing is a potent predictor among whites and blacks, as is neighborhood crime among whites and Hispanics.

The view that excessive force is common (model 3) is amplified, for all three groups, by the following: living in high-crime neighborhoods, having personal or vicarious experiences of abuse, and frequent exposure to negative media portrayals of the police. The view that police brutality is common is also heightened among whites and Hispanics who live in disadvantaged neighborhoods, while community policing decreases this perception among whites and blacks.

Finally, model 4 reports findings for corruption. Here, personal experiences with police mistreatment and media exposure increase the odds of perceiving police corruption among all racial groups. For instance, whites who have experienced police abuse are about four times more likely than those without such experience to say they have seen an act of police corruption (odds ratio = 3.980); similarly, Hispanics exposed to media accounts of police misconduct are two-and-a-half times more likely than those with less exposure to have observed corruption. For blacks, feeling safe (at night) reduces these odds; for whites and Hispanics neighborhood crime increases, and for whites community policing decreases, the likelihood of seeing corruption as common in their neighborhood or city.

In sum, although several variables shape citizen assessments of the scope of police misconduct, some factors are particularly important. Salient in most models for most groups are (1) personal and vicarious experiences, (2) exposure to media accounts of policing problems, and (3) residence in high-crime neighborhoods. Each of these factors increases the chances that police misconduct will be viewed as widespread. In addition, (4) misconduct tends to be viewed as less of a problem in areas where residents report that community policing exists, which is exactly what advocates of community policing would predict. Community policing seems to reduce the chances of police mistreatment of citizens and to improve relations with residents.

OBSERVATIONS OF MISCONDUCT

People sometimes directly *observe* police officers engaging in some type of wrongdoing, reducing trust in the police (Son et al. 1997). This section of the chapter presents qualitative data offering additional insights into the nature of police misconduct. The accounts that follow are illustrative of the kinds of misconduct people have witnessed in their local area as well as how they feel about what they have seen.

Although a substantial number of people believe that police corruption occurs in their city (Figure 2.1), most people have never directly observed any corruption. Corruption usually involves a transaction between cops and citizens in settings that are invisible to third parties (National Research Council 2004:269). Still, a minority of Americans have witnessed corruption in their city (3 percent of whites, 8 percent of Hispanics, 10 percent of blacks) or neighborhood (2, 4, and 6 percent, respectively). We asked these respondents to describe what they had seen.

Recall that the questionnaire defined corruption broadly as "any corrupt activities, such as taking bribes or involvement in the drug trade." In answering this question, some people cited acts that were not corrupt per se but instead involved some other type of misconduct. Included here are actions such as harassment, traffic violations, drinking while on duty, lying, abusive language, and brutality. For example, two of our teenage respondents had witnessed excessive force:

> I saw a police officer manhandle a little boy who was the wrong person he was looking for. He slammed his neck on the car and the little boy hadn't done anything. (UMC black male, 13)

> This white police officer just started to hit the man for no reason, threw him on the car, kneed him on the back of his leg so the man would fall, and then kicked him. (MC black female, 17)

Some respondents had observed or heard about a wide variety of acts of misconduct:

> I've seen police plant narcotics on innocent people, people who were supposed to be taken into custody get beaten up, police keeping people's identification, police mistakenly raiding the wrong house, get sued by the innocent victims, and then turn around and threaten the people with arrest. (LC black woman, 58)

Others had also witnessed compound abuses:

> An officer searched a vehicle but couldn't find anything illegal. So the driver was given a ticket even though he was not speeding. . . . When the driver [a young black male] questioned the violation, the officer became very nasty, trying to provoke the driver to become violent. (MC black male, 26)

The following analysis focuses on corruption, because that was the subject of our open-ended question. The main types of corruption mentioned by our respondents were drug offenses, bribery, and sexual misconduct.

Drug Corruption

The policing of drug crimes invites police corruption, because the drugs and drug money are fairly easy to pilfer and because the victims are offenders with little credibility should they decide to complain to other officers (Newburn 1999). Drug-related corruption thus offers the twin benefits of high opportunity and low accountability.

Of the 640 officers convicted of corruption nationwide during 1993–1997, nearly half were involved in drug-related crimes (General Accounting Office 1998). Vice squad officers are at high risk for drug-related corruption (Rubenstein 1973:387–390); the temptation is great to trade confiscated drugs for information from informants, to plant drugs on suspects, to use the drugs, or to sell them for profit. These are the same types of drug-related corruption identified in a recent report by the General Accounting Office (1998).

The Mollen Commission found that drug-related corruption became rife in New York City with the advent of crack cocaine in the 1980s. The traditional view that drug graft was "dirty money" that should be shunned by officers was replaced with "a wide spectrum of drug-related corruption" – including cops using or dealing drugs, stealing from street dealers, and ongoing partnerships with traffickers, including efforts to "assist, facilitate, and strengthen the drug trade" (Mollen Commission 1994:15). The commission presents plenty of evidence of such corruption in New York City. Of course, New York is not alone in this, though the NYPD has been investigated more frequently by commissions of inquiry than any other police department in the country. An example of a corrupt officer in another city who fit the profile sketched by the Mollen Commission is Shawn Verbeke, who worked in Washington, DC. In court, he admitted to routinely shaking down drug dealers at nightclubs, seizing their Ecstasy and methamphetamines, selling the drugs while in uniform, and using the drugs while at work (Markon 2004).

Drug-related acts were the most frequent type of corruption observed by our respondents. People had witnessed each type of drug corruption sketched above: (1) theft of drugs or drug money from suspects, (2) sale of confiscated drugs by officers, (3) planting drugs on citizens to justify an arrest, and (4) officer use of drugs. African Americans were especially likely to say they had personally observed drug-related police corruption, followed by Hispanics – perhaps because black neighborhoods are more likely to host street-level drug markets than are Hispanic or white neighborhoods (Ousey and Lee 2002).

Perhaps the most commonly observed offense is when a police officer *confiscates drugs in lieu of an arrest.* Respondents typically assumed that the officer simply pocketed the drugs and did not turn them in:

> An officer arrested a friend of mine who had marijuana on him. The officer took the weed and stuffed it in his pocket, and never charged my friend with possession of the substance. (LC black male, 25)

> Taking drugs, money, and stolen articles instead of making an arrest. I've seen weapons confiscated and the person released within minutes. (MC black male, 59)

> The police will often stop drug traffickers, take the drugs, let the person go, bust them the next time, and repeat this again and again. (MC black male, 44)

Another type of corruption involves officers who *sell confiscated drugs*. One person had witnessed "cops busting a drug spot, pocketing some of the money, and selling some of the confiscated drugs at other drug spots" (LC Hispanic male, 22), and another had "seen officers exchange drugs and money with hoods on the streets" (MC black male, 33).

Some respondents recounted observations of police *planting drugs* on a suspect prior to making an arrest. One middle-aged black woman had seen officers "plant drugs on guys and lie in court to get a conviction." A similar account follows:

> If they don't like you, they will stop you and tell you to get on the car because you fit the profile of a person they looking for . . . and then they will check your pockets and put some drugs on you and say "look what we found." (LC black male, 31)

Others had seen *police use drugs* in public or in private settings, and a few admitted using drugs with officers. One respondent stated, "Seven police officers were arrested for trafficking. [They] would be at a known neighborhood crackhouse. I never saw any arrests being made, and it sure is strange seeing people from opposite sides of the war being friends" (MC Hispanic male, 26). Another person stated,

> One police officer I know, when he busts people, he takes part of the evidence to an old woman's house, who sells it for him and she gets part of the profit. Another police officer I know took me over to his house and started smoking a joint and had a sack of weed next to him. (MC white female, 20)

Finally, some people defined as corruption instances where police fail to intervene in a crime situation, such as when they simply drive by an open-air drug market without stopping or when they engage in some suspicious activity:

> The girl next door to me was dealing drugs out of the house. I saw a lot of activity coming and going. She was sexually involved with a local policeman whose squad car was parked there frequently. The car was always backed in so we could not see the license plate. (MC white female, 51)

Bribery

Bribery is as old as policing, and it is the first thing that comes to mind when most people think of corruption. Respondents reported instances where officers had accepted or asked for bribes or other payoffs, and a few stated that they had bribed an officer to avoid some type of sanction. Although most had seen or experienced an isolated act of bribery (a "corruption event"), others had witnessed ongoing illicit activities, such as bribes to watch a business, making illegal bets with bookies, or seeing officers enter a gaming house without making an arrest (a "corruption arrangement") (Sherman 1978). Corruption arrangements seem to be more easily detected by police supervisors than corruption events, though individuals are more likely to make a complaint about a nonconsensual event than a consensual arrangement (Sherman 1978:43). Perhaps the most common bribery scenario takes place during routine traffic stops, which offer officers an opportunity for gain in return for not writing a ticket or making an arrest:

> I was with a friend who got pulled over late at night. The officer told him that if he had any money or drugs he would let him go. My friend told him that he did not have any, so he went to jail. (LC Hispanic male, 25)

Some people who lack direct knowledge of corruption nevertheless infer it from circumstances, such as the incongruity between a cop's modest salary and conspicuous consumption: "The old neighborhood I lived in had a policeman's house, and they were always having renovations, flashy cars, late-night parties. It all looked very expensive for one source of income" (LC Hispanic male, 26).

Sexual Misconduct

Respondents described incidents of sexual misconduct that ranged
from having sex in police cars, to attempts to extract sexual favors
from female motorists, to consorting with prostitutes. Most of these
respondents are women. Perhaps the most common type of sexual
misconduct is trying to extort sex in return for not enforcing the
law. One respondent had seen a "cop getting oral sex from a prostitute in Grand Rapids, Michigan" (LC white female, 15), and another
described her own experience: "After being arrested for having four
parking tickets, I was encouraged to engage in oral sex to avoid going
to jail" (MC white female, 44). Another respondent told us that he
had "seen police officers release attractive women in exchange for the
woman's phone number. The officer looks to receive sexual favors for
his 'generosity'" (UMC black male, 33).

Extracting sexual favors from prostitutes in exchange for their
freedom was witnessed by several people, like the man who had seen
officers "with prostitutes for over 20 minutes in alleys, on several occasions" (UMC black male, 52). Another person reported that "a neigh-
bor was a prostitute and several officers visited for long times and at
regular intervals" (LC Hispanic female, 59).

CONCLUSION

This chapter began with an examination of Americans' overall confidence in the police. Our research shows that the two most robust
predictors of general satisfaction are how well local police deal with
crime and whether officers are believed to be frequently engaged in
misconduct in one's neighborhood or city. These factors influence the
views of whites, blacks, and Hispanics alike.

Police effectiveness in fighting crime (as perceived by respondents)
increases overall satisfaction with police among each group. This is
what we would expect, because the public considers crime-fighting
the core function of the police – even though officers actually spend
more time maintaining order than dealing with crime. It would be
surprising indeed if views on police effectiveness in crime control did
not affect global satisfaction with the police.

Where police misconduct is regarded as widespread in one's city or
neighborhood, overall satisfaction with the police department suffers

in the eyes of all groups. People who believe that officers are frequently involved in corruption, verbal abuse, brutality, and unjustified street stops hold their local police in low esteem. It seems logical that negative police practices like these would dampen approval of the police. By contrast, positive practices, such as community policing, should boost overall satisfaction, and this is indeed the case for whites and blacks.

Turning to the chapter's main theme – the issue of police misconduct – race matters greatly. In each of the race-only baseline models, blacks are the most likely to perceive misconduct and whites are the least likely. Most whites doubt the existence of misconduct, or see it as an isolated problem. Whites tend to feel that police are rarely involved in corruption, excessive force, verbal abuse, and improper stops of citizens. Blacks and Hispanics are more inclined to believe that such misconduct is a problem and one that is *very common* in their city and residential neighborhood – not limited to a few rotten apples but instead symptomatic of a larger "rotten barrel." Moreover, those who view police misconduct as prevalent in their local area are also prone to generalize from this to overall assessments of the police, amplifying dissatisfaction with their perhaps rotten police department. This has important implications for the fundamental legitimacy of a police agency and for people's willingness to trust and cooperate with the officers they encounter.

Based on our findings and other research, blacks and Hispanics are at heightened risk of mistreatment by police. What is more, they are vulnerable to *repeated* instances of abuse. In other words, misconduct is not simply a matter of racial disparities in the occurrence of abuse; disparities also exist in the recurrence of abuse. It is possible that people who have had several experiences of this kind are more disturbed by them and thus more inclined to relate them to friends, family members, and others. In other words, multiple personal experiences may increase the odds that others will vicariously experience police abuse – a "multiplier effect" that is likely more pronounced in the social networks of Hispanics and African Americans than of whites.

Furthermore, the distribution of these experiences varies not only between the three groups but also within them. Our findings show that one subgroup faces *triple jeopardy* based on a combination of race, age, and gender: Young minority males are significantly more likely than older minority males, same-age minority females, and white males to report having experienced mistreatment by an officer.

The information presented in this chapter shows that police misconduct is more complex than a simple gap between whites and the two minority groups. As noted, Hispanics perceive more police abuse than whites but less than blacks. Considerably fewer Hispanics than blacks believe that all four types of misconduct are a problem. This disparity helps address one unanswered question in the literature on police-minority relations – that is, whether blacks and Hispanics share a minority-group perspective versus a white majority-group perspective, or whether perceptions take the form of a white–Hispanic–African American racial hierarchy. When it comes to the types of police abuse examined in this chapter, blacks and Hispanics do differ significantly, consistent with the racial-hierarchy thesis.

To further explore these racial differences, we identified several influences on public perceptions. First, both personal and (usually) vicarious experience sharply heighten perceptions of police misconduct for all groups. Second, residents of neighborhoods with community policing are less likely to believe that police misconduct is widespread in their city. This finding is consistent with the few studies that provide some evidence that community policing actually reduces police misconduct (Greene 1999; Terrill and Mastrofski 2004).

Third, crime plays a role. The belief that crime is a serious problem in one's neighborhood almost always increases the odds that police misconduct will be viewed as pervasive. Why this connection? High-crime neighborhoods are the sites where police-community relations tend to be problematic. Residents of such areas are more vulnerable to being stopped on the street, verbally abused, and physically roughed up (Smith 1986; Fagan and Davies 2000; Kane 2002; Terrill and Reisig 2003), and corruption also thrives in such communities (Mollen Commission 1994). Police appear to cast a wide net of suspicion in neighborhoods that they view as especially troublesome, resulting in more aggressive and indiscriminate treatment of residents. Such typifications of residents of high-crime neighborhoods may thus increase the aggregate level of police misconduct toward those residents. These patterns may help to explain the association between the neighborhood crime situation and citizen perceptions of police misconduct.

Fourth, the mass media: Repeated exposure to media reports on police abuse is a strong predictor of citizens' assessments of each type of police misconduct. As a general rule, people who frequently hear or read about incidents of misconduct, as presented in the media, are inclined to view such misconduct as widespread. A few previous studies, cited in Chapter 1, suggest that single incidents involving brutality or corruption reduce approval of the police (e.g., the Rodney King beating in Los Angeles), and our research reconfirms and broadens this finding with regard to persons who are frequently exposed to such media coverage over time. The fact that we have only a single-item, self-report measure of media exposure limits the conclusions that can be drawn, but the congruence of our media findings with those reported in other studies lends credence to our results. Although it is usually overlooked by researchers who study popular attitudes toward the police, the mass media appear to play a very important role, as subsequent chapters will also show.

In a nutshell, *beliefs about police misconduct are strongly and consistently influenced by citizens' contacts with officers (both personal and vicarious), by neighborhood crime, and usually by the existence of community policing and mass media representations of the police.*

According to the group-position thesis, racial and ethnic minorities should be more inclined than whites to believe that police misconduct is a serious and prevalent problem in America. Whites should be more predisposed to discount or deny allegations of police misconduct, reflecting their basic group affinity with the police. These predictions are generally supported by both the quantitative and qualitative findings presented in this chapter.

CHAPTER THREE

Racially Biased Policing

This chapter examines four types of racialized policing: discrimination against minority individuals, discrimination against minority neighborhoods, racial prejudice among police officers, and racial profiling during traffic stops.[1] Like the misconduct examined in the previous chapter, the frequency and scope of racially biased policing remains unknown. Despite a recent flurry of studies of racial profiling during traffic stops, there are no reliable estimates of how many stops are motivated entirely or largely by the drivers' race. Similarly, we do not know how often police discriminate in other ways against individuals because of their race. Almost no studies have investigated whether the race of officers affects citizen attitudes toward the police, despite the conventional wisdom that officers' race does make a difference. Although racial prejudice among officers is thought to be common-place (Jefferson 1988:522) and likely influences their behavior at least to some degree, the extent of racial animus on the part of police is opaque.

Citizens' views of racialized policing may be considered just as important as the objective reality of policing. Behavior perceived as racially motivated may increase the frequency of face-to-face altercations between minorities and officers and generate broader distrust of the police. Such perceptions also may make people less inclined to call the police to report crimes, to cooperate with police investigations, and to consider police work as a career. In short, the belief that policing is

[1] We use the terms "racial bias" and "racialized policing" to refer to these four types of bias, while recognizing that differential treatment of individuals and neighborhoods may or may not reflect outright racially motivated discrimination.

racialized and thus unjust can have serious ramifications for both the public and the police.

The U.S. Justice Department is unequivocal in its position that policing should be racially neutral: "Law enforcement officers should not rely on generalized stereotypes, attitudes, or beliefs about the propensity of any racial, ethnic, or national origin group to engage in unlawful activity.... Agencies should have a clear and widely disseminated policy prohibiting law enforcement officers from discriminating" (U.S. Department of Justice 2001). Similarly, most Americans, regardless of race, are opposed *in principle* to racially biased law enforcement. According to a national poll, over three-quarters of the public believe it is the responsibility of the federal government to ensure that the police and the courts treat minorities and whites equally, even if this policy would mean higher taxes (Kaiser 1995).

But this begs the question of whether people view the system as *actually dispensing unequal justice.* We know that whites and blacks differed on this issue in years past. For example, in a 1977 poll, large majorities of African Americans felt that blacks received inferior police protection from crime and that police officers discriminated against blacks, whereas only about a quarter of whites agreed (Harris 1977). White skepticism of claims about racial bias in the criminal justice system is consistent with the group-position thesis and with whites' well-documented doubts about claims of discrimination in other spheres, such as housing, employment, and education (Hochschild 1995; Schuman et al. 1997). What we do not know is the *extent* to which whites see racialized policing as obsolete today and whether they are more inclined to believe that it exists in some areas than in others. It is possible, for example, that media reporting on the issue of racial profiling has sensitized whites to this problem to a greater extent than other types of racial injustice.

Both popular accounts and research studies suggest that African Americans are acutely attuned to the problem of racial discrimination in many areas of American life – housing, education, jobs – and a substantial number of Hispanics hold the same views (Sigelman and Welch 1991; Kluegel and Bobo 2001). Several polls also show that many Americans are convinced that the criminal justice system does not mete out equal justice. Less clear, however, are the *sources* of these views – that is, the factors that account for similarities and differences in the views of whites, blacks, and Hispanics.

Ordinary citizens are not alone in believing that racial bias is a problem in American policing; a number of police officers agree. One-fourth of Los Angeles police officers, for instance, agreed with the following survey question: "Racial bias on the part of officers toward minority citizens currently exists and contributes to a negative interaction between police and the community" (Christopher Commission 1991:69). Do officers in other departments feel similarly? It depends in part on the officer's race. According to a survey of 925 officers in 121 police departments, 12 percent of white officers and 51 percent of black officers said that police "often treat whites better than blacks and other minorities" and poor people worse than middle-class people. Almost no white officers (5 percent) but a majority of black officers (57 percent) thought that "police are more likely to use physical force against blacks and other minorities than against whites in similar situations" (Weisburd and Greenspan 2000).

This chapter examines the following issues:

- Are blacks and Hispanics more likely than whites to believe that racially biased policing is widespread? If so, do these racial differences persist after controlling for other variables?
- Do Hispanics differ from blacks in their attitudes toward and experiences with racially biased policing? If so, do these differences take the form of a black–Hispanic–white racial hierarchy?
- Does personal experience with discriminatory treatment by an officer increase the belief that biased policing is widespread? If so, does this vary by racial group?
- Do neighborhood crime and socioeconomic conditions shape citizen assessments of biased policing? If so, does this vary by racial group?
- Chapter 2 showed that exposure to media reports on police wrongdoing strongly influences public opinion regarding police misconduct. Is media exposure also a predictor of views on racialized policing?

This chapter presents both quantitative data, which help identify the contours and determinants of citizens' attitudes, and qualitative data, which provide a deeper, more nuanced understanding of how

Hispanics, blacks, and whites think about and, in some cases, experience racialized policing. Respondents' views were measured by four sets of questions; the questions within each set were standardized and summed to create four separate indices:

- *Disparate treatment of individuals*: "Do you think the police in your [city/neighborhood] treat whites and blacks equally, do they treat whites worse than blacks, or blacks worse than whites?" Parallel questions inquire about Hispanics as the comparison group.
- *Disparate treatment of neighborhoods*: The police typify different neighborhoods, which may lead to disparate patterns of behavior in different neighborhoods and indiscriminate treatment of residents based on police stereotypes of the community. We asked: "In general in the United States, do you think that police services in white neighborhoods are better, worse, or about the same as in black neighborhoods?" A parallel question asked for a comparison between white and Hispanic neighborhoods.
- *Police prejudice*: Respondents estimated how common racial or ethnic prejudice is among police officers in different contexts: throughout the United States, in their city, and in their neighborhood.
- *Racial profiling*: Several items addressed profiling: (1) Respondents were asked, "Since many drivers engage in minor traffic violations like speeding, it is sometimes hard to tell why some drivers get stopped by the police while others do not. Do you think that black drivers are more likely to be stopped by the police than white drivers for the same types of violations?" Parallel questions compared Hispanic and white drivers and Hispanic and black drivers. (2) Replicating an item from a 1999 Gallup poll, we asked respondents whether they approve or disapprove of profiling: "There have been reports that some police officers stop drivers from certain racial groups because they think members of these groups are more likely to commit crimes. This is known as 'racial profiling.' Do you approve or disapprove of the use of this practice?" (3) Respondents were then asked a follow-up question (not in the earlier Gallup poll) that tapped the firmness of their approval or disapproval of profiling. Those who disapprove of profiling were presented with a hypothetical condition: "Suppose that studies show that racial profiling helps to catch criminals. If this is true, would you still

disapprove of racial profiling?" Likewise, those who approve of profiling were asked: "Suppose that studies show that racial profiling
does not help to catch criminals. If this is true, would you still
approve of racial profiling?" (4) Finally, we asked people to esti-
mate the scope of profiling (widespread or not widespread) in different contexts: respondents' neighborhood, city, and the nation as
a whole.[2] All indices are coded such that high scores reflect greater
perceived bias.

PERCEPTIONS AND EXPERIENCES OF RACIALLY
BIASED POLICING

Do people believe that police in their city and neighborhood treat
individual whites and minorities differently? Most blacks and Hispanics
believe that police in their city treat blacks worse than whites; three-
quarters of blacks and just over half of Hispanics take this view. Roughly
the same percentages think that police treat Hispanics worse than
whites. Whites tend to take the opposite view: Three-quarters of whites,
for instance, believe that police in their city treat whites the same as
the two minority groups. Some whites are rather adamant about this
(as documented later in the chapter), and for others, equal treatment
is an article of faith:

> I would hope that society has progressed beyond racial prejudices
> and preferences, and that police in my community would treat all
> people based on what they say and do, without regard to their skin
> color. (MC white male, 35)

Whites' belief in police equanimity is related to the fact that most
whites simply do not witness discrimination toward minorities and is
also rooted in whites' deeper confidence in the criminal justice system,
per the group-position thesis. Some whites, however, are quite certain
that discrimination is a reality. An example is a man who grew up in

---

[2] Alphas for the four indices are .91, .88, .86, and .73, respectively. The racial profiling
index does not include the two hypothetical follow-up questions on approval of
profiling, because they were asked only of subsamples of respondents. Also excluded
from three of the indices (profiling, individual discrimination, neighborhood bias)
are the questions comparing blacks and Hispanics, because each index is a measure
of disparities between whites and minority groups.

an all-black neighborhood, where he was in a position to compare his experiences with those of black kids: "I grew up the only white kid in my neighborhood, and I was treated differently by the police. They would smile at me and scowl at my friends" (UMC white male, 25).

When asked to compare police treatment of blacks and Hispanics, most respondents conflate the two minorities and see them as receiving equal treatment at the hands of the police. It is important to remember, however, that this "equal treatment" means worse treatment in comparison to whites.

A second set of questions pertains to disparities in police service to neighborhoods populated by different racial groups. These items differ from the above question in that they tap differential police treatment of *neighborhoods.* This issue has rarely been explored in public opinion surveys, but one poll found that 74 percent of blacks and 41 percent of whites believed that police protection in black neighborhoods was worse than in white neighborhoods (Gallup 1993:34). In our research, the majority of whites think that police practices are roughly similar across neighborhoods, and only a third think that police services are worse in black neighborhoods than in white neighborhoods. By contrast, a majority of blacks (78 percent) and Hispanics (60 percent) believe that black communities receive inferior treatment, and almost identical percentages hold the same view about Hispanic neighborhoods. "Worse" treatment can range from the fairly benign (e.g., longer delays in responding to calls, lack of follow-up after a crime) to severe abuses of power. One of our black respondents focused on the latter:

> Black and white officers are more aggressive, use more force, and shoot more in black neighborhoods. These same officers are less aggressive, use less force, and shoot less in white neighborhoods. (MC black male, 38)

When asked whether police services differ between black and Hispanic neighborhoods, however, most people see little disparity. Three-quarters of Hispanics and more than four-fifths of whites and blacks see no differences in police treatment of the two minority communities. Interestingly, more blacks than Hispanics feel that police discriminate against Hispanic neighborhoods.

Police practices may reflect not only racial bias but also class bias. It is well known that government agencies are far more attuned and responsive to the interests and demands of the affluent than to working-class people, a fact that is engrained in American popular culture. It should come as no surprise, therefore, if many people perceive class bias in the criminal justice system, and a recent national poll found that three-quarters of Americans believed that the police "treat wealthy people better than the less well-off" (CSR 2000).

Our survey asked a question about class bias toward neighborhoods, in order to determine whether people are predisposed to accept or doubt the existence of *any* kind of police discrimination or whether they are convinced that one type of discrimination (class or race) is more prevalent. We asked: "In general in the United States, do you think that police services in low-income neighborhoods are better, worse, or about the same as in high-income neighborhoods?" Fully 77 percent of blacks, 63 percent of Hispanics, and 47 percent of whites believe that low-income neighborhoods received inferior police service. Blacks and Hispanics, in other words, are just as likely to perceive police class bias as racial bias against neighborhoods, whereas whites are significantly more likely to perceive class disparities. Many whites acknowledge that policing is not an impartial enterprise, but for them it is class, more than race, that drives unequal justice. In our qualitative data, some of our white respondents volunteered that they had been victims of class discrimination: "I have not been the victim of racial profiling but there is a definite 'economic profiling.' If you're poor you're not serviced or treated well by the police!" (LC white female, 49).

How common is racial prejudice among police officers? British criminologist Tony Jefferson (1988:522) concludes that, "All the major British and North American studies, from the early post-war period on, agree that negative, stereotypical, prejudiced, and hostile attitudes to blacks are rife amongst police officers." To call it "rife" is probably exaggerated; yet, the existence of police prejudice should not be surprising, since officers live in a society with a long history of racism and hold the same stereotypes about minorities that exist in the wider population.

It is possible to hold prejudiced attitudes yet not *act* on them – a "prejudiced nondiscriminator" in Robert Merton's terms. Hence, a person with racial animus does not necessarily treat people of other races unfavorably. We do not know how many police officers fit this profile and how many, by contrast, are "prejudiced discriminators," whose attitudes and behavior are both racially biased. A study of three cities found that, after controlling for situational factors, highly prejudiced officers were more likely than nonprejudiced officers to arrest black suspects (Friedrich 1979), but since these data were originally collected in the mid-1960s (Black and Reiss 1967) it is impossible to know if the findings still apply today.

Americans' perceptions of police prejudice have almost never been explored in public opinion surveys, but a 1995 national poll found that 54 percent of whites and 65 percent of blacks thought that "racist feelings" were common among police officers (*Washington Post* 1995). From our research, it is clear that many Americans believe that police prejudice is either very or fairly common in the United States. Indeed, a substantial number of minorities take the view that police prejudice is *very common* throughout the nation: 60 percent of blacks, 46 percent of Hispanics, and 20 percent of whites subscribe to this position. As for one's own city, almost half of blacks and a third of Hispanics say that police prejudice is very common there (compared to only 8 percent of whites), whereas more than a third of blacks and a quarter of Hispanics say the same for their own neighborhood (compared to 4 percent of whites). Many other respondents regard police prejudice as "somewhat common" in all three contexts, indicating that police prejudice is regarded as a problem by very many Americans.

When people think of police prejudice, most seem to have white officers in mind. As one interviewee put it, "A lot of white officers are prejudiced and corrupt by nature, whereas a black officer I would hope has more compassion for people of several races because of his or her history" (MC black female, 27). Some respondents, however, also thought that black and Hispanic officers were prejudiced in their own distinctive ways – an issue covered later in this chapter. And some whites used their own bad experiences with the police as a basis for the generalization that the police are *not* prejudiced:

> California police don't have prejudice toward anyone. My husband and I got beat up by the police right before the Rodney King incident. They didn't charge us with anything, and didn't have anything to charge us with. The San Diego cops beat us both pretty much senseless. (UMC white female, 48)

Turning to the issue of racial profiling in traffic stops – there is no doubt that it exists, but how widespread is it? A few studies report no race differences in stops, but do find that, when stopped, blacks are more likely than whites to be searched. Most other studies, some cited in Chapter 1, have found that blacks and Hispanics are stopped out of all proportion to their numbers in the local population, to the number of them driving in an area at the time of the study, or to the local crime rate. The reported racial disparities are sometimes so large as to constitute prima facie evidence of racial bias, suggesting that police use drivers' race as a proxy for criminal propensity. The seriousness of the problem is especially apparent when we take into account the poor success rates in finding contraband (guns, drugs, stolen merchandise, open container of alcohol) or other evidence of crime. Several studies have found that the "hit rates" for blacks and Hispanics are either similar to or lower than for whites (Harris 1999; Cordner, Williams, and Velasco 2002; Harris 2002). The findings from these observational studies are consistent with self-reports from two national surveys of people who had been stopped by police, which found that searches of whites yielded higher hit rates than searches of Hispanics or blacks (Bureau of Justice Statistics 2001, 2005). This suggests that if police want to increase their hit rates, they should stop more white motorists.

Do people consider racial profiling a problem? The answer is a resounding *yes*. There is substantial agreement across groups that profiling is wrong: 91 percent of blacks, 77 percent of Hispanics, and 73 percent of whites disapprove of the practice. Moreover, those who disapprove of profiling tend not to alter their positions when confronted with the hypothetical possibility that profiling "works." We asked disapprovers whether they would still disapprove of the practice if it could be shown "that racial profiling helps to catch criminals." Majorities of each group said they would still disapprove – 75 percent of blacks, 62 percent of Hispanics, and 57 percent of whites (see Figure 3.1).

Respondents who initially approved of profiling were asked an analogous hypothetical question – whether they would still approve of profiling if studies showed that it "does not help to catch criminals." The approvers were more likely to change their views than the disapprovers when confronted with this counterevidence: A minority

Figure 3.1. Opinions on racial profiling

Percent

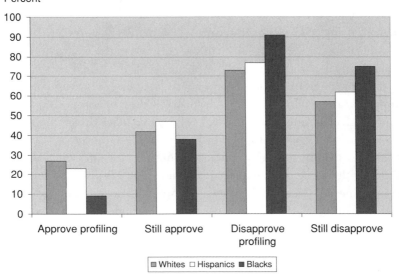

Note: Respondents who initially approved of profiling (the first set of bars) were asked whether they would still approve of profiling if studies showed that it "does not help catch criminals" (the second set of bars). The second set of bars, "Still Approve," is thus a subset of the first set. Similarly, respondents in the third set of bars, "Disapprove Profiling," were asked whether they would still disapprove if it could be shown "that racial profiling helps catch criminals." "Still Disapprove," the fourth set of bars, is thus a subset of the third set.

of each group would continue to approve of the practice (Figure 3.1), but a majority of black (62 percent), Hispanic (53 percent), and white (58 percent) approvers said they would no longer endorse profiling if it was shown to be ineffective in catching criminals. Approval of profiling thus appears to be softer than disapproval. Still, some people remain convinced that profiling does help police fight crime. This view is held by whites more than by minorities, but one affluent black woman told us: "It's irritating to be racially profiled, but the alternative is more rampant crime."

Not only do most Americans reject racial profiling in principle, but they also see it as pervasive. The overwhelming majority of blacks (92 percent) and Hispanics (83 percent) believe that profiling is widespread in the United States. Most blacks (8 out of 10) and Hispanics (6 out of 10) also believe that profiling is pervasive in their

own city, and a majority of blacks and near-majority of Hispanics also
see it as widespread in their own residential neighborhood. Whites
tend to compartmentalize profiling: It is seen as widespread outside
their own city (70 percent) but only half as many (35 percent) think it
is widespread in their city – in striking contrast to the vast majority of
blacks and Hispanics. That only 18 percent of whites see it as common
in their own neighborhood is probably because so many white neighborhoods are predominantly or exclusively white in composition.

Most African Americans (8 in 10) believe that black drivers are more
likely than whites to be stopped by police for the same kinds of traffic
violations; two-thirds of Hispanics, but only one-third of whites, agree.
Virtually the same percentages also believe that Hispanic drivers are
more vulnerable than white drivers. But, when asked to compare blacks
and Hispanics, fewer people perceive any disparity: One-fifth of whites,
43 percent of Hispanics, and 56 percent of blacks believe blacks are
more likely to be stopped than Hispanics, but the remainder believe
that both minority groups are at risk, particularly when the officer is
white. As a Hispanic respondent remarked,

> When a black or Hispanic officer stops a citizen, it is because he or
> she has violated some traffic law. When a white officer stops a black or
> Hispanic citizen, it is not because he or she has violated a traffic law –
> it is because of their race. If a black or Hispanic person is driving
> a fancy car, in the white officer's mind it is a stolen car. Blacks and
> Hispanics are not allowed to have good, fancy cars; we are treated
> like second-class citizens. (UMC Hispanic female, 49)

Is the white-minority perception gap mirrored by an experiential
gap? In one nationwide poll, four times more blacks than whites
(35 vs. 8 percent) said they had been treated unfairly by police specifically because of their race (Gallup 1995). Our research also found a
large gulf separating minorities and whites when it comes to their personal experiences. Many Hispanics and blacks, but almost no whites,
believe that they have been the victims of discrimination. Figure 3.2
shows the number of people who believe they have been "treated
unfairly by police specifically because of your race." Nearly 4 out of
10 blacks and a quarter of Hispanics say this has happened to them
in their own city, and a substantial minority (about one-quarter of
blacks and one-sixth of Hispanics) also say it has happened in their

Figure 3.2. Experiences of biased policing

Percent

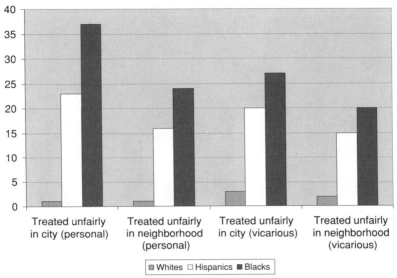

Treated unfairly | Treated unfairly | Treated unfairly | Treated unfairly
in city (personal) | in neighborhood (personal) | in city (vicarious) | in neighborhood (vicarious)

▨ Whites ▢ Hispanics ▮ Blacks

Note: Respondents were asked if they (personal) or someone else in their household (vicarious) have ever felt that they were "treated unfairly by the police specifically because of your/their race." Respondents' city and neighborhood are mutually exclusive categories.

neighborhood. A significant number of blacks and Hispanics have experienced this vicariously, through another member of their household (Figure 3.2). As discussed later in this chapter, many of those who felt that they had been discriminated against identified the culprit as a white officer. As one person told us, "White officers usually talk down to me, make demeaning comments, and act very bullish" (MC black female, 39).

The disparity is not only racial, however. Similar to our findings in Chapter 2 regarding misconduct, both age and gender also play key roles in shaping personal experiences of discrimination. When the sample is broken down into different age and gender categories, it becomes clear that racial discrimination by the police is something that acutely affects *young black and Hispanic males*, based on their self-reports. As Figure 3.3 shows, black and Hispanic men between the ages of 18 and 29 are much more likely than same-age white males to report that police have treated them unfairly because of their race,

Figure 3.3. Experiences of biased policing, young males

Percent

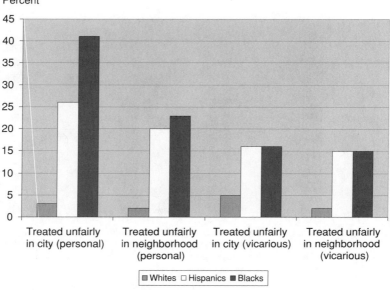

| | Treated unfairly in city (personal) | Treated unfairly in neighborhood (personal) | Treated unfairly in city (vicarious) | Treated unfairly in neighborhood (vicarious) |

■ Whites □ Hispanics ■ Blacks

Note: Young = ages 18–29. Respondents' city and neighborhood are mutually exclusive categories.

and about one-sixth of young black and Hispanic men say this has happened to someone else in their household. Similar numbers of blacks and Hispanics say they have experienced this injustice in three of the cases shown in Figure 3.3, but on one – personal experience of unfair treatment in one's city – young black males are at special risk. Young black men are also much more likely than young black women to say they have been victimized in this way: 41 versus 23 percent say this has happened to them in their city (data not shown in a figure).

With regard to racial profiling, a substantial number of African Americans (43 percent) and Hispanics (26 percent) say that they have been "stopped just because of" their race or ethnic background (Figure 3.4). A good number of Hispanics (24 percent) and blacks (35 percent) also say that this has happened to someone in their household. Although these figures are based on citizens' *perceptions* of reality, their magnitude does suggest that racially biased stops are not confined to a small fraction of the population (see also Amnesty International 2004). And, even if some of this treatment is not racially motivated,

Figure 3.4. Experiences of racial profiling

Percent

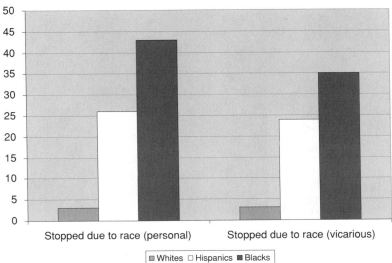

Stopped due to race (personal)   Stopped due to race (vicarious)

☐ Whites ☐ Hispanics ☐ Blacks

Note: Respondents were asked if they (personal) or someone else in their household (vicarious) ever felt that they were stopped by the police just because of their race or ethnic background. The stop may have occurred anywhere in the country, including the respondents' city and neighborhood.

individuals' perceptions of the situation remain consequential: They may lead to ill feelings or escalate into verbal or physical clashes with officers.

Age and gender also affect the odds of being racially profiled. Specifically, young black men appear to be especially vulnerable, compared to young white and Hispanic men (Figure 3.5). Half of young black men say they have been stopped solely because of their race, compared to a third of their Hispanic counterparts and only 3 percent of whites, and young black men are twice as likely to experience this as young black women (23 percent). Other research confirms our finding that young minority males are uniquely at risk of racial profiling. A 1999 Gallup survey, for instance, documented a similarly huge gulf between the experiences of young black men and women and between young black and white men (Weitzer and Tuch 2002).

Only 1–3 percent of whites say that they have ever been treated unfairly because of their race, and 3–5 percent report that they have

Figure 3.5. Experiences of racial profiling, young males

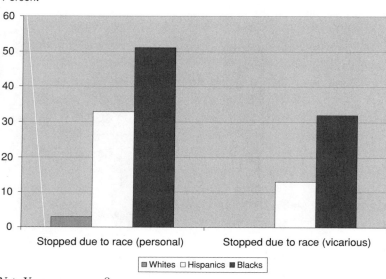

Note: Young = ages 18–29.

been racially profiled during a traffic stop. Why might some whites feel they have been profiled? One circumstance that may foster this belief is when a white motorist is stopped by a minority police officer. Another type of situation is one in which a white person appears to be "out of place" in a particular area, such as a minority neighborhood. Rubenstein's (1973:263) study of Philadelphia police officers noted, "When a patrolman sees a white person he does not know in a black neighborhood, he thinks the person is there to buy either drugs or sex." Some whites who testified at Amnesty International's (2004:2) recent hearings on racial profiling believed they had been stopped in minority neighborhoods because they were profiled as drug buyers.

In sum, race and ethnicity matter greatly in citizens' assessments and experiences of police racial bias. On almost every issue, blacks are much more inclined than whites to perceive racial disparities in policing, to disapprove of the disparities, and to say that they have personally experienced discriminatory treatment. Hispanics occupy an intermediate position between blacks and whites, on most issues. A racial hierarchy of group perceptions and experiences is evident.

EXPLAINING CITIZEN VIEWS OF RACIALIZED POLICING

Group differences in perceptions and experiences of racialized policing, documented above, are congruent with other research and
with the group-position thesis. Yet key questions remain: Do race
differences persist after taking account of other factors that might also
influence citizen attitudes and experiences in this area? What other
factors besides race shape views of police bias? And, central to the focus
of the book, do the factors that shape views of racially biased policing
differ for whites, African Americans, and Hispanics? To answer these
questions, we turn to our multivariate results.

The four models in Table 3.1 present findings for police treatment of
individuals and neighborhoods, police prejudice, and racial profiling
for the combined sample as well as for each racial group separately. In
every case, significant group differences exist in the race-only baseline
models and persist when other variables are taken into account. In
all models, blacks and Hispanics are more likely than whites to adopt
a critical view of the police and, consistent with the racial hierarchy
scenario, Hispanics' assessments are intermediate between the views
of whites, who are less negative, and blacks, who are more negative
(the black-Hispanic differences are statistically significant in all models
except police prejudice, where blacks and Hispanics are equally critical
of the police). The most consistent predictors in the full models are
neighborhood crime, media exposure, and personal experience with
discriminatory treatment by an officer.

We are especially interested in how the explanatory factors impact
views among each racial group. The race-specific columns in Table 3.1
provide the answer. Model 1 presents results for disparate treatment of *individual whites and minority group members.* The belief that
this kind of treatment is common increases among those blacks
and Hispanics who feel that crime is serious in their neighborhood;
it decreases among blacks who feel safe in their community during the day; personal experience with police discrimination substantially heightens perceptions of bias among blacks and Hispanics,
while vicarious experience does so among Hispanics; and exposure
to media accounts of police misconduct increases perceived police
bias among all three groups. The media and personal experience

TABLE 3.1. *Perceptions of police bias*

	Total sample		Whites		Blacks		Hispanics	
	b	beta	b	beta	b	beta	b	beta
Model 1. Bias against individuals								
Black	.680***	.237	—	—	—	—	—	—
	(.080)		—		—		—	
Hispanic	.439***	.157	—	—	—	—	—	—
	(.067)		—		—		—	
Neighborhood crime	.095**	.073	.010	.007	.148*	.126	.225***	.192
	(.033)		(.065)		(.061)		(.057)	
Safety (day)	-.063	-.037	-.131	-.063	-.261**	-.173	-.001	-.001
	(.052)		(.110)		(.092)		(.081)	
Safety (night)	-.021	-.016	-.076	-.052	.051	.042	.048	.045
	(.040)		(.079)		(.075)		(.071)	
Concentrated disadvantage	-.001	-.001	-.001	-.001	-.035	-.035	-.069	-.069
	(.028)		(.048)		(.048)		(.048)	
Personal experience with bias (1 = yes)	.431***	.154	-.078	-.017	.600***	.300	.656***	.308
	(.078)		(.230)		(.101)		(.101)	
Vicarious experience with bias (1 = yes)	.139	.046	.060	.012	.058	.028	.265**	.119
	(.080)		(.243)		(.097)		(.100)	
Community policing (1 = yes)	-.027	-.013	-.009	-.005	-.089	-.044	-.139	-.069
	(.044)		(.084)		(.091)		(.085)	
Media exposure	.261***	.188	.343***	.232	.149**	.117	.252***	.200
	(.031)		(.062)		(.056)		(.053)	
N of cases (unweighted)	1,458		526		440		492	
Constant	-1.050		-.357		-.631		-1.634	
R² (adjusted)	.285		.082		.187		.278	

TABLE 3.1. *Perceptions of police bias (continued)*

	Total sample		Whites		Blacks		Hispanics	
	b	beta	b	beta	b	beta	b	beta
Model 2. *Bias against neighborhoods*								
Black	.558*** (.085)	.195	—	—	—	—	—	—
Hispanic	.356*** (.072)	.127	—	—	—	—	—	—
Neighborhood crime	-.085* (.036)	-.065	-.209*** (.065)	-.150	.091 (.060)	.078	.113 (.062)	.096
Safety (day)	-.002 (.055)	-.001	-.175 (.111)	-.084	.249** (.090)	.165	.256** (.089)	.196
Safety (night)	-.072 (.042)	-.056	-.069 (.079)	-.048	-.209** (.073)	-.174	-.070 (.078)	-.065
Concentrated disadvantage	.023 (.030)	.023	.035 (.048)	.035	-.039 (.047)	-.039	.060 (.053)	.060
Personal experience with bias (1 = yes)	.279*** (.083)	.100	.053 (.230)	.011	.355*** (.098)	.177	.401*** (.111)	.188
Vicarious experience with bias (1 = yes)	.054 (.085)	.018	.252 (.244)	.051	-.083 (.095)	-.041	.087 (.110)	.039
Community policing (1 = yes)	-.044 (.047)	-.022	-.079 (.084)	-.039	.052 (.089)	.026	-.144 (.093)	-.072
Media exposure	.280*** (.033)	.202	.301*** (.062)	.204	.419*** (.054)	.330	.231*** (.058)	.183
N of cases (unweighted)	1,458		526		440		492	
Constant	-.645		.375		-2.296		-1.472	
R² (adjusted)	.182		.072		.227		.130	

(*continued*)

TABLE 3.1 *Perceptions of police bias (continued)*

	Total sample		Whites		Blacks		Hispanics	
	b	beta	b	beta	b	beta	b	beta
Model 3. Police prejudice								
Black	.304***	.106	—	—	—	—	—	—
	(.074)		—		—		—	
Hispanic	.193**	.069	—	—	—	—	—	—
	(.063)		—		—		—	
Neighborhood crime	.097**	.074	.045	.032	.071	.061	.228***	.195
	(.031)		(.059)		(.055)		(.054)	
Safety (day)	.042	.024	.012	.006	.150	.100	.062	.048
	(.048)		(.101)		(.083)		(.077)	
Safety (night)	−.044	−.034	−.033	−.023	−.144*	−.120	.043	.040
	(.037)		(.072)		(.068)		(.067)	
Concentrated disadvantage	.083**	.083	.145***	.145	.073	.073	−.099*	−.099
	(.026)		(.043)		(.044)		(.045)	
Personal experience with bias (1 = yes)	.651***	.233	.914***	.194	.656***	.328	.756***	.355
	(.072)		(.209)		(.091)		(.096)	
Vicarious experience with bias (1 = yes)	.319***	.107	.451*	.091	.169*	.083	.348***	.156
	(.074)		(.222)		(.088)		(.095)	
Community policing (1 = yes)	.054	−.027	−.050	−.025	−.097	−.048	−.115	−.057
	(.041)		(.077)		(.082)		(.080)	
Media exposure	.353***	.254	.395***	.267	.362***	.286	.296***	.234
	(.029)		(.056)		(.050)		(.050)	
N of cases (unweighted)	1,458		526		440		492	
Constant	−1.153		−.762		−2.294		−1.982	
R² (adjusted)	.383		.237		.336		.350	

TABLE 3.1 *Perceptions of police bias (continued)*

	Total sample		Whites		Blacks		Hispanics	
	b	beta	b	beta	b	beta	b	beta
Model 4. Racial profiling								
Black	.612***	.213	—	—	—	—	—	—
	(.078)							
Hispanic	.334***	.120	—	—	—	—	—	—
	(.066)							
Neighborhood crime	.137***	.105	.104	.074	−.014	−.012	.326***	.278
	(.033)		(.063)		(.061)		(.056)	
Safety (day)	−.037	−.021	−.144	−.069	.023	.015	.114	.087
	(.051)		(.108)		(.092)		(.080)	
Safety (night)	.035	.027	.068	.047	−.118	−.098	.067	.062
	(.039)		(.077)		(.075)		(.070)	
Concentrated disadvantage	.050	.050	.069	.069	.118*	.118	−.050	−.050
	(.028)		(.047)		(.048)		(.047)	
Personal experience with bias (1 = yes)	.413***	.148	.210	.045	.509***	.254	.681***	.319
	(.076)		(.225)		(.101)		(.100)	
Vicarious experience with bias (1 = yes)	.251***	.084	.544*	.109	.243**	.119	.308**	.138
	(.078)		(.238)		(.097)		(.099)	
Community policing (1 = yes)	−.012	−.006	.005	.002	−.045	−.023	.014	.007
	(.043)		(.082)		(.091)		(.084)	
Media exposure	.237***	.171	.278***	.189	.210***	.166	.190***	.151
	(.030)		(.060)		(.056)		(.052)	
N of cases (unweighted)	1,458		526		440		492	
Constant	−.950		−.267		−.984		−2.361	
R² (adjusted)	.317		.118		.185		.293	

Note: Standard errors in parentheses; estimates are net of controls for education, household income, gender, age, city-suburban residence, and region; *p < .05; **p < .01; ***p < .001.

effects are among the strongest in the model, as indicated by the standardized coefficients associated with these two variables. Overall, blacks' and Hispanics' neighborhood crime situation, personal experience with discriminatory policing, and exposure to media accounts of police misconduct are key explanations of beliefs about disparate treatment of minority individuals; for whites, by contrast, only media exposure is important.

Model 2 reports findings on disparate police treatment of white and minority *neighborhoods*. As above, exposure to media reports of police misconduct strongly amplifies beliefs among each racial group that police treat neighborhoods differently, while personal experience with police discrimination inflates blacks' and Hispanics' perceptions of unequal treatment across neighborhoods. For whites, neighborhood crime decreases and media exposure increases these views. The remaining variables generally have weak or inconsistent effects on opinions regarding police practices in neighborhoods populated by different racial groups.

The third model in Table 3.1 explores views regarding *police prejudice*. Media exposure and personal and vicarious experience of police discrimination are the most consistent predictors, increasing the belief among whites, blacks, and Hispanics alike that police officers are racially prejudiced. Feeling unsafe in one's neighborhood at night increases blacks' perceptions of police racial prejudice and living in a neighborhood with a serious crime problem does so for Hispanics. For whites, living in areas of concentrated disadvantage heightens the belief that prejudice among officers is common, but for Hispanics residence in such areas decreases these beliefs.

Regarding *racial profiling* (model 4), residence in areas of concentrated disadvantage increases blacks' perception that profiling is prevalent; neighborhood crime does so for Hispanics; and media exposure and personal and vicarious experience with police bias *strongly* amplify the perception that racial profiling is both widespread and unacceptable among all groups (with the exception of personal experience among whites). For whites, again, few of the predictors are important determinants of attitudes toward profiling.

An important question is whether racialized policing has implications for general confidence in the police. Chapter 2 identified variables that shape global satisfaction with the police, and here we consider whether these general views are also affected by attitudes or experiences regarding the specific issue of racially biased policing. Using as independent variables the full set of predictors in Table 3.1 in addition to perceptions of the four types of racial bias, our analyses (not shown in a table) indicate that: (1) among whites, attitudes regarding police racial bias do not affect overall satisfaction with the police; (2) among blacks, those who believe that police officers are racially prejudiced have less overall satisfaction with the police; and (3) among Hispanics, overall satisfaction is reduced among those who believe that police are biased against minority neighborhoods and those who believe that police officers are racially prejudiced. Thus, among minority group members, but not among whites, one or another type of police bias does influence global opinion of the police.[3]

To summarize our findings: Overall, fewer of the explanatory factors shape whites' perceptions of racially biased policing than is true for blacks and Hispanics, but *the two most consequential factors for all three groups are mass media reporting and personal experience with discriminatory treatment.*

IS OFFICERS' RACE IMPORTANT?

Another vantage point from which to understand policing is in terms of the racial or ethnic background of officers rather than citizens. The racial and ethnic composition of police forces has been a contentious issue in many multiracial and multiethnic societies, such as South Africa, Israel, and Northern Ireland (Enloe 1980; Weitzer 1985, 1990, 1995). It is also an issue in Europe, where the Council of Europe takes the position that a model police force is one that is representative:

> The composition of police forces should normally be representative of the community it serves. This diversification of recruitment will establish a more trusting climate between the police and the different population groups. In addition, it will give the police in general a more accurate, more respectful, and more sensitive vision of the various ethnic and racial groups. (quoted in Zauberman and Levy 2003:1077)

---

3 The direction of causality could be the opposite – that is, the general assessment might be prior to the specific perception of bias – but our presumed causal ordering is equally plausible and consistent with other studies.

   In America, the racial complexion of police forces and the presence
of white officers in minority neighborhoods have long been sources
of friction. In the 1960s, police were lambasted as agents of white
supremacy, an "occupation force" in black neighborhoods deployed
to control and oppress residents (Levy 1968; Sherman 1983). Both the
President's Commission on Law Enforcement (1967) and the Kerner
Commission on Civil Disorders (1968) advocated diversification on
the grounds that black officers would help to defuse tensions with
residents, promote more impartial law enforcement, and enhance
the image of the police in minority communities. Since the 1960s,
some police departments have become much more diverse, while others have made less progress and remain subject to the same criticisms leveled decades ago. For example, a Boston community leader,
Reverend Eugene Rivers, recently complained about the underrepresentation of African Americans in the Boston Police Department: "The
time has come in the City of Boston for a real conversation regarding
race and diversity throughout the entire BPD. It is not good policing
to have the racial composition of the police force appearing as though
they are an alien occupying force in the black community" (quoted in
Smalley 2005).
   Today, diversity is an article of faith in government and law enforcement circles. It is the official position of the Justice Department and
other leading organizations like the Police Foundation and the Police
Executive Research Forum that racial and ethnic diversification – ide-
ally, proportional representation in each jurisdiction – fosters more
respectful and cooperative police-citizen interactions and pays symbolic dividends in building minority confidence in the police. As the
U.S. Department of Justice (2001) proclaims, "A diverse law enforcement agency can better develop relationships with the community it
serves, promote trust in the fairness of law enforcement, and facilitate
effective policing by encouraging citizen support and cooperation.
Law enforcement agencies should seek to hire a diverse workforce."
   Racial and ethnic diversification is seen, in short, as enhancing both
equal justice for citizens and legitimation of the police. Although both
are certainly plausible consequences of diversification, whether diversity actually produces these positive outcomes is a largely untested
claim. Do citizens really care about the racial composition of police

Figure 3.6. Perception that officers' race affects their behavior

Percent

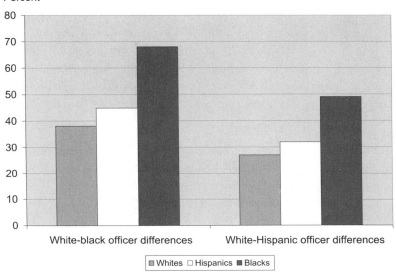

White-black officer differences	White-Hispanic officer differences

▨ Whites ☐ Hispanics ▪ Blacks

Note: The question asks whether there are differences in the ways in which officers act toward citizens.

departments or about the race of officers working in their community, as the conventional wisdom holds? Do they believe that white and minority officers act differently toward civilians? A couple of studies address this issue. A 1981 Milwaukee poll found black residents divided on the question of whether black officers treat blacks more fairly than white officers: 32 percent agreed and 38 percent disagreed (Dresner et al. 1981), and a more recent study found black residents of Washington, DC, to be similarly split on this issue (Weitzer 2000b). But most studies never bother to investigate citizens' experiences with and views of officers of different races. Instead, police are treated as a monolithic group.

We asked respondents whether they thought there were differences between different-race officers in the way they "act toward citizens." Figure 3.6 shows that there is a clear white–Hispanic–African American hierarchy in perceived behavioral differences between white and minority officers. Of the three groups, blacks are most inclined to believe that white and black officers (68 percent) and white and

Hispanic officers (49 percent) differ in their actions toward citizens.
Fewer Hispanics and whites take this view.

   To say that there are differences between white and minority officers
begs the question of what the differences consist of, and whether they
are innocuous or invidious. Respondents who perceived differences
were asked a follow-up question, "What are the differences?"[4] This
question yielded narrative responses from 189 whites, 223 Hispanics,
and 321 African Americans; responses clustered around two dominant
themes:

- A contrasting depiction of white and black officers. Respondents
  in all three groups (though blacks more so) characterized white
  cops as tough/arrogant/insensitive and black cops as courte-
  ous/respectful/ understanding. Hispanic officers were viewed more
  positively than negatively, with attributes similar to those of black
  officers.
- References to both racism and racial solidarity were used to account
  for behavioral differences between white and minority officers.
  Among all three groups, but especially among blacks, white officers
  were indicted for holding racist beliefs or engaging in discriminatory
  practices. Several respondents saw police racism as part and parcel
  of the larger racial order in American society. Hispanic and black
  officers were generally not seen as racist or as racially motivated in
  their treatment of citizens.

White, Black, and Hispanic Officers: Similarities and Differences
Nicholas Alex's classic study of black officers in New York distinguished
between "professionals," who treat black and white civilians similarly,
and "hardliners," who act harshly toward minority citizens in order to
assert authority or compel respect (Alex 1969:154–160). If black officers differ in their interactional styles along a professional-hardliner
continuum, then it is possible that citizens will have varying experiences with such officers as well as diverse opinions of them. By contrast,

---

[4] Some respondents chose to compare the behavior of white and black officers, others
   chose to focus on the behavior of just one race of officer, and some, contrary to the
   intent of the question, focused on the treatment of civilians without commenting
   on the race of officers, or spoke of what they saw as influencing police behavior in
   general. We make use of all three types of responses.

it is equally possible for citizens to view officers more monolithically. Such perceptions would be consistent with studies that find that black and white officers behave similarly at work (Riksheim and Chermak 1993; National Research Council 2004). This is the *blue cops* position – the idea that the color of the uniform is the only color that matters, not one's skin color.

Of course, the behavior of blue cops of different races can be similarly good or similarly bad. Several respondents who see no difference between officers of different races are convinced that black officers have been tainted by their occupational association with white officers. They "have to prove something to their white colleagues" (LC black female, 60) and "are always showing off for the white police" (LC black male, 31):

> A lot of black cops want to fit in the police department, and they act differently when they get on the police force. (LC black female, 31)

> Minority officers in the presence of these [white] officers are not empowered to do the right thing, but are encouraged to play along if they want to survive. (MC black male, 39)

And some based their views on personal experiences:

> I am a young black woman, and I have honestly had better experiences with cops that were of a different race than I have had with cops of the same race. (MC black female, 25)

Several Hispanics also took the blue cops position:

> I don't think police officers are prejudiced against different races anymore. Officers treat their own race just as bad at times. Officers can be dicks no matter what. I believe it's in their nature. (MC Hispanic female, 25)

> Most white and the majority of black [officers] act like Gestapo. They need training on how to talk to people. (MC Hispanic male, 67)

Others took the view that minority citizens were discriminated against by *all types of officers*. Regardless of officers' race, "Minorities are treated like second-class citizens, while whites are treated as royalty" (UMC black male, 38). When it comes to treatment of minorities, this segment of the population regards all cops as blue and abusive.

However, among those who answered this open-ended question, two-thirds of blacks and about half of Hispanics do see important differences between black and white officers – depicting black officers as empathetic, attentive, fair, tolerant, sensitive, friendly, and respectful. In stark contrast to these positive attributes, white officers were seen quite negatively by many minority citizens. Their demeanor toward citizens was portrayed as "aggressive," "hostile," "tough," "pushy," and "mean." The following statements elaborate on these differences:

> White officers seem to want to be in charge and just give orders. Black officers seem to use common sense and talk to people to see what the problem is before yelling or just throwing you down and asking questions later. (LC black male, 18)

> White male officers are more apt to use deadly force against citizens than black officers, more apt to use excessive force, period, and are more apt to use ugly language toward citizens. (LC black woman, 68)

> Black police don't shoot people, nowhere as much as white officers do, and most of the [victims] are black men.... That is what caused the race riots here in Cincinnati a couple of years ago. (LC black male, 57)

According to our interviewees, one thing that makes black officers more sensitive to citizens is their own experience as members of an oppressed minority group in America:

> Black officers are more empathetic and sympathetic towards citizens. Black officers are taught, by virtue of their racial background, not to have bias or prejudice, whereas their white counterparts are not. Black officers are taught...not to lump everyone into one category.... White officers are taught that certain people *always* behave a certain way. (MC black male, 33)

People from all three racial groups argued that each type of officer is more comfortable around, can better relate to and communicate with, and understands the culture of same-race civilians. Many stated this categorically, as a natural condition requiring no further explanation, whereas others pointed to in-group acculturation and racial bonding as well as tenuous or unfavorable relations with out-groups – just what group-position theory would predict. In sociological terms, there is more *social distance* between different-race officers and citizens than when both share the same racial background. Minority respondents declared that "whites do not understand blacks and do not care to," whereas minority officers were praised for "listening," "understanding," and treating minority civilians with respect and fairness. Whites echoed these sentiments, "Black officers are more sympathetic toward their own; ditto with whites" (MC white male, 26), and "every race develops a rapport with their own kind. It's simply natural for that to happen" (MC white male, 65).

Studies have found that black officers do indeed have a better understanding of black civilians than do white officers (Decker and Smith 1980), though most research finds that this does not necessarily translate into more sensitive behavior (National Research Council 2004). One exception – lending support to the views of respondents cited in the previous paragraph – is a study of Indianapolis and St. Petersburg, which found that black officers working in black neighborhoods were more inclined than white officers to engage in activities supportive of residents, such as offering information, providing assistance, comforting victims, making referrals to other agencies, and behaving respectfully (Sun and Payne 2004). At the same time, black officers were also more likely to use physical force against citizens in conflict situations. But, again, most other research finds that white and minority officers tend to behave similarly.

Personal experience also shapes opinions:

> From my experience, white officers are usually more arrogant and less polite than black officers. They tend to feel that the badge gives them more power and authority than what is mandated by law. (MC black male, 36)

> I've only been stopped by white officers. On one occasion, a white officer tried to plant a .38 revolver in my car. On another occasion, a white officer tried to search my car for narcotics for no apparent reason. (LC Hispanic male, 29)

> White officers stop black people in my mother's neighborhood for no reason. I got a new truck a year ago. I went to my mom's house to visit. Two white police officers stopped me and asked where I was going. I ask the police why he stopped me. The officer said my truck

[a Highlander] was a high-theft truck. I told the officer that is bullshit.
He did not ask for a license or anything. The officers then let me go
without saying why I was stopped. (MC black female, 36)

Vicarious experience also plays a role:

A white officer normally acts superior to minorities. This comes from
observation [of my] extended family and friends. A minority officer
will normally be more open, friendly. (MC Hispanic female, 39)

My husband grew up in St. Louis and he talks about how he and his
friends were always stopped by white policemen just because [of his
race]. I'm sure this continues to happen across the U.S. (MC black
female, 32)

Such experiences can have a ripple effect on those who are told
about it:

To be stopped by officers for no reason and prejudged can cause ill
feelings from good citizens, leaving them no choice but to bad mouth
officers because of this unfair treatment. (MC black female, 47)

People who have heard such "bad mouthing" and are sympathetic
to the victim may have a vicarious experience of being unjustly
stopped.

The mass media is another source of these beliefs. Some people
made reference to videotapes of police beatings shown on the news,
while others cited specific TV programs:

You notice the difference if you watch the show *COPS*. White officers
seem to get very upset with the criminals if they run or resist. Black
officers seem to have more patience, and it takes more to make them
upset towards the criminals. (MC black female, 35)

You don't see many black officers beating on minorities as you see
white officers doing. That's not an opinion; it's a fact that has been
documented in videos on the news. (MC black female, 35)

Several white respondents also mentioned the media as a basis for
their judgments about white cops' mistreatment of blacks:

I think of people like [LAPD officer] Mark Fuhrman, the Rodney
King brutalizers, the white officers who shoot blacks, and the Louima
case in New York. In neighboring Hartford and other places in

Connecticut, we have had cases of white officers shooting blacks, not the other way around. (UMC white female, 76)

You see on television [white cops] beating up on criminals. Probably they deserve it, but it makes one sick to watch them beating on them. We are not there to see what happened to make them do that . . . but they are law officers, so they should try to hold their tempers. (LC white female, 83)

Even if the citizen deserves to be roughed up, this elderly white woman was disturbed by what she saw on television.

Still, whites generally are not inclined to criticize white officers. A few thought that white cops are sometimes reluctant to act against minority civilians for fear of being accused of racism: "White officers are afraid to do anything against a minority for fear of repercussions, whereas other officers don't have that limitation" (MC white male, 64). But some whites do describe white officers as rude, condescending, arrogant, and aggressive, and black officers as polite, courteous, and respectful:

Black officers show more respect toward people than white officers do. They are friendlier and have better manners. They don't intimidate until they feel a need to, rather than right from the beginning like white officers do. (UMC white male, 41)

Black and Hispanic police are kinder and more understanding and compassionate than whites. Many white police officers are bullies. I've personally known three white officers in my life and they had bullying personalities. (UMC white female, 60)

Many Hispanics adopted the same binary model and used the same categorical terms to describe white and minority officers. White cops were depicted as arrogant, aggressive, rude, ruthless, and racist, whereas minority officers are more sensitive. A number of Hispanic respondents believe that, because of their shared experiences as members of a minority group, both black and Hispanic officers are more inclined to understand, listen to, and be tolerant of minority civilians: "My observation is that officers of color are more empathetic to all citizens" (UMC Hispanic male, 46). Another stated, "Hispanic officers belong to a minority group, so they will behave accordingly,

being very careful to treat people fairly" (MC Hispanic male, 41).
Furthermore,

> Black officers can relate to the trials and tribulations of inner-city
> youth because many of them come from the same neighborhoods,
> went to the same schools, and face the same type of prejudice that
> the citizens they serve do. (MC Hispanic male, 45)

A few Hispanics inverted the white-black paradigm, characterizing black officers negatively and white officers positively. They criticized black cops for being "harder on people" and acting as though
they had "something to prove." One Hispanic woman stated that
white officers were "more gentle and have a better knowledge of the
job." A few black respondents made similar comments, but, unlike
whites and Hispanics, they offered reasons that included the pressures minority officers face working within a white-dominated police
department.

Although some Hispanics grouped black and Hispanic cops
together, others viewed Hispanic officers as distinctive and rated them
much more positively than did blacks and whites. Hispanic officers
were depicted as more impartial than white officers in dealing with people of other races, and as "friendlier," "nicer," "humane," and "empathetic" toward citizens. As one person stated, "White officers treat most
minorities like crap. Latino cops treat you with respect" (LC Hispanic
woman, 42).

> Hispanic officers are friendlier toward Hispanics. . . . This does not
> mean Hispanic officers are lenient. Personally, I am less afraid if an
> Hispanic officer stops me on the road. (UMC Hispanic female, 54)

Such upbeat views about Hispanic officers are not universally held,
however. A black woman put it this way:

> Hispanic officers are more likely to show a superior attitude. Although
> most officers act that way and understandably so, the Hispanic officers
> show more of that attitude, especially in a black neighborhood. (MC
> black female, 67)

Some Hispanic respondents also accused Hispanic cops of being
"harder on their own," engaging in "profiling their own race," being
"overly aggressive" toward blacks, and needing to "prove something"

to fellow officers, which makes them "more aggressive." One man reasoned that, "because they now have a badge, they forget where they came from."

Although not frequently mentioned, people in all three groups raised the issue of a language barrier between Spanish-speaking people and officers who do not speak Spanish. According to our respondents, Spanish-English differences created "misunderstandings," "frustration," and "barriers" to communication. One woman spoke from personal experience: "With Hispanic officers we find that, since we speak Spanish, they are always polite and accommodating" (MC Hispanic female, 77).

Some people think cops discriminate not only against racial and ethnic minorities but also against lower-class people. For some, social class trumps race:

> Unless they are dealing with a citizen who is educated, they come down on the individual like they are worthless. If they sense that the individual is educated and knows their rights, then they are treated with the utmost respect. This is not right. (MC Hispanic female, 57)

Others pointed to the intersection of race and class:

> A white officer acts more powerful against a black or Hispanic citizen, especially if the citizen is economically poor or deprived. Unfortunately, this happens too often here in the lower Rio Grande area. A poor, uneducated Hispanic will be stopped more often than a poor, uneducated white person. The white race wants to be superior over any other race! (LMC Hispanic female, 78)

One way of summarizing the accounts presented above is to highlight the kinds of explanations people offered for both similarities and differences between officers of different backgrounds. Similarities were explained by occupational pressures and peer socialization, where job demands and police subculture outweigh officers' racial identities. For these reasons, cops are blue – not black, white, or brown. By contrast, officer differences were accounted for both in terms of the racial bonding argument (i.e., better relations between same-race officers and citizens) and the group-position argument (predicting tensions between different-race officers and citizens).

Three additional explanations were offered to account for behavioral differences between officers: police racism toward minorities, "rational discrimination" by those officers who tend to presume that minorities are crime-prone, and characteristics of neighborhoods populated by different racial groups.

Police Racism. Nearly a third of black respondents who responded to this question believed that racism explains differences in the conduct of white and black cops. Most focused on the racial animus of white officers, and others cited institutionalized racism throughout the criminal justice system or American society. Among these respondents, almost half emphasized white cops' disposition to presume black criminality and to engage in racial profiling, and over a third described other discriminatory behaviors or simply asserted that white police acted on the basis of racism, prejudice, and stereotypes. Some explained mistreatment by white officers by mentioning white supremacy, such as "looking down at poor blacks" and "still thinking of blacks as slaves," whereas others related this to the larger racial hierarchy in America: "White officers are more likely to use racial profiling because they are members of the dominant group and are acting out racist beliefs" (MC black female, 26).

A sizeable number of black respondents made reference to *institutional racism* affecting both white *and* black officers:

> Black police can only harass their own people. That's the way the system is. Black police are victims of a racist society. (LC black female, 44)

> Some commanding officers place more importance on the arrest of blacks (versus whites) and that's one reason why the jails are filled with more blacks than whites. (MC black male, 35)

> White officers treat blacks bad and black officers treat blacks bad. There is no justice for the poor black man. (MC black woman, 40)

One important aspect of institutionalized racism, and a central tenet of conflict theory, is officials' greater accountability to white than to minority citizens. Whereas whites have clout when it comes to the police, black powerlessness is the norm:

> Both white and black officers are probably more courteous to white citizens. The reasons are fairly obvious for white officers and white

citizens, but I think that black officers would fear more repercussions from white citizens than black citizens who voice complaints. Blacks usually feel they have no recourse when it comes to authority. Blacks feel that white complaints will be heard, not theirs. (MC black woman, 31)

African Americans are not alone in seeing racism as the main reason why white and black cops differ. Although blacks mention racism more frequently, several whites and Hispanics also labeled white officers as bigoted, racist, and prone to profiling; they were convinced that racial prejudice "still prevails," is "very much alive," or is "everywhere." For several white respondents, racism is a fact of life that inevitably affects policing: "There is going to be some racism in any situation," or, as another person put it, "We will never become a nation of equals. There will always be prejudice." In the minds of many people, racialized policing is a tough nut to crack because it is embedded in a larger system of racial inequality in American society.

A number of whites thought that racism was not, however, the monopoly of white cops alone. "Reverse discrimination" or "reverse racism" also exist. These whites claim that black cops mistreat whites because, as officers, they have the power to do so. A few whites who described discriminatory behavior on the part of black cops suggested that the motive was "payback" for historical mistreatment of blacks:

Black and Hispanic officers feel they have to get even with whites, and white officers think all blacks and Hispanics are criminals. (LC white female, 33)

Black officers are unfairly unbiased towards black offenders, and seem to think of harassing whites as payback. (UMC white female, 43)

"Unfairly unbiased" probably does not mean that officers should be biased but instead that black officers treat black offenders leniently. One white woman living in a mostly black neighborhood had this to say:

Racial profiling can be just as prevalent by black officers toward white people and Hispanics as the other way around, and I do know something about that in this area [a community that is 90 percent black]. (LMC white female, 65)

Black respondents did not make the reverse discrimination argument, but several Hispanics argued that *both* white and black officers are inclined to favor civilians of their own race, and mistreat different-race civilians – for payback or other motives. Some Hispanics, therefore, see the race-of-cop issue similarly to the way many whites view it, in terms of group solidarity and intergroup conflict. Interestingly, Hispanic officers were seldom accused of reverse discrimination or any other kind of racism. As one man stated, "I never met a racist Hispanic officer" (UMC black male, 63).

Presumption of Criminality. Minority respondents complained that police, and white officers in particular, view individual blacks and Hispanics with suspicion, if not a presumption of wrongdoing. Black respondents, for instance, stated that "white officers assume that you are engaging in a criminal activity" or are "prone to crime," or "they feel most black people steal and don't work, so they treat most black people alike." This contrasts sharply with the presumption of innocence afforded white folk:

> Blacks are guilty until proven innocent, while whites are innocent until proven guilty. (MC black male, 38)

Some argued that the presumption of criminality applied not only to blacks but also to other minority groups:

> Most white officers look at all minorities as a crime waiting to occur. (MC Hispanic male, 40)

> White officers often anticipate that people of other races will be confrontational and that they have something to hide or were doing something illegal. For instance, the racial profiling issue. (MC black female, 48)

> White officers treat blacks and Hispanics differently because most crimes and gangs [involve these] people, and the police are used to this. They treat all blacks and Hispanics they pull over as a potential gang member in cities where there is heavy gang violence just because gangs are mostly made up of people of these races. (UMC Hispanic male, 48)

Some whites see police treatment of racial groups in a different light altogether. In line with the group-position thesis, these whites think that officers who pay special attention to minorities are engaged in

rational discrimination. If minorities are indeed committing a disproportionate number of street crimes, it only makes sense for the police
to target them:

> It may be a fact in a certain city that the majority of the crimes are
> being committed by a particular race. If this is true, that race may be
> looked at more closely [by police]. . . . I don't think that is necessarily
> racial profiling; they are not looking at a white person because in
> that city they aren't typically committing as many crimes. (MC white
> female, 39)

This respondent also noted that it would be equally rational to target
whites if the police were looking for a serial killer, since most serial
killers are white. The respondent seems unaware of the fact that serial
murder is an extremely rare event, that whites as a group are not
targeted in these investigations, and therefore that the pursuit of a
serial killer is hardly equivalent to routine, institutionalized discrimination against minorities.

Neighborhood Context. Another explanation for behavioral differences
among officers centers on the neighborhoods in which they work.
More whites than blacks or Hispanics invoked neighborhood-type
explanations, and there is a subtle difference, by race, in these narratives. Drawing again on the idea of rational discrimination, many
whites linked policing to the amount of street crime in a community, with high-crime translating into a need for aggressive policing
in those areas. Although some respondents thought that neighborhood context influenced the behavior of all officers, most singled out
white officers as being especially prone to treat residents of minority
neighborhoods harshly. The imputed tendency of white officers to typify neighborhoods thus helps explain behavioral differences between
white and minority officers:

> It depends on the area. The tougher the neighborhood and higher
> crime, the tougher attitude the police would have to have. It's not a
> bad thing to adapt to the particular area. (MC white female, 44)

> It depends upon the neighborhood these officers are in. In the
> higher-crime areas, the officers have to act/react differently than a
> lower-crime area. I believe in a low-crime area, the citizens are treated
> with more respect. (UMC white female, 48)

In cities with large areas of poor minorities, officers become callous and treat people unjustly because of the high crime in that area. (MC white female, 68)

A few respondents blamed the residents of such communities, who are seen as uncooperative or even hostile to authority figures:

Newspapers report abuse by white officers against minorities in areas such as Los Angeles and Miami, but I tend to think those are isolated cases. It must be frustrating to deal with neighborhoods where citizens close ranks against law officers instead of regarding them as helpers seeking to maintain order. (MC Hispanic female, 74)

Unlike whites, blacks did not necessarily see differential policing as a logical response to neighborhood differences but instead as more unwarranted and invidious:

White officers seem to fear black neighborhoods. They seem to assume that all black neighborhoods have high crime. Black officers are a little more relaxed when they enter a black neighborhood. (MC black female, 38)

When white cops encounter blacks in ritzy areas, they radio for backup and stop them and question and search – acting like they are out of place. In black neighborhoods they feel they can lord it over anyone. Black officers try to talk to those they stop with respect, but are mindful of physical altercations. (MC black female, 64)

It depends on the neighborhoods as to how cops act. In this town, there is one housing development that has a bad reputation – when officers go into that neighborhood they act differently than when they go into other neighborhoods. All people living in that neighborhood are not bad, but good citizens. It's just that they live where they can afford to. (MC black female, 56)

The subtext here is that officers must avoid stereotyping all residents of troubled areas – what is known in the literature as "ecological contamination":

White officers in minority neighborhoods feel like they're there to pacify the area, and not there to protect the citizens. This is too bad because if they noticed the good citizens as well as the bad, they could make good allies. (LC Hispanic male, 29)

White officers treat economically depressed areas like the "wild, wild West." They fail to view the residents as people and rather [see them]

Figure 3.7. Preferred type of officers in neighborhood

Percent

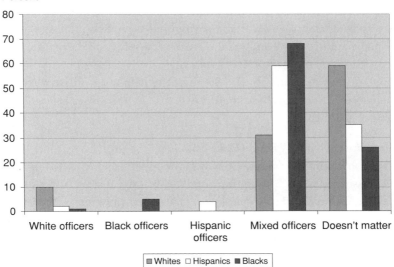

Note: The question asks: "If you had a choice, would you prefer to have mostly white officers assigned to your neighborhood, mostly black officers, mostly Hispanic officers, a mix of officers of different races, or doesn't it matter?"

as obstacles. Black and Hispanic officers, who often live in the same neighborhoods that they police, will treat the residents as people and neighbors, not as accessories to the perpetrators they may be pursuing. (UMC Hispanic male, 37)

Should Officers' Race Determine Neighborhood Deployment?

Comparison of officers of different races in terms of their behavior toward people is related to but analytically distinct from citizens' preferences regarding where such officers should be deployed. A few, older studies examined opinions on whether black officers should be assigned to black communities. Only a minority of blacks in Detroit (12 percent), Baltimore (28 percent), and Milwaukee (33 percent) wanted exclusively black officers assigned to their communities (Aberbach and Walker 1970; Wallach and Jackson 1973; Dresner et al. 1981).

Our survey asked whether people would prefer to have officers in their neighborhoods who are mostly white, mostly black, mostly Hispanic, a mix of races, or "doesn't it matter"? For minorities, the race of officers assigned to their neighborhoods is a salient issue. Figure 3.7

shows that most minority individuals adopt a *race-conscious* approach: 59 percent of Hispanics and 68 percent of blacks want officers of diverse races in their communities. By contrast, 6 out of 10 whites take an ostensibly *color-blind* view, saying that race-of-cop does not matter. In what follows, we analyze the reasons people hold these different views, based on their responses to our open-ended, follow-up question: "Why would you prefer that?"[5] Some of the responses mirror views of behavioral differences described above, but the responses also yielded distinct insights.

The Unpopularity of Single-Race Policing

Few people want officers exclusively of their own race or any other race to be assigned to their neighborhoods. Given the history of race relations in America and sour memories of all-white policing in America's ghettos and barrios, it is not surprising that minorities are not eager to be policed by white officers. Almost no Hispanics (2 percent) or blacks (1 percent) want only white officers assigned to their neighborhoods, and those few who do said it was because they lived in a largely white neighborhood. More surprising, perhaps, is their rejection of the idea of policing by same-race officers. Only 5 percent of blacks and 4 percent of Hispanics want most officers assigned to their neighborhoods to be of the same race as the residents.

No whites wanted most officers in their areas to be black or Hispanic, but they are somewhat more likely to display an own-race preference. Of the one-tenth of whites who prefer mostly white officers in their neighborhoods, most do so because they live in a white neighborhood and believe in "matching law enforcement with the population" (MC white male, 55). Another said:

> I wouldn't mind officers other than white, but our community is mostly white and I know most of the applicants for our department are white. I wouldn't want the department to go to crazy lengths to recruit minorities. (MC white female, 50)

5 Answering "a mix of races" or "doesn't matter" might appear to be the socially acceptable responses. However, in answering our follow-up question, respondents gave specific reasons, sometimes grounded in observations or personal experiences, for their preferences for the race of officers assigned to their communities and for their evaluations of officer behavior in the preceding section. The reasons provided suggest that respondents were not simply giving socially acceptable answers to these questions.

About a fifth of whites who preferred white officers did so because of expected mutual rapport and understanding or because they would feel more comfortable around white cops:

> They would be more likely to understand where I am coming from since I am white. I don't care if it's a black officer, I have nothing against them. It's just that white people understand each other, just like black people understand each other better. (MC white female, 66)

Of the 5 percent of blacks who want black officers assigned to their communities, most cited the same reasons: more understanding, greater rapport, or living in an all-black community. But some added that they thought black officers are fairer than white cops:

> Cleveland is an extremely segregated city. . . . I cannot trust my safety to someone who openly considers me an unworthy neighbor. There is an extreme lack of respect in this city, and as a result I personally don't trust other races. (LMC black female, 32)

White officers do not understand blacks who live in poor areas and "resent being put into those places," whereas black officers:

> usually come from low-income families so they seem to understand the day-to-day fight to survive. The white cops from middle- to upper-income families see low-life's running rampant in the street. (MC black male, 45)

But other minority respondents were convinced that minority officers do not necessarily act differently than white officers:

> I prefer an individual that is going to uphold the law truthfully, rather than worry about someone of my own race. Who's to say that I will be treated fair just because it's someone of my own race? I don't think so. (MC black male, 20)

> I would like them to be Hispanic, but there are some [Hispanic officers] that think they are better than us, and some white or black police treat us better than our own people. (LC Hispanic female, 24)

Among the 4 percent of Hispanics who prefer Hispanic officers, the reasons mirror those of their black and white counterparts, but some Hispanics added that they expected communication benefits from Spanish-speaking officers:

> There are many Hispanics living around here. That's one big reason. I'm sure that there are times that a Hispanic person gets pulled over and really isn't able to communicate with the officer.... An officer who can speak Spanish would be able to explain the situation. (MC Hispanic male, 21)

Blue Cops

One quarter of blacks, 35 percent of Hispanics, and 59 percent of whites selected the "doesn't matter" option when asked about the preferred race of officers in their neighborhoods. The majority of these respondents embraced the nonracial, blue-cops idea. Most whites, blacks, and Hispanics who chose "doesn't matter" did so because they wanted qualified and well-trained officers, regardless of race. We were frequently told that "a cop is a cop," that "color doesn't matter," that what matters is "quality rather than the race," that blue officers are "a race of their own," and that "an officer in uniform is the color of the law."

Some whites who took the blue cops position were motivated by their opposition to hiring officers on racial or ethnic grounds:

> I believe in equal opportunity, but not in affirmative action. The best qualified people should work on the police force (or any business) so that it can operate at maximum efficiency. (MC white male, 34)

> I work with police officers and I find that as long as they do their job it doesn't matter which racial background they have. I do not believe that different racial groups should get extra points simply based on that racial group. Grading qualifying tests differently based on race and gender is unfair. It should be based strictly on qualifications! (MC white female, 45)

Some Hispanics agreed:

> Any police officer should be competent and the requirements should be the same for all minorities. Just to meet a ratio with incompetent minorities would be unfair for everyone. Equality. If you require a certain amount of college for whites, it should be the same for all the races. (MC Hispanic female, 63)

Blacks were more favorable toward affirmative action:

> For many years the preferences were against people who were not white just because they were not white. Most officers were white and they had the inside track on recommending their relatives and friends. This was an artificial barrier against a mixed force, so an artificial barrier removal system has to be put in place. (MC black female, 48)

Other reasons for the view that race of officer does not matter included the "I am not a racist" refrain. Whites were inclined to argue that race-of-cop was irrelevant to them because *they* personally were not bigoted:

> It just doesn't matter. I'm color-blind. (MC white female, 81)

> I'm not a racist; as long as it's a good cop, I don't care about race. (MC white female, 32)

> I have no prejudice. I would only hope that any officer is fully qualified to wear the badge. (MC white female, 72)

Very few blacks and Hispanics cited their own race-neutrality as a reason for arguing that race-of-cop is unimportant.

Neighborhood context shaped the understandings of a similar proportion of Hispanics, blacks, and whites. Whites who noted that their community was all-white, "safe," or "good" saw officers' race as immaterial. Race of officer might be more salient, they claimed, in neighborhoods with a different racial complexion or high crime rate:

> As long as they are trained to do their job and are good at their job. We live in an all-white neighborhood.... If I lived in Baltimore, I'm sure I would feel very different. (UMC white female, 26)

One white woman thought that Hispanic and black officers would be better prepared to understand the "customs of the neighborhood," which she believed were different in minority communities.

Minority respondents who mentioned their community agreed that officers' race mattered more in minority neighborhoods or racially diverse neighborhoods than in areas that are predominantly white:

> My community is mostly white, so I don't care what race pulls me over or assists in crime fighting. But if I was in a predominately minority

community I would want a minority officer assisting. (MC Hispanic
female, 27)

Racially Mixed Policing

Respondents think that mixed-race patrols offer several advantages.
These rationales are remarkably similar to those documented in two
previous studies: one of residents of Washington, DC (Weitzer 2000b)
and the other of police officers in New York City (Leinen 1984:183–
189). Leinen found that a majority of officers strongly supported black
and white teams, and both studies found that mixed teams were valued for three reasons: (1) their *moderating effect* on officers of each
race, (2) their *edifying effect* on officers (each officer helps the other
learn about different-race individuals, cultures, or neighborhoods),
and (3) a *symbolic effect*, where mixed teams personify racial integration in the police force, embody good race relations more generally,
or serve as role models for residents of racially diverse cities. Mixed
teams may have the added bonus of deracializing citizens' interpretations of questionable incidents and thus preempting conflict. If a case
of excessive force, for instance, involves white officers only, it is easier
to construe it as racially motivated.

Judging from these two studies, police and citizens see the advantages of racially mixed teams of officers in very similar ways, and our
qualitative data corroborate this:

- *Educational*: Mixed patrols help to educate each officer in the dyad
  about different communities, cultures, and races and are therefore
  better positioned to understand the concerns of residents of diverse
  neighborhoods;
- *Pragmatic*: Mixed patrols help to equalize the behavior of different-
  race officers and thus foster more impartial treatment of citizens;
- *Symbolic*: Mixed patrols symbolize racial and ethnic equality and integration both in the police force and in the larger society. There
  are thus symbolic dividends in having racially integrated authority
  figures.

A number of respondents combined these themes in their answers:

Balance is good, creates a greater possibility of them learning from
each other, and understanding the mixed community better. (MC
Hispanic male, 45)

My neighborhood is very diverse, so if we have a diverse police force, then the people in the neighborhood wouldn't be discriminated against. People of the same race can relate to each other and understand each other more than a different race. Diversity would balance out the racism. (MC Hispanic female, 16).

For most minority citizens, integrated teams of officers were seen as a means of furthering racial justice. Such teams were associated with "impartiality," "fairness," "less profiling," and "checks and balances."

With a mix of races on the police force, the people in the African American communities will feel more confident that they are not discriminated against when it comes to arrests, [in contrast to] the all-white police department we currently have. (MC black female, 56)

In the past five years, we have seen several high-profile cases in the media involving white police officers who violated the rights of minorities. Of the officers found guilty, there were eyewitness accounts by officers of color as well as whites. In the cases where all [officers] involved are white, the officers were exonerated or given light sentences because the prosecutor's case is further weakened by not having credible witnesses. (MC Hispanic male, 60)

Both minority and white respondents believe that mixed patrols would help to *enhance understanding* between police and the communities they serve. A Hispanic man observed:

You can't ask a black cop to defuse a situation in a Hispanic family if he does not have proper knowledge or understanding, especially if he cannot speak Spanish. Same for a Hispanic cop going to a Chinese home with a serious problem. (LMC Hispanic male, 38)

Black respondents were more likely than whites or Hispanics to argue that integrated teams were a means of edification, *educating officers* about the cultures and neighborhoods of other racial and ethnic groups:

It would be better for the police officers; they would be exposed to diversity among the human family; they would have to learn to work together, support each other on the job; change many attitudes and beliefs about people who are different. This could go toward developing better relationships between the police department and the community. Then we could have true community policing. (LC black female, 61)

Officers can get to know the backgrounds of different ethnic groups by working together. This would help in knowing why some situations are as they are. Things that are common in one racial background may not be common in another racial background. Working together can help bring an understanding of these differences. (MC black male, 70)

Symbolic benefits take two forms. First, racially diverse officers (like the unpopular all-minority officers) is seen as a way of neutralizing minority complaints. Referring to racial profiling, one low-income white man stated, "A mix of officers might make it harder for that kind of complaint to stick." Another respondent echoed this view and envisioned other advantages as well:

A mix is not only fair but it would keep people from complaining about not having officers of their race on duty in their neighborhoods. I do believe these officers could handle some situations better than white officers. It is a known fact that, at times in my city, white officers have been afraid to go into some neighborhoods to take care of a complaint. Officers of the same race as those [causing] a problem probably could do a better job in a lot of situations simply because they understand their race better. And so many people resent white officers handling calls that they are apt to be more troublesome. I personally don't care what race an officer is as long as they act in the manner a police officer is supposed to, but I believe a more even mix of races would be better for a city. (LC white female, 64)

A few minority respondents expressed similar views – that mixed teams would deracialize police-citizen encounters:

It's a good idea, because if you get stopped you would not think it was because of your race. (MC Hispanic female, 59)

So that the community won't have the excuse that they were treated differently because of race. (LC Hispanic female, 46)

It would cut down on the incidence of both actual and perceived prejudice, as well as giving the people of the community someone they feel can relate to who may be more understanding of their situation. It would cut down some on the mistrust of "The Man" found in a lot of poor or minority neighborhoods. (MC black female, 30)

A second type of symbolic dividend is that racially diverse teams convey to the public the value of racial integration and unity, and consequently help to build trust in authority figures:

> With a mixture of officers on the force for any city, you not only get the benefits of learning different cultures in order to better understand a community, but you also get the benefits of teaching our youth that people of all races can peacefully work for one common goal and that is to protect the rights of everyone. (LMC black female, 26)

> I believe in diversification for the police department, so that they reflect the population they serve and hopefully understand different cultures. And for the citizens and young people to see people who look like them. (MC black female, 51)

These findings, coupled with those of the polls cited above, lend very little support to policies of assigning officers of only one race to neighborhoods in multiracial cities. Most respondents reject not only the idea of being policed exclusively by other-race officers but also by same-race officers. Both policies are seen as regressive. Integrated teams, by contrast, are quite popular, because of their anticipated practical and symbolic benefits.

CONCLUSION

We began this chapter by posing several questions about whether and how race shapes citizen views of police bias. We asked, first, whether minorities are more likely than whites to believe that racially biased policing is a problem, and we found that both blacks and Hispanics are indeed more apt than whites to take this view. Furthermore, in three of our four models, blacks are significantly more likely than Hispanics to perceive racially biased policing. This finding lends further support to the *racial-hierarchy* pattern documented in Chapter 2. On the issues of both police misconduct and racialized policing, "minority group" perceptions are far from monolithic. African Americans and Hispanics differ significantly on these two key issues.

One reason why the two groups differ on perceptions of police bias is because of their differential personal experience with racialized policing, which, in turn, may be related to their differential visibility. For instance, blacks may be more vulnerable than Hispanics to traffic stops by police because their skin color heightens their visibility. Another important influence is the two groups' dissimilar histories of incorporation in American society and the associated differences in their overall relationship with criminal justice and other institutions. But further research is needed to more fully account for black-Hispanic differences in their contemporary relations with police.

Americans are overwhelmingly opposed in principle to racially biased law enforcement, but principled support for equal justice does not necessarily mean that one believes the system dispenses unequal justice. Many whites believe that the police treat citizens impartially, not unfairly. Over three-quarters feel that police treat minorities the same as whites; a substantial majority take the same view of minority and white neighborhoods; among whites who believe that police officers are prejudiced, most take the mild, "somewhat common" position; and only one-third of whites believe that police engage in racial profiling of minority drivers.[6] That many whites are skeptical about police discrimination, or see it as isolated and episodic rather than widespread, mirrors their views of racial discrimination elsewhere in American society (Hochschild 1995:60, 279; Schuman et al. 1997). In one poll, for instance, only 17 percent of whites – compared to 44 percent of blacks – thought that blacks are discriminated against "a lot" in America (*Washington Post* 1997). For most whites, racial discrimination in general, and police discrimination in particular, is not a serious problem. Minorities, by contrast, perceive racial discrimination in a wide range of institutional arenas, including housing, employment, and education (Hochschild 1995; Schuman et al. 1997).

We also asked if blacks and Hispanics are more likely than whites to report being victims of discriminatory treatment by the police, and again the answer is yes. Members of both groups are significantly

---

[6] The exception to this pattern is the 70 percent of whites who believe that racial profiling is widespread in the United States (but not in their city or neighborhood). Curiously, whites are twice as likely to believe that profiling is widespread than to believe that blacks or Hispanics are stopped more frequently than whites – an apparent contradiction.

more likely than whites to say that they have personally been discriminated against by the police and that this has happened to another member of their household. Although fewer Hispanics than blacks report these kinds of experiences, the percentage of Hispanics who do so is considerably closer to that of blacks than it is to whites – departing somewhat from the racial hierarchy pattern. Furthermore, the pattern of these experiences varies within as well as between the three groups. The triple jeopardy finding documented in Chapter 2 regarding the confluence of race, gender, and age also applies to racially biased policing, with young minority males especially at risk.

Of course, a person's subjective experience of police bias is not necessarily equivalent to actual discrimination – because the sheer exercise of police authority (typically in a brusque and authoritarian manner) may be construed as racial bias by citizens (Wilson 1972; Sykes and Clark 1975). But, as is true for racial discrimination in other spheres, there is at least a rough aggregate correspondence between actual practice and minorities' reported experiences of police treatment. Our respondents' self-reports are consistent with evidence from police records and street observations of police-citizen interactions, which indicate that police indeed tend to target minorities, who are viewed with a high degree of suspicion and as having criminal propensities. Minorities tend to be stopped more often than whites (Fagan and Davies 2000; Harris 2002) and treated more harshly in encounters (Hepburn 1978; Smith 1986; Kane 2002; Terrill and Reisig 2003). Similarly, the high percentage of blacks and Hispanics who believe that police prejudice is widespread in the nation is consistent with research on police officers themselves (Jefferson 1988:522).

To explore group differences in more detail we examined several possible explanatory factors. For blacks and Hispanics, neighborhood crime concerns and personal experience with police bias play key roles in the perception that racialized policing is common. Vicarious experience has the same effect in at least one model for each racial group (with one exception, bias against neighborhoods). Research shows that a similar pattern is evident in discrimination in other arenas, such as jobs and housing. One study, for instance, found that blacks, Hispanics, and Asians who felt that they had personally experienced

job discrimination were more likely to perceive this kind of discrimination against their entire racial or ethnic group (Kluegel and
Bobo 2001).

A second key theme is the mass media's role in shaping perceptions. Repeated exposure to media reports on police abuse (i.e.,
excessive force, verbal abuse, corruption) is a strong predictor of
the belief that racialized policing exists, is widespread, and is unacceptable. Media effects are extremely robust – operating for all three
racial groups in all four models. People who frequently hear or read
about incidents of police misconduct, as transmitted by the media, are
inclined to conclude not only that misconduct itself is prevalent (as
reported in Chapter 2) but also that racially unjust policing is common. The mass media appears to be an important determinant of those
perceptions.

As indicated earlier, much of the literature on police-citizen relations documents race differences but does not adequately identify their
sources. Our extension of the group-position thesis holds that views
of social and legal institutions will be influenced by group interests
and perceived threats. Dominant groups should perceive the police
as an institution allied with their interests, whereas minorities should
be more inclined to view the police as contributing to their subordination. These predictions are generally supported by our findings.
Whites tend to minimize or discount the existence of racialized policing and perhaps view charges of police racism as a threat to a revered
institution. Blacks are inclined to believe that police bias is common,
and many Hispanics share this view. Both groups are interested in
ensuring that police minimize abuses of citizens, and particularly of
minority citizens, who are disproportionately the recipients of mistreatment. Thus, blacks and Hispanics appear to believe that their group
interests would be advanced by greater controls on police.

In sum, the greater tendency for blacks and Hispanics to believe that
racially biased policing is a problem is largely a result of their disproportionate adverse experiences with police officers and their concerns
with neighborhood crime. For whites, by contrast, the only consistent
predictor across the four areas is media exposure. Thus, compared to
whites, the path leading to blacks' and Hispanics' perceptions of racialized policing is more complex and nuanced. Views are thus shaped by

racial differences not only in general group-position relationships but also in real or perceived group vulnerability to abusive police practices, which is reinforced by both personal and (to a lesser degree) vicarious experience. In policing, as in other institutions, the evidence is clear: Race is a major fault line in how citizens view the world. In the next chapter, we explore preferences for a range of policies designed to ameliorate abusive and unjust police practices.

CHAPTER FOUR

Reforming the Police

It is very difficult to overhaul any large institution. Organizational culture and institutionalized practices are not conducive to change. Such bureacratic inertia is the norm for police departments as it is for other organizations. The history of policing is filled with instances in which police forces – throughout the world – succeeded in foiling or diluting reforms (Weitzer 1985, 1995; Goldsmith 2005).

Still, major change has occurred in some nations over the past three decades, usually precipitated by one or more of the following: a disturbing scandal; sustained pressure from the media, political leaders, or civil rights groups; a change in the leadership of the department; or outside intervention by some authority (Sherman 1978; Weitzer 2005). Under the right conditions, progressive changes can enhance the quality of police service and improve relations between cops and the communities they serve. Policies on the use of force are a good example. The number of citizens killed by police has declined as police departments nationwide have tightened their policies on use of firearms (Brown and Langan 2001). And, although it does not happen frequently, investigations of police departments by blue-ribbon commissions or by an executive agency have resulted in some meaningful reforms. In 1994 the U.S. Justice Department was empowered by law to initiate "pattern-or-practice" litigation against police departments accused of systematic violation of citizens' rights – and this power has been used successfully to force reforms in several urban police departments (Walker 2005).[1] Britain's Home Office has been even more active in its attempts to restructure police forces throughout the nation (see, e.g., Home Office 2004).

One might expect to find broad support in America for core principles of good policing (such as responsive, respectful, and impartial practices) because it is easy to endorse police integrity and professionalism in the abstract. But what specific kinds of reforms receive the greatest public support? Surprisingly, this question has seldom been investigated. Almost all of the research on citizen perceptions of policing problems, and police misconduct in particular, centers on the misconduct itself and not on corrective measures that might help to reduce it or to improve policing more generally. It seems to be assumed that the public overwhelmingly favors reforms: Who wouldn't want to improve the police? But this is an untested assumption. Little is known about the level of public support for specific kinds of reform or about the social forces influencing public evaluations of proposed reforms. Contrary to conventional wisdom, a substantial segment of the public may be opposed to certain kinds of changes, especially those construed as interfering with police work or viewed as politically motivated. For instance, in 1966, after an intense campaign by police and other opponents of a civilian review board in New York City, a majority of New Yorkers (63 percent, and whites especially) voted against the creation of such a board in a citywide referendum. Civilian review of the police appears to be more popular today, but the New York experience and subsequent conflicts over civilian review in other cities illustrate how changes (in this case, in accountability) can be construed negatively, as straitjacketing the police. On other issues, public support may vary from enthusiastic to lukewarm.

Why is it important to examine the level of popular support for reforms? First, such knowledge may be useful in informing public policy. Where demands for a specific change are intense and widespread,

---

[1] Lawsuits filed in the past 10 years against several cities were settled by consent decrees or agreements that require a police department to implement a set of reforms, overseen by a monitor to ensure compliance with the agreement. The first such consent decree was negotiated in Pittsburgh in 1997, and an independent evaluation found that major, positive changes in the city's police department resulted (Davis, Henderson, and Ortiz 2005).

this may be symptomatic of a problem that needs to be addressed. If implemented, the reform may help to reduce the amount of misconduct or improve police practices more generally. Second, certain kinds of reform may boost public confidence in the police. Whether or not the change (e.g., hiring more minority officers) actually affects police practices, it may be symbolically meaningful to the public, with a resulting overall improvement in the legitimacy of the police. Third, reforms may increase citizens' willingness to cooperate with officers, especially when the changes lead to concrete and visible improvements in how officers treat people. This chapter explores public perceptions of several kinds of reforms and the key determinants of citizens' preferences.

MAJOR TYPES OF REFORM

Good policing is based on a set of ideals that include equal justice, the use of minimum force against citizens, and accountability. But how are these standards to be institutionalized, and how are departures from them best remedied? In the United States, the remedies most frequently advanced include racial diversification, policies that enhance procedural justice, new mechanisms of accountability, and community policing. Such policies are motivated by the twin goals of making the police more reflective of and responsive to the public, on the one hand, and reducing police lawlessness or abuse of power, on the other. Of course, these policies are not exhaustive of the types of reforms that have been advocated. Indeed, another type of change departs from these liberalizing reforms by expanding police powers or intensifying crime control efforts. This chapter examines each of these policies.

Racial Diversification

Our discussion of racially biased policing in Chapter 3 examined the issue of officers' racial backgrounds in terms of similarities and differences in the behavior of different-race officers and the kind of officers people want assigned to their neighborhoods. Here, we explore the larger policy of racial diversification of police departments.

The principle of proportional representation, or matching the racial composition of a police department to that of the city, is now widely accepted in American political and law enforcement circles. The U.S. Department of Justice (2001), for instance, proclaims, "A diverse law enforcement agency can better develop relationships with the community it serves, promote trust in the fairness of law enforcement, and facilitate effective policing by encouraging citizen support and cooperation. Law enforcement agencies should seek to hire a diverse workforce." Although several police departments are now majority-black (e.g., Atlanta, Detroit, Washington) or majority-Hispanic (e.g., El Paso, Miami) in composition, most remain unrepresentative of their city's populations (Bureau of Justice Statistics 2004). Underrepresentation is especially glaring in elite units and in the senior ranks of most departments.

The notion that a police department's image and/or operations will be improved by greater racial diversity is an assumption that rarely has been tested. A few studies, as well as findings presented in Chapter 3, suggest that people are divided on whether police officers of different racial backgrounds behave differently toward citizens – but this is a different issue than the questions of whether diversification is valued in principle and how it affects the overall standing of a police department.

It has been hypothesized that "a department with more black officers behaves differently from a department with fewer black officers. As blacks comprise a larger portion [or the majority] of a police department, they may become less isolated and more influential in shaping the values and culture of the entire police department" (Sherman 1983:221), with potentially positive consequences for both police behavior and citizen opinion of the department. Yet, research testing this proposition is almost nonexistent. In one city with a majority-black police department (Washington, DC), two-thirds of both whites and blacks rated the department's overall job performance as excellent or good, and roughly half of each group gave the police high marks on their honesty and integrity (Weitzer 1999). A study of Detroit found that blacks residing in four neighborhoods rated the police department more favorably than whites (Frank et al. 1996), but a citywide survey found that black residents were far less satisfied with the police. In fact, "the dramatic change in the racial composition of Detroit's police force did not enhance blacks' satisfaction and may have reduced whites' satisfaction.... Both blacks and whites were massively dissatisfied" (Welch et al. 2001:147). Moreover, blacks living in the largely white suburbs were happier with the police than their counterparts living in the city of Detroit.

Little is known about the impact of police diversification in other cities or about public assessments of it. This chapter explores several aspects of such diversification. Do people view it as a good thing? Should more minority officers be hired? Should they be deployed in minority communities?

Procedural Justice

Research indicates that people are sensitive to whether or not they receive procedural justice. They expect fair and courteous treatment from police officers. When police maintain a professional demeanor – listening to people, being polite and respectful, explaining their actions, treating people fairly – this increases citizen satisfaction with the immediate encounter as well as more general confidence in the police (Tyler 1990; Tyler and Huo 2002). Such treatment can also improve citizens' demeanor and reactions to officers, and the chances of cooperation. Officers who treat citizens unfairly or disrespectfully are less likely to obtain compliance (Wiley and Hudik 1974; Mastrofski, Snipes, and Supina 1996; Tyler and Huo 2002).

Unfortunately, it appears that procedural justice is lacking in many police-citizen encounters. A significant number of people feel that they have not been treated fairly by an officer. About one-third of blacks and one-quarter of Hispanics in California, for example, reported that the police had not used fair procedures when dealing with them in an encounter (Tyler and Huo 2002:149). Practices designed to reduce procedural injustice are one important area of reform.

Research on procedural justice has focused on fairly general measures of officer behavior, such as fair and respectful treatment. Little research has explored public attitudes toward specific reforms that might increase procedural justice. We examine people's assessments of three such procedures: requiring officers to explain to people the reasons for their actions, requiring officers to apologize to citizens whom they have stopped and found no incriminating evidence, and reading people their *Miranda* rights (the latter is not technically a reform but instead retains an existing practice, in effect since the landmark 1966

Supreme Court decision, *Miranda v. Arizona*). Explaining one's actions and apologizing for mistakes are related to two aspects of procedural justice (Leventhal 1976) – giving citizens information with which to understand police actions (which may give citizens the opportunity to state their case) and the correctability of decisions (apologizing for mistakes). Many officers fail to do these simple things. The officer typically is "reluctant to reveal his reasons for stopping people because he sees his cues as private knowledge which, if it were generally known, would aid criminals and make his work even harder than it is" (Rubenstein 1973:264). The *Miranda* rule also represents correctability, by rendering inadmissible confessions obtained in violation of proper procedures.

Accountability

Police accountability has long been a contentious issue in the United States. According to Human Rights Watch (1998:33), "Consistently lacking [in American cities] is a system of oversight in which supervisors hold their charges accountable for mistreatment." Among the reasons for inadequate accountability are leadership failure, weak departmental and external oversight, and ineffectual civil remedies and criminal prosecutions.

If a civil suit for an incident of police abuse results in an award by the court or a financial settlement, the money paid to the victim typically comes out of the city's general funds, not the police department's budget. The police department thus pays no financial price for its officers' misconduct. Moreover, the officers implicated are rarely punished in civil cases. An analysis by Gannett News Service of 100 lawsuits in 22 states between 1986 and 1991 (totaling $92 million in awards) found that, of the 185 officers involved, no action was taken against 160 of them, 17 were promoted, and only 8 were disciplined (cited in Human Rights Watch 1998:82). The Christopher Commission (1991) in Los Angeles and other investigations document the same pattern of officer impunity. New York City, for example, routinely pays out millions of dollars to settle claims against the NYPD ($27.3 million in 1996), yet neither the officers involved nor the department was held liable: "The officers named in their lawsuits almost always continue working without scrutiny or punishment" (Sontag and Barry 1997:A1). Detroit paid out a total of $188 million in settlements from 1987 to 2004 ($45 million in 2002–2004 alone), and 60 percent of the accused officers had been charged in previous lawsuits (Swickard 2005). As a rule, civil suits have little appreciable impact on police practices: "Cities continue to pay large amounts without examining, acknowledging, or correcting the police activities that led to the lawsuits" (Human Rights Watch 1998:80). Taxpayers are penalized, not the deviant officers.

Criminal prosecution is another type of external accountability, but one that is rare and limited to either the most serious cases or to cases where prosecutors have a good chance of securing a conviction. Proving criminal intent is extremely difficult, particularly in cases alleging use of excessive force, though easier in cases involving corruption. Criminal prosecution is not used often enough to be an effective check on misconduct or to induce reform in a police department, and the occasional successful prosecution does not appear to affect other officers' conduct (Walker 2005:35). And because criminal cases involve individual officers or "rotten apples," they are not likely to result in organizational reform of a "rotten barrel."

What about internal police department mechanisms of accountability? A majority of Americans lack confidence in the capacity of internal, departmental oversight mechanisms to control officers effectively. When asked in a Harris poll whether police officers would be "too lenient" in investigating complaints against fellow officers, an affirmative answer was given by 62 percent of whites, 58 percent of Hispanics, and 70 percent of blacks (Harris 1992). External mechanisms of accountability are widely regarded as superior. A national survey found that 58 percent of whites and 75 percent of blacks wanted authorities external to the police to investigate and discipline officers accused of brutality against citizens (*New York Times* 1991). And some leading scholars agree: "Police cannot be impartial when investigating other police, and even when they are, they are unlikely to be credible" (Skolnick and Fyfe 1993:227).

This does not necessarily mean that citizens will be satisfied with existing mechanisms of external oversight. A civilian complaint review board, for instance, may have greater public credibility than an oversight system within a police department, but boards with low substantiation rates (the norm for civilian review) also raise public concerns

(Goldsmith and Lewis 2000). Moreover, persons with firsthand experience of such boards are often dissatisfied with both the process and the outcome. In New York City, for instance, two-thirds of those who had filed complaints with the city's civilian review board were dissatisfied with their experience, and 84 percent of those whose complaints had been fully investigated were dissatisfied (Sviridoff and McElroy 1989). But the most serious deficiency of such boards is that they are limited to reviewing complaints against individual officers on a case-by-case basis, rather than larger organizational policies and practices that give rise to officer misconduct – in other words, the symptoms rather than the causes of abuses of police power.

Still, civilian review boards can play a valuable role. First, even if most police chiefs fail to use the information provided by the boards as evidence of larger problems that need to be remedied, they could do so. A board's reports can be used to identify patterns in complaints and track changes over time and place; a spike in complaints in a precinct may signal a problem in need of attention. Second, the very existence of such boards sends a message to officers that they are not free of external oversight. Even if a board substantiates only a few complaints, the fact that some are sustained may serve as a deterrent to both the guilty officer and to other officers. Finally, civilian review may have symbolic value for the public, showing that the police are under external oversight. As Skolnick and Fyfe (1993:230) write, "only an independent investigative body can allay public suspicions of the police." Virtually no studies have examined whether a civilian review board actually heightens public confidence in a city's police force (Walker 2001).

In addition to civilian review boards, this chapter examines four other changes designed to enhance police accountability:

Video cameras in police cars: A number of police departments have installed video cameras in cars to monitor police-citizen encounters. It is not known how many departments have installed such cameras, but in 2000, the Justice Department's Office of Community Oriented Policing Services (COPS) awarded $12 million to 41 police agencies to purchase a total of 2,900 in-car cameras. Recently, the Seattle, Washington, police department decided to equip all patrol cars with digital cameras. Not only will the cameras document police behavior and misbehavior, but they also are expected to help build citizen trust in the police, according to Seattle's mayor, Greg Nichels. City Councilman Nick Licata echoed this view when he predicted that, with cameras in all cars, "we will begin to see the community recognize their importance in providing police accountability" (Castro 2004). The same benefits are expected from cameras in Milwaukee, according to the city's Commission on Police-Community Relations, which investigated ways of reducing police-citizen tensions (Diedrich 2005), and in Los Angeles, where the federal monitor who oversees the LAPD draws the same connection between cameras and minority confidence: "The LAPD needs to come up with a way to assure its citzens that minorities are not singled out. We believe cameras in police cars is one of the ways you can do that" (Winton 2005). There is no research on whether this fairly new innovation actually affects officer behavior during street stops, but Amnesty International (2004) has called for all police cars to be equipped with such cameras in order to enhance the visibility of and better scrutinize police behavior.

Early warning systems: Both the U.S. Department of Justice (2001) and the Commission on Accreditation for Law Enforcement Agencies take the position that police departments throughout the nation should implement early warning systems to identify "at-risk" officers. These systems consist of computerized records of each officer's history of citizen complaints, use of firearms, civil suits, and other indicators of questionable performance. Early warning systems are designed to identify deviant officers and then intervene with counseling, retraining, or discipline. About one-quarter of America's urban police agencies now have such early warning systems, and it appears that they have at least some capacity to check police misconduct. An evaluation of Miami, Minneapolis, and New Orleans (Walker, Alpert, and Kenney 2001) found that early warning mechanisms reduced police misconduct in each city. When problem officers were flagged, prompt interventions followed, helping to curb bad behavior. Pittsburgh's early warning system has enhanced officer accountability as well (Davis, Henderson, and Ortiz 2005).

Recording information on people stopped by officers: To prevent racial profiling, many states and cities now require officers to record the race (and other demographic information) of all motorists they stop, in addition to the reason for the stop, whether a search or arrest was made, and whether contraband or other evidence of a crime was found. The U.S. Department of Justice (2001) endorses this practice, and the Commission on Accreditation for Law Enforcement Agencies now requires its member police agencies to collect and analyze such information. Requiring officers to document who they are stopping and to justify their actions in writing could reduce improper stops. Because such data-recording requirements are recent, it is too early to assess their effects, but it is possible that collecting this information will help prevent racial profiling. Of course, much depends on how the information is used by superior officers. Like early warning systems and videotaped encounters, data on citizens stopped by officers are of value only if supervisors are prepared to use the information to hold patrol officers accountable.

Stronger punishment for officers guilty of serious misconduct. Instances of police misconduct are typically hidden from public view, and few incidents are reported to police officials, civilian review boards, or the courts. When unlawful acts or other types of misconduct are discovered, how should these officers be treated? Does the American public believe that such officers are typically treated too leniently or that just punishments are meted out in most cases?[2] Do people want stiffer sanctions to be imposed? Increasing the severity of punishment differs from the other remedies in its generality: It involves less a specific institutional or operational change than a more general commitment to the principle of ensuring that sanctions are meaningful and proportionate to the type of misconduct. It is included in our study because it is important to know whether and how the public evaluates the punishment of wayward police officers, based on their general understanding of the sanctions typically applied. If many citizens believe that bad cops are often treated with kid gloves and if they favor more severe punishment, this would add further impetus – along with existing supporting evidence – to the need to address this deficiency in the area of police accountability.

---

[2] There is considerable consensus in America regarding the relative seriousness of crimes committed by civilians, but much less agreement about the exact punishments warranted for particular crimes (Rossi and Berk 1997).

Community Policing

Community policing is the most widely touted institutional reform in recent years and has become increasingly popular. In fact, it has been heralded "the most important development in policing in the past quarter century" (National Research Council 2004:85). Community policing generally means officers working with residents to identify neighborhood conditions that foster crime and then to formulate solutions. As a proactive approach, it departs from the traditional practice of responding to incidents after the fact. Examples include regular police-community meetings, foot patrols, police mini-stations, and programs for youth.

During the Clinton administration, the federal government trumpeted community policing and promoted it with grants to police departments throughout the country. The Violent Crime Control Act of 1994, for instance, created the Office of Community Oriented Policing Services within the Justice Department and authorized $8.8 billion over 10 years to support community policing initiatives in cities throughout the country, including the hiring of 100,000 officers. These funds have now been spent and nearly 90,000 officers were hired.

Most police chiefs claim that their departments practice community policing, and about two-thirds report that at least some of their officers practice community policing full time (National Research Council 2004:104–105). However, cities vary considerably in the degree to which community policing exists and in the degree to which officers accept it. In many places community policing is marginalized, relegated to a few officers or to a community relations branch that operates independently of most police officers.

In some other cities – for example, San Diego, Savannah, Portland – community policing is much more integrated throughout the police department as a philosophy and practice guiding all officers. Chicago's Alternative Policing Strategy (CAPS) is another example. Begun in 1993, key elements of CAPS include assigning officers to a permanent beat to increase their knowledge of neighborhood problems, intensive training of officers in solving neighborhood problems (e.g., vandalism, prostitution, crack houses), regular formal meetings between residents and officers, and ongoing review of program outcomes.

Wesley Skogan's 10-year evaluation of CAPS found that police became more responsive to community concerns, neighborhood crime and disorder decreased, people became less fearful of crime, gang problems were reduced, and residents expressed greater confidence in the police (CCPEC 2004). This research suggests that community policing, although no panacea, can be effective when a police department sees its implementation as a long-term process and commits sufficient resources to it. Unfortunately, most community policing programs do not live up to these requirements. They are fragmented, marginalized, and underfunded.

Although community policing has been embraced, at least in principle, by police executives throughout the United States, little is known about citizen attitudes toward it. A few studies find that residents, and particularly minority residents, are less than enthusiastic about community policing programs, either because they were seen as intrusive and unwelcome, were imposed by officers in a top-down manner, or because residents feared retaliation from offenders who discover that they are working closely with the police (Grinc 1994; Williams 1997). Other research, however, indicates that community policing can improve residents' attitudes toward the police (Trojanowicz 1983; Skogan 1994; Skogan and Hartnett 1997; Reisig and Parks 2003; CCPEC 2004) and perhaps reduce citizen complaints against officers (Greene 1999). A survey of residents of 12 cities found overwhelming support (86 percent) for community policing among residents who said community policing did not exist in their neighborhoods (Bureau of Justice Statistics 1999:28–30). A few other polls have found substantial public support for particular types of community engagement, such as foot patrols, community meetings, and school programs.

In addition to the issue of public support for the *principle* of community policing and for specific types of community policing, little is known (aside from the studies just cited) about whether *existing programs* actually live up to their promise of improving police-citizen relations. Chapter 2 reported that black and white residents of neighborhoods with community policing had greater overall satisfaction with the police than residents of neighborhoods lacking community policing, and this chapter examines the determinants of popular support for community policing itself.

Intensified Policing

The reforms discussed earlier are designed to make the police more responsive to citizens and more accountable for their actions. A very different kind of change would *intensify and bolster* law enforcement. Such intensification of policing is not necessarily inconsistent with reforms that would liberalize policing (Block 1970). In other words, people might favor both more policing and more sensitive policing in their neighborhoods. The two would be inconsistent only in cases where a particular change in one area undermines, or is viewed as undermining, a practice in another area – for example, where crime control contradicts due process (Skolnick 1966; Packer 1968). An example would be a change that would infringe on people's rights, such as overturning the *Miranda* decision or allowing cops to stop and frisk people without reasonable suspicion of wrongdoing.

Historically, underenforcement of the law was a serious problem in minority communities. Four decades ago, a blue-ribbon commission concluded that many blacks wanted increased law enforcement, as well as sensitive and just policing, in their communities: "The strength of ghetto feelings about hostile police conduct may even be exceeded by the conviction that ghetto neighborhoods are not given adequate police protection" (Kerner Commission 1968:307). Is this concern with underpolicing and desire for increased policing still evident in minority communities today?

Our research examined popular support for three types of changes in the direction of intensified law enforcement: more car patrols, more police surveillance of high-crime areas, and stopping and searching more people on the street.

* * * * *

This chapter investigates popular support for police reform. First, we examine how Americans view various innovations. How much support is there, among blacks, whites, and Hispanics, for each type of change? Second, we explore the determinants of citizen preferences. In other words, is support for reform amplified by demographic or ecological factors, citizen experience with officer abuse, exposure to media reports of police misconduct, and belief that misconduct occurs frequently in one's city or neighborhood? And, third, we present qualitative data on reforms that respondents volunteered to us, that is, changes they would like to see in their city's police department that were not explicitly mentioned in our questionnaire. Our dependent variables are as follows:

Racial Diversification. To measure support for diversification, we created an index using several questions related to the composition of the police. Respondents were first asked: "Do you think that minorities should be given preferences in hiring so that a police department will have a similar racial makeup to the racial makeup of that city?" We then asked whether hiring more minority officers or assigning more minority officers to minority communities would "improve the police department or police services in your city." The items are coded such that higher scores reflect more positive opinion about the efficacy of the reforms. Finally, we inquired about racial proportionality: "Do you think that it's a good idea for the racial makeup of a city's police department to be similar to the racial makeup of that city?" The latter question is analyzed separately.

Procedural Justice. Three procedural justice issues were examined. Regarding police conduct during stops, respondents indicated whether they agreed or disagreed with two statements: "When a police officer stops a person on the street or in a car, the officer should be required to explain to the person the reason for the stop," and "When a police officer stops a citizen and searches the citizen or his or her vehicle and finds no evidence of a crime (such as drugs, weapons, stolen items), the officer should be required to apologize to the citizen for the inconvenience of the search." A third item asks about whether the *Miranda* rule should be retained: "Police officers should continue to read all persons whom they interrogate their *Miranda* rights."[3] All items are coded such that higher scores reflect a stronger preference for procedural justice.

Accountability. A number of questions address accountability – both whether a particular monitoring mechanism should be created and the kinds of sanctions that should be applied to deviant officers.

---

[3] The lead-in to this question provided background on the rule: "The law currently requires officers to inform persons whom they interrogate of their 'Miranda rights' (the right to remain silent, to consult with an attorney before speaking to the police, and to be informed that anything they say may be used against them in court)."

Respondents were asked whether the following would improve either the police department or police services in their city – stronger punishment for officers who engage in misconduct against citizens; a computerized early warning system in the police department to help identify officers who receive multiple complaints from citizens; installing video cameras in all police cruisers to monitor officer behavior; and punishment of officers guilty of using excessive force against a citizen (excessive force is defined in the question as "more force than is necessary under the circumstances"). Each of these items is coded such that high scores reflect more enthusiasm for the reform. Not part of the accountability index, and discussed separately below, is a question on mandating police recording of information on drivers during traffic stops and two questions about independent civilian review boards: Respondents who reported that their city has no such board, or that they do not know if one exists, were asked if they wished their city had one; and another question, asked only of those who said a civilian review board does exist in their city, about whether they thought the board "helps to reduce the amount of police misconduct against citizens."[4]

A final set of accountability items pertains to sanctions against officers who use excessive force. Respondents who said that officers who use excessive force should be punished were asked what kind of punishment should be meted out – a reprimand or warning from the police chief; demotion to a lower rank; fired from the police department; criminal charges and prosecution in court; and imprisonment if prosecuted and found guilty.

Community Policing. Types of community policing examined in the survey include police meetings with the community, programs for school children, and foot patrols. Respondents were asked whether they thought each would "improve a lot, improve somewhat, not improve much, or not improve at all either the police department or police services in your city."[5] High scores indicate improvement.

---

[4] Because this question was asked only of those who reported that a review board exists in their city, including it in the index would have resulted in a large loss of cases.

[5] Respondents who said that community policing does not exist in their neighborhood were asked if they want it. Because this item was asked only of a subsample, it was not included in the index to avoid a large loss of cases.

Figure 4.1. Support for racial diversification

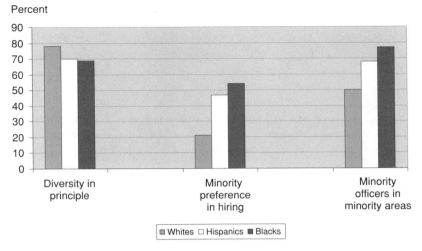

Percent

Intensified Policing. Another set of changes would intensify law enforcement: Respondents were asked whether they favored increasing the number of officers patrolling the streets in police cars, more police surveillance of areas where street crimes occur frequently, and stopping and searching more people on the street.[6]

POPULAR SUPPORT FOR REFORM

Racial Diversification

An overwhelming majority of the American public endorses the principle of racial diversification in policing, agreeing that a city's police department should be similar to the racial composition of the city. Whites are somewhat more likely than minorities to support this principle – nearly 8 out of 10 whites do so, compared to 7 out of 10 Hispanics and African Americans (see Figure 4.1).

When we asked respondents to tell us why they do or do not support the racial proportionality principle, their responses revealed a much more nuanced set of perspectives than a simple "yes"/"no" answer

---

[6] Alphas for the five standardized item indices are, respectively, .68, .60, .67, .75, and .68. We do not create an index of the type-of-punishment items, so no reliability coefficient was calculated.

allows. Among those who said that it is not a good idea for a police department to reflect the racial makeup of its host city, most said that police recruitment should be color-blind, and that "merit" and "qualifications" should always trump racial considerations. This was the view of two-thirds of the whites who oppose proportional representation, as well as a substantial number (but not a majority) of Hispanics and blacks:

> The most qualified candidate for the job should get the job, regardless of anything else! If a duck were the most qualified for the job, he should get it. (LMC white male, 64)

> A lot of very good, non-bigoted, intelligent, dedicated persons will be overlooked [in a hiring system based on racial proportionality]. The focus should be on quality. (LC black female, 71)

> This would encourage police departments to start discriminating in hiring, solely based on race. If they don't have an adequate percentage of Hispanic officers and they need to hire 50 new recruits, a majority of those new recruits will be Hispanic to help the police force hit its quota, whether they were the best-qualified applicants or not. Police departments (as all other things in life) should hire based on merit, not on racial preference or to mirror the race of the community. (LMC white male, 29)

A sizeable group of these respondents felt that a policy of racial matching might result in discriminatory hiring, favoritism, or other racially unfair practices. Many of these statements are reminiscent of arguments, well documented in previous studies, against affirmative action in other jobs:

> Race or ethnic background should not be a part of the hiring or firing of police officers. . . . If this is taken into consideration, it then becomes "racial profiling" in its own right. Good officers are passed over because they are of one race or another, not just for lack of training, experience, or other factors that should be on the top of the list. (LC white female, 58)

> Forced integration in any situation causes resentment among coworkers and the public. It doesn't work in schools; why would it work in the workplace? (LC Hispanic female, 47)

> With all the talk of freedom from racial inequality, why would you specifically staff a department that you want to be free from such

thinking strictly by racial differences? I've done police work for thirty years and know that if you want your officers to quit thinking of racial or gender differences, quit emphasizing them yourself. Make hiring, promotions, and staffing [decisions] on the basis that we're all just people. (MC white male, 52)

Others were concerned that in majority-white cities racial matching in hiring would only perpetuate white domination in the police department. The best remedy according to these respondents would be equal representation, not proportionality:

If the majority of the citizens are of one particular race and the force is a representation of the community, one race will always be in the minority [on the police force]. I think that the makeup should be as close to 50–50 as possible. (UMC black male, 34)

In other words, although the principle of racial proportionality is usually discussed as a means of achieving racial justice or improving police-community relations (indeed, most respondents see it in these terms), some people noted that its efficacy depends on the racial complexion of the city in question.

Another reason for skepticism regarding diversification is that officers' race is a dubious predictor of good policing – a point made in Chapter 3. According to this logic, officers of all races are equally prone to engage in bad behavior, so basing hiring or deployment on race is a faulty premise to begin with. More blacks and Hispanics than whites were skeptical that police would behave any differently even if the department reflected the racial composition of the host city. These respondents also gave little credence to the idea that a racially diverse police force would have symbolic benefits, a major theme among those who value the principle of racial diversity.

The vast majority of our respondents, however, take a much more optimistic view of racial diversification (Figure 4.1). Among those who said that it is "a good idea" for a police department to reflect the racial makeup of its city, most said that this would improve police-community relations by promoting understanding between officers and residents, whereas others believed it will curb racially biased practices or simply consider it a fair policy. The three racial groups did not differ on these themes, but they did vary somewhat in the outcomes they expected diversity to produce – such as improving police behavior, enhancing community confidence in police, or changing internal workings of the police department. One important sidebar is that many respondents do not specifically identify advantages of *proportional representation* but instead discuss the benefits of racial and ethnic *diversity*.

Of the three main themes, improving police-citizen understanding was the one most often mentioned by members of all three groups. "People of the same race and background generally have a better understanding of each other" (UMC black male, 45), and with minority representation on the force, "maybe the police would understand the plight of the people they deal with" (UMC black female, 36). These respondents believe that shared race and ethnicity means a shared culture and, as a result, same-race officers would help to improve police relations with minority communities:

> Certain races have customs that are not understood by others not of their race, and if there is a person who understands the customs then the situation would be handled better. For example, Hispanics like to hang in large groups and sit outside and talk, play cards or dominoes, and they aren't dealing drugs or gambling. But an officer of another race who isn't familiar might suspect something and check them, disrespect them, think that they are doing something wrong, and waste time on people who are just relaxing after work or spending time with friends and family. (MC Hispanic male, 26)

Most people simply assume that same-race understanding is natural, but a few base their opinion on personal experience:

> Because there are cultural differences they may be better at understanding and relating. I witnessed a domestic violence episode where the victim would speak to the officer of his ethnic background but would not speak freely to the other [white] officer. (LC white male, 31)

A third of those who favor racial diversification reasoned that it would curb discriminatory police practices:

> It helps to reduce prejudice and also it helps everyone to understand each other's differences and similarities. Also, a suspected criminal will most likely feel more comfortable with someone of his own race

and maybe be more cooperative. It is a great idea to help prevent racial profiling. (MC white female, 39)

Black cops in a black-majority city are less likely to be prejudiced against their own race and that goes for the Hispanic cops in Hispanic-majority cities. (LMC Hispanic male, 26)

People also value the symbolism of minority representation. For some whites, diversity is useful in taking the heat off of white officers. There would be "no room for complaints about white brutality from the blacks. Let them scream about their own race for a while and file lawsuits against their own color," or "there's a good chance a minority officer will stop a minority person. That makes it harder for the person stopped to yell 'profiling' or 'prejudice'" (LC white male, 88). Blacks and Hispanics pointed to other symbolic benefits: It "makes the community feel more like the police are there to protect and [not] as an occupation and pacification force" (LC Hispanic male, 29).

Finally, a smaller group of respondents simply thought that either diversity or proportional representation was "fair." Not only was diversification the right thing to do to promote equal opportunity within the police department, but it was also expected to result in fairer treatment of members of the public.

Some people talk about all three advantages – understanding, prevention, and fairness – illustrated by the following account:

A police officer who is from the same background . . . will be more familiar with the psyche of those people, thus gaining better communication, cooperation, and respect from that community. Second, if police officers are matched in a community of the same ethnic background, there are far less likely to be lawsuits and complaints of discrimination, prejudice, and mistreatment of criminals within that community. This saves the taxpayers money and frees the court system up for legitimate complaints. Third, it is a wonderful role model for a community's young people to see police officers of their own ethnicity and to know they too may become a police officer one day – that it is not just for some other race. It also may help kids to listen more carefully to a police officer of their own ethnicity. . . . The kids can't say "he doesn't understand what it is like to grow up here." (UMC white female, 32)

Two related questions are whether police departments should give minorities preferences in hiring and whether more minority officers should be assigned to minority neighborhoods? Although 8 in 10 whites support the principle of racial diversification, when it comes to implementing the principle by giving minorities preferences in hiring, white support plummets to 21 percent. In contrast, about half of blacks and Hispanics support preferential hiring (Figure 4.1). On the second question, fully 77 percent of blacks and 68 percent of Hispanics favor assigning more minority officers to minority neighborhoods (Figure 4.1). It is important to note that this is a general question asking whether more minority officers should be deployed and thus differs from the specific issue, discussed in Chapter 3, of whether the officers assigned to neighborhoods should be exclusively of one race or mixed teams. As a general principle, there is overwhelming support, especially among blacks and Hispanics, for deploying more minority officers in minority neighborhoods.

Procedural Justice

Most people strongly favor policies that would increase fair and respectful police practices. People are almost unanimous in the view that officers should be required to explain to people the reasons why they have been stopped. Around 90 percent of all three groups see this as valuable. Similarly, over three-quarters of each group also believe that cops should be required to apologize for the inconvenience of a stop if they find no evidence of wrongdoing.

Miranda rights have been controversial in recent years, opposed by conservatives who believe *Miranda* interferes with police investigations. Police, however, have largely adapted to *Miranda* and now see it as a routine police procedure; most officers do not believe it weakens their ability to elicit confessions from suspects (Thomas and Leo 2002). And, despite opponents' claims that *Miranda* "handcuffs" the police, the vast majority of Americans support these rights. In our national survey, a striking 91 percent – from each racial group – endorse *Miranda*, and the majority of these people *strongly* support it. This level of approval is almost identical to other recent polls. In one, 94 percent of Americans thought that officers should be required to inform persons they arrest of their Constitutional rights (Gallup/CNN/*USA*

Figure 4.2. Support for greater monitoring

Percent

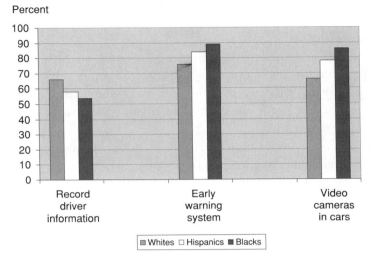

Today 2000), and in another, 86 percent agreed with a recent Supreme Court decision upholding *Miranda* (Princeton 2000). Despite occasional efforts to weaken or overturn it, the *Miranda* rule enjoys almost unanimous popular support in America.

Accountability

As a general rule, people strongly approve of police accountability – whether it involves greater monitoring and oversight or stiffer punishment of deviant cops. Regarding monitoring, one policy – currently being implemented in a number of state and local police agencies – is to require officers to record information on every driver they stop (i.e., race, gender, age, reason for stop, etc.). We asked respondents whether this policy would "help to prevent profiling." Interestingly, as Figure 4.2 shows, more whites than blacks or Hispanics believe that this would reduce profiling – 66 percent, 54 percent, and 58 percent, respectively – suggesting that minorities are somewhat less sanguine about the prospects of deterring profiling simply by recording information on drivers. A counterpart question asked whether people thought collecting this information would "interfere with police work": 18 percent of blacks and 26 percent of whites and Hispanics subscribe to this view. One respondent thought that the recent *publicity* about racial

profiling, even where monitoring hasn't been implemented, hinders
police work: "Because of all the hype regarding racial profiling, the
police department in our city is often too soft on criminals" (UMC
Hispanic female, 59).

Two other reforms, designed to enhance monitoring, are early warning systems that flag rogue officers and the installation of video cameras in police cars. Americans overwhelmingly favor both; most blacks
and Hispanics, but also a substantial majority of whites, value these
innovations (Figure 4.2).

Although police unions have fought the creation of civilian review
boards in several cities in years past, today such boards exist in many
big cities. These boards are resented by some officers, and especially
by white cops. According to a Police Foundation survey of 925 officers
throughout the nation, only 33 percent of white officers, compared
to 70 percent of black officers, agreed that "civilian review boards are
an effective means of preventing police misconduct" (Weisburd and
Greenspan 2000).

In our survey, the majority of the public – and especially minorities –
approve of the creation of civilian review boards in cities without them.
About 8 out of 10 Hispanics and African Americans see the need for
civilian review of their city's police. However, in cities that currently
have civilian review boards, whites are more confident than the other
two groups that the board helps to reduce police misconduct (see
Figure 4.3): 84 percent of whites compared to 57 percent of blacks
believe that their review board curbs abuses by their city's cops. Such
skepticism may stem, in part, from a sense that their city's review board
does not substantiate a sufficient number of cases or is insufficiently
powerful:

> There should be an office of a special prosecutor to handle these
> types of cases. The civilian complaint review board has no teeth. This
> agency should be an arm of the special prosecutor. (MC Hispanic
> male, 60)

When it comes to the issue of sanctioning misconduct, most
Americans believe that wayward officers should be punished. A recent
Gallup poll, for instance, found that 80 percent of the public thought
that officers who engage in wrongdoing should be prosecuted and

Figure 4.3. Support for more accountability

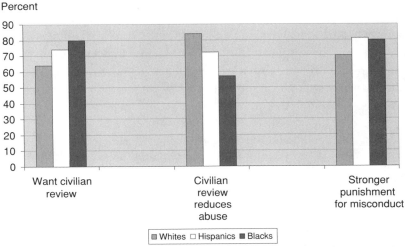

Percent

Note: "Want civilian review" was asked only of people who say that their city does not have a civilian review board: the question asked whether the respondent thought an independent civilian review board "would improve either the police department or police services in your city." "Civilian review reduces abuse" was asked only of people who say that their city already has a review board, and the question asked whether the board "helps to reduce the amount of police misconduct against citizens." "Stronger punishment" was asked of all respondents, and specified "stronger punishment for officers who engage in misconduct against citizens."

punished.[7] Some police departments are rather intolerant of serious officer misconduct, but many Americans are convinced that adequate punishment is the exception rather than the rule. The latter view is likely influenced in large part by media reports on individual cases of cops who are treated with impunity, as well as more general exposés such as a report in the *Los Angeles Times* on December 9, 2005 headlined "Police Are Rarely Prosecuted Unless Case is Bulletproof."

---

[7]   The fact that four-fifths took this view is striking given the somewhat loaded question wording, which is sympathetic to police: "Some people feel that the job police officers perform is so difficult and important that it is wrong to second guess them by prosecuting or punishing them for wrongdoing which occurs in the course of their job performance. Would you agree or disagree that it is wrong to prosecute and punish police officers?" (Gallup 1999). A more neutrally worded question might have yielded even greater support for this type of accountability.

Such points were echoed by our respondents. As one stated, "When police do serious things wrong, 98 percent of the time they do not get punished, not even a reprimand" (MC Hispanic female, 64), and another cited specific examples: "We had the Diallo [shooting] case, the Louima [beating] case, and many more, but in both of these cases the cops got off with a smack on the hand. If that was a citizen that did that to a cop, he or she would be in jail rotting" (MC Hispanic male, 24). Echoing this complaint:

> Our newspaper discovered that several officers have in excess of 5 and as many as 15 reprimands, loss of pay, and other minor punishment for use of excessive force. I believe that by the fifth infraction the officer should be dismissed. We have very strong laws to deal with citizens who dare assault a police officer. Some police officers use this law as a weapon. If you so much as raise your arm to defend yourself from a baton, you are charged with assaulting a police officer. (MC Hispanic male, 69)

> Police should be prosecuted to the full extent of the law. Examples are slamming a kid's head onto a car hood after he has been subdued and in handcuffs, and shooting an unarmed man 40 times [referring to Amadou Diallo in New York] while he tries to enter his apartment. (MC Hispanic male, 65)

Another Hispanic man thought that police who commit crimes should receive "double the punishment" of what a citizen would receive, because they are sworn to uphold the law rather than violate it.

Most people believe that stronger punishment for officers who mistreat citizens will improve policing (see Figure 4.3), and blacks and Hispanics are more inclined to believe that such punishment will improve policing "a lot." A separate question asked about excessive force, conduct that almost everyone feels warrants punishment – 93 percent of blacks, 92 percent of whites, and 86 percent of Hispanics. It seems difficult to argue that such officers deserve no punishment at all.

Respondents were provided with options as to the kind of punishment that would be appropriate for officers who have used excessive force (more than one sanction could be selected; these data are not displayed in a figure). Blacks generally favor the stiffer sanctions, especially the most severe (imprisonment of an officer who is found guilty), whereas whites tend to favor the most lenient punishment (a reprimand or warning from the police chief). As one white woman reasoned, "I don't feel a policeman should go to jail for excess force unless he caused the death of someone deliberately" (MC white female, 60). And another stated,

> Sometimes an assailant does things that force the officer to use "excessive force." . . . Depending on each case of excessive force, the police officer should be dealt with accordingly. . . . You can't use the same punishment for each incident. (UMC white female, 18)

Community Policing

Aside from the reforms discussed earlier, most of which can be described as attempts to curb police misconduct, other changes might help to increase the *sensitivity and responsiveness* of police to citizens. Community policing is a major example of this. A national survey of police officers found that half believed that community policing reduces incidents involving excessive force (Weisburd and Greenspan 2000). The American public also endorses community policing. A 1998 survey of 12 American cities that found 86 percent of residents of areas lacking community policing wanted it practiced in their neighborhoods (Bureau of Justice Statistics 1999). We replicated this question in our national survey and found that 70–80 percent of our three groups favor it (see Figure 4.4). With regard to specific community policing practices, the vast majority of all three racial groups favor police-community meetings, police programs for schoolchildren, and foot patrols on the streets, though blacks are slightly more inclined to favor these practices (Figure 4.4).

Another example of more sensitive policing is sensitivity training itself. The Police Foundation survey discovered that fully three-quarters of police officers believe that training in "human diversity or cultural awareness" would help prevent police abuse of authority (Weisburd and Greenspan 2000). We asked our respondents whether more sensitivity training would improve treatment of minorities. Most thought that it would indeed help (84 percent of blacks, 75 percent of Hispanics, 60 percent of whites), with 57 percent of blacks and 39 percent of Hispanics saying it would help "a lot." Another item asked

Figure 4.4. Support for community policing

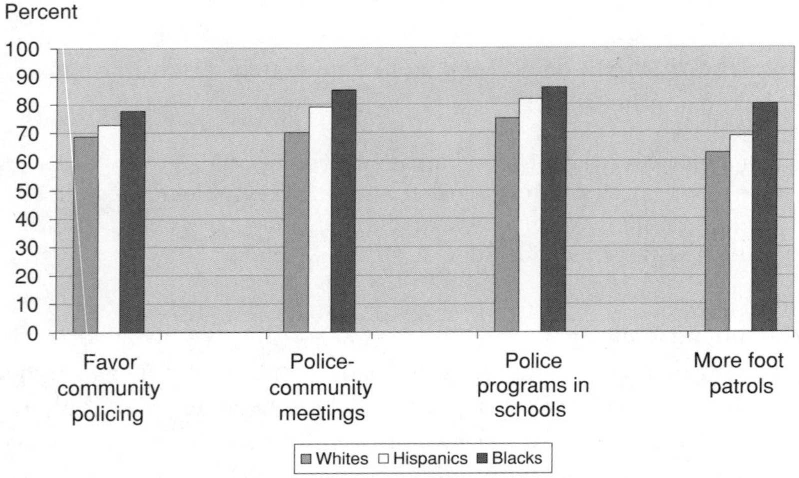

Percent

Note: "Favor Community Policing" means that respondent wants it in his or her neighborhood; this question was asked only of respondents who said their neighborhoods do not have community policing. The other questions were asked of all respondents.

about requiring officers in Spanish-speaking areas to learn Spanish. More than two-thirds of all three groups thought that this would improve matters, with a plurality of blacks and Hispanics saying this would help "a lot."[8]

Intensified Policing

It is possible to favor policing that is both sensitive toward citizens and more intensive in fighting crime. The two are not necessarily contradictory, although they often are in practice. Depending on *how* police expand their efforts to control crime, this may or may not

[8] Two other changes, that have the potential to increase sensitivity toward the public, were presented to respondents: hiring more female officers and replacing the chief of police. A majority of Hispanics and blacks, but only one-third of whites, believe that hiring more women will have at least some positive effect. Replacing the chief of police is an item that clearly does not apply universally across the country. There is likely to be significant variation from city to city in public ratings of chiefs' job performance and, hence, in the desirability of replacing their chief. Still, it is noteworthy that 16 percent of whites, 31 percent of Hispanics, and 39 percent of African Americans believe that replacing their city's police chief would improve policing at least somewhat.

Figure 4.5. Support for intensified policing

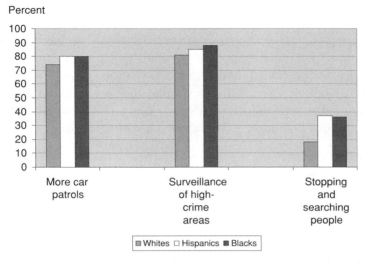

Percent

infringe on people's rights and interfere with the goal of treating people respectfully and fairly. People who live in high-crime communities, for instance, have called on the local police to simultaneously crack down on street crime and treat residents with more respect. At police-community meetings in such neighborhoods, residents often clamor for much more vigorous law enforcement and are very critical of what they see as police unresponsiveness to calls from residents regarding ongoing problems in their neighborhoods (Weitzer 1999; CCPEC 2003:34–42).

In our survey, intensified policing was measured by three items: more car patrols, more surveillance of areas where street crimes occur often, and stopping and searching more people on the street. The first two changes receive widespread support across the board, changes that are expected to improve policing either somewhat or a lot (see Figure 4.5) – although minorities are more likely than whites to believe that more car patrols and more surveillance will improve matters "a lot" in their city. In evaluating the three practices, people seem quite cognizant of individual rights. The one change that might violate those rights – stopping and searching more people on the street – is rejected by a majority of all three groups. Although an appreciable minority of Hispanics and blacks favor more street stops, only 8 percent and 10 percent, respectively, say that this would improve policing "a lot."

In sum, in striking contrast to many whites' opinions that minorities want to straightjacket the police, our research shows that blacks and Hispanics are quite supportive of robust police efforts to fight crime. They overwhelmingly endorse more car patrols and more police surveillance in their cities. At the same time, they are also interested in curbing police misconduct, as this and other chapters abundantly show. They favor both more policing and more humane policing.

WHAT INFLUENCES REFORM PREFERENCES?

The results presented earlier indicate that race matters in citizen evaluations of a host of reforms in policing. To further explore how race shapes reform preferences, we begin again by examining a baseline model containing only race. Results of the race-only model (not shown in a table) confirm that blacks are significantly more supportive than whites of *every* reform initiative; that Hispanics also support each initiative (except procedural justice) more strongly than whites; and that blacks are more supportive than Hispanics of reform in the areas of racial diversification, police accountability, and community policing (blacks and Hispanics do not differ significantly from each other on procedural justice or intensified policing). Thus, on every issue except procedural justice and intensified policing, Hispanics' support for reform is intermediate between that of blacks, who are most supportive, and whites, who are least so. This is largely consistent with the racial hierarchy thesis.

But what accounts for these differences among whites, African Americans, and Hispanics? And are there other factors besides race that shape views of police reform? Table 4.1 provides answers to these questions. As in earlier chapters, our purpose is to clarify not only how race shapes reform preferences alone but also in concert with our other key explanatory factors. Models 1 through 5 in the table present findings on racial diversity, police accountability, community policing, procedural justice, and intensified policing, respectively. Model 1 (racial diversity) includes two variables not used in the other models, variables based on two questions asking respondents to compare

white and minority officers' behavior toward citizens: "In general
in the United States, do you think there are differences in the way
white officers and black officers/Hispanic officers act toward citizens?"
(1 = yes). Because these questions tap citizens' perceptions of behavioral differences in officers of different races, they may be especially
relevant to understanding popular views on diversification of police
departments.[9]

The coefficients in the total sample columns of Table 4.1 indicate
that, once the additional variables are taken account of, blacks continue to favor police diversification more strongly than whites, but
the two groups do not differ on the other reforms; Hispanics remain
more likely than whites to support reforms in the areas of racial diversity, community policing, and intensified policing, but not in the other
two areas.

The most consistent predictors in the combined sample are perceptions of misconduct and media exposure: Citizens who perceive
police misconduct in their city or neighborhood and who are exposed
to media reports of police misbehavior express more support for *all*
reforms in Table 4.1. Those residing in areas of concentrated disadvantage show heightened enthusiasm both for community policing and
intensified policing, and respondents who think that white and Hispanic officers act differently toward citizens are more likely to endorse
police racial diversification.[10]

Having established that race differences persist in some models
and disappear in others after controlling for additional factors, we

9 We do not know whether respondents who answered these questions affirmatively
   believe that white officers behave better or worse than minority officers, just that
   behavioral differences are acknowledged.
10 Research has found that perceived discrimination against minorities increases support for changes in racial policies (Tuch and Hughes 1996a, 1996b; Hughes and
   Tuch 2000; Kluegel and Bobo 2001). Do beliefs about racially biased policing similarly influence support for reforms designed to increase sensitivity to minority group
   members? To address this question, we examined the impact of the four measures
   of police bias discussed in Chapter 3 (as well as the other independent variables)
   on three other policy measures – recording of driver information, requiring police
   officers in Spanish-speaking areas to learn Spanish, and more sensitivity training –
   (results not shown in a table). Although recognition of police bias does not shape
   views of the efficacy of recording driver information to deter racial profiling, it did
   increase support for the policies of requiring Spanish and sensitivity training. Thus,
   the perception that police bias exists is an important predictor of support for two
   significant reforms that may improve the treatment of minorities.

TABLE 4.1. *Reform preferences*

	Total sample		Whites		Blacks		Hispanics	
	b	beta	b	beta	b	beta	b	beta
Model 1. Diversification								
Black	.448***	.153	—	—	—	—	—	—
	(.086)		—		—		—	
Hispanic	.393***	.143	—	—	—	—	—	—
	(.068)		—		—		—	
White-black police diff's (1 = yes)	-.051	-.025	-.115	-.056	.260*	.124	.052	.026
	(.067)		(.128)		(.128)		(.110)	
White-Hispanic police diff's (1 = yes)	.262***	.121	.257	.113	.087	.043	.293**	.143
	(.070)		(.136)		(.122)		(.114)	
Concentrated disadvantage	.023	.023	-.012	-.012	.047	.047	.060	.060
	(.030)		(.045)		(.048)		(.047)	
Perceived misconduct	.179***	.179	.127**	.127	.265***	.265	.145**	.145
	(.031)		(.054)		(.055)		(.053)	
Personal experience with misconduct (1 = yes)	-.125*	-.056	-.106	-.045	-.126	-.062	-.076	-.037
	(.061)		(.116)		(.111)		(.104)	
Vicarious experience with misconduct (1 = yes)	.170**	.071	.204	.076	.021	.010	.124	.059
	(.061)		(.119)		(.108)		(.103)	
Media exposure	.172***	.125	.129*	.089	.183**	.152	.349***	.280
	(.034)		(.065)		(.061)		(.056)	
N of cases (unweighted)	1,498		589		468		513	
Constant	-.487		-.051		-.679		-1.169	
R² (adjusted)	.197		.053		.151		.201	

154

TABLE 4.1 *Reform preferences (continued)*

	Total sample		Whites		Blacks		Hispanics	
	b	beta	b	beta	b	beta	b	beta
Model 2. Accountability								
Black	.159 (.085)	.054	—	—	—	—	—	—
Hispanic	.112 (.067)	.041	—	—	—	—	—	—
Concentrated disadvantage	.023 (.030)	.023	.012 (.042)	.012	.001 (.047)	.001	.155*** (.048)	.155
Perceived misconduct	.275*** (.030)	.275	.343*** (.050)	.343	.207*** (.054)	.207	−.048 (.054)	−.048
Personal experience with misconduct (1 = yes)	.006 (.061)	.002	−.076 (.108)	−.033	.101 (.111)	.050	.113 (.106)	.055
Vicarious experience with misconduct (1 = yes)	.006 (.061)	.002	.071 (.110)	.026	−.193 (.107)	−.093	.120 (.105)	.057
Media exposure	.236*** (.033)	.172	.159** (.060)	.109	.348*** (.058)	.290	.438*** (.056)	.351
N of cases (unweighted)	1,691		605		487		523	
Constant	−.422		−.096		−1.124		−1.317	
R² (adjusted)	.205		.177		.152		.171	

(*continued*)

155

TABLE 4.1 *Reform preferences (continued)*

	Total sample		Whites		Blacks		Hispanics	
	b	beta	b	beta	b	beta	b	beta
Model 3. Community policing								
Black	.143 (.090)	.049	—	—	—	—	—	—
Hispanic	.186** (.071)	.068	—	—	—	—	—	—
Concentrated disadvantage	.113*** (.031)	.113	.046 (.045)	.046	.152** (.050)	.152	.186*** (.049)	.186
Perceived misconduct	.125*** (.032)	.125	.085 (.054)	.085	.173** (.056)	.173	-.003 (.055)	-.003
Personal experience with misconduct (1 = yes)	-.008 (.064)	-.004	-.093 (.117)	-.040	.225* (.115)	.111	.156 (.108)	.075
Vicarious experience with misconduct (1 = yes)	.074 (.064)	.031	.192 (.118)	.071	-.269* (.111)	-.129	.065 (.107)	.031
Media exposure	.147*** (.035)	.107	.098 (.064)	.067	.145** (.061)	.121	.347*** (.057)	.278
N of cases (unweighted)	1,696		605		489		527	
Constant	-.648		-.544		-.594		-1.019	
R² (adjusted)	.106		.046		.077		.140	

TABLE 4.1 Reform preferences (continued)

	Total sample		Whites		Blacks		Hispanics	
	b	beta	b	beta	b	beta	b	beta
Model 4. Procedural justice								
Black	.048	.016	—	—	—	—	—	—
	(.092)		—		—		—	
Hispanic	.076	.028	—	—	—	—	—	—
	(.073)		—		—		—	
Concentrated disadvantage	-.047	-.047	-.020	-.020	-.062	-.062	.090	.090
	(.032)		(.044)		(.048)		(.051)	
Perceived misconduct	.076*	.076	.119*	.119	.088	.088	-.194***	-.194
	(.033)		(.053)		(.055)		(.056)	
Personal experience with misconduct (1 = yes)	.019	.008	-.054	-.023	.065	.032	.121	.059
	(.066)		(.116)		(.113)		(.112)	
Vicarious experience with misconduct (1 = yes)	.234***	.097	.377***	.140	-.106	-.051	.263*	.125
	(.066)		(.117)		(.109)		(.110)	
Media exposure	.149***	.109	.065	.045	.324***	.270	.259***	.208
	(.036)		(.064)		(.059)		(.058)	
N of cases (unweighted)	1,703		608		493		520	
Constant	-.535		-.332		-1.345		-1.044	
R² (adjusted)	.057		.062		.118		.083	

(continued)

157

TABLE 4.1 *Reform preferences (continued)*

	Total sample		Whites		Blacks		Hispanics	
	b	beta	b	beta	b	beta	b	beta
Model 5. Intensified policing								
Black	-.063	-.021	—	—	—	—	—	—
	(.090)		—		—		—	
Hispanic	.212**	.077	—	—	—	—	—	—
	(.071)		—		—		—	
Concentrated disadvantage	.115***	.115	.080	.080	.130**	.130	.146**	.146
	(.031)		(.044)		(.050)		(.051)	
Perceived misconduct	.094**	.094	.065	.065	.151**	.151	.008	.008
	(.032)		(.053)		(.057)		(.056)	
Media exposure	.102**	.074	.051	.035	-.012	-.010	.307***	.246
	(.035)		(.063)		(.061)		(.058)	
Personal experience with misconduct (1 = yes)	-.041	-.019	-.094	-.040	.163	.081	.009	.005
	(.065)		(.115)		(.117)		(.112)	
Vicarious experience with misconduct (1 = yes)	-.006	-.002	.007	.002	-.368***	-.178	-.033	-.016
	(.064)		(.116)		(.112)		(.110)	
N of cases (unweighted)	1,703		609		489		529	
Constant	-.103		.148		.299		-.765	
R² (adjusted)	.102		.076		.056		.087	

Note: Standard errors in parentheses; estimates are net of controls for education, household income, gender, age, city-suburban residence, and region; * $p < .05$; ** $p < .01$; *** $p < .001$.

now address the key question of how these factors shape each racial group's views of police reform. The race-specific columns in Table 4.1 provide the answer. In model 1, we note first that neither question about behavioral differences between different-race officers influences whites' views on racial diversity. In other words, whether or not whites believe there are behavioral differences between white and minority officers, it does not influence whether they think racial diversification is a good thing. The pattern is different for blacks and Hispanics. Blacks who perceive behavioral differences between white and black officers, and Hispanics who perceive such differences between white and Hispanic officers, are more likely than same-race peers to prefer diversity on their police force. These differences regarding the importance of the behavioral variables are all that distinguish the views of minority from white respondents.

Model 2 summarizes findings for police accountability. Overall, there are few racial differences. The most salient factors are perceptions of misconduct and exposure to mass media accounts of police misbehavior.[11]

Regarding community policing (model 3), the differences between whites and minorities are especially marked. None of the explanatory factors significantly impacts whites' views of the efficacy of community policing; among blacks, however, all do (though the direction of the effect for vicarious experience is counterintuitive). Among Hispanics, media exposure and concentrated disadvantage both heighten support for community policing.

What about procedural justice (model 4)? Whites who see misconduct as common and who have vicariously experienced police abuse are more likely to support procedural justice reforms. For blacks, media exposure is the only factor that matters, while Hispanics are influenced by perceived misconduct (though not in the expected direction), media exposure, and vicarious experience.

---

[11] We also ran a separate analysis for the question asking what kind of punishment respondents would favor for police officers who have used excessive force against a citizen. The only strong predictor in this analysis was exposure to media reports on police misconduct. People frequently exposed to such reports were more likely to support several of the specified types of punishment.

Model 5 pertains to intensified policing. Among whites, none of the predictors significantly impacts their support for this change. Blacks' support for more vigorous crime control is heightened among those who perceive widespread misconduct by local cops and who live in areas of concentrated disadvantage (those who have vicariously experienced misconduct express disfavor with intensified policing); for Hispanics, media exposure and concentrated disadvantage tell the story. That people living in neighborhoods with high levels of socioeconomic disadvantage support intensified policing is understandable in light of the high crime rates that typically afflict these communities, rates that might be reduced by more robust police activity.

In sum, citizen experiences with police officers seem to matter little insofar as their reform preferences are concerned. As indicated earlier, the evidence is somewhat mixed regarding the effect of police-citizen contact on larger attitudes toward the police. While negative contact influences general satisfaction with the police, it is by no means a necessary condition for the formation of either general or specific attitudes. And general attitudes may influence specific views (e.g., police reform) irrespective of one's personal or vicarious experiences with officers. Our research shows that preferences regarding police reform are shaped by larger views of the police, which seem to transcend one's experiences with officers.[12]

Especially important is the role of the mass media in influencing opinion about the desirability of police reform. Particularly for blacks and Hispanics, those who are frequently exposed to media reports of incidents of misconduct are apt to support reforms. It appears that *frequent exposure to such reports leads people (and especially minorities) to*

---

[12] In Chapter 2, we found strong effects of personal experience on perceptions of police misconduct, leading us to suspect that the effect of experience on views of police reform might be indirect, operating through perceptions of misconduct. In other words, perhaps it is not one's experience alone that affects evaluations of reform. Instead, it may be when personal experience is generalized to a larger belief that police misconduct is rife that the experience conditions reform preferences. To examine this possibility, we decomposed the total effect of the two experience variables on reform into direct and indirect components. We found that experience with misconduct increased support for reforms indirectly through perceptions of misconduct among whites in models 2 and 3, among blacks in model 5, and among Hispanics in models 1 and 5. This suggests that experience with the police does play some indirect role in shaping citizens' reform preferences.

conclude that there are serious problems with their police department, problems that require sweeping changes. The media play an important role in stoking demands for reform not only among people who are often exposed to reporting of policing problems but also, according to other studies, in the wake of a single controversial incident. For example, in the aftermath of the 1991 Rodney King beating in Los Angeles and repeated rebroadcasting on television of the videotaped beating, a growing number of city residents favored reforms. These included replacing the combative chief of police, Daryl Gates, and creating a civilian review board. Similarly, in the wake of a major corruption and brutality scandal in the LAPD's Rampart Division in 2000, also heavily covered by the local media, a majority of city residents favored appointment of an independent monitor to scrutinize the department and to oversee implementation of other reforms (Weitzer 2002). Media coverage of a single incident can therefore have a major impact on the public's assessment of the need for reform, just like the effect of serial media coverage of disparate events and problems.

Also important in several models is neighborhood context. Support for police accountability is heightened among Hispanics living in areas of concentrated disadvantage, and support for community policing and for intensified policing is strengthened among both blacks and Hispanics living in such areas. The latter finding supports the argument that minorities living in poor neighborhoods desire both *more robust policing and more sensitive policing* in their communities. In the remainder of the chapter we discuss our qualitative findings.

WHAT OTHER REFORMS ARE DESIRED?

Although the policies examined above are wide-ranging, they are not exhaustive of all conceivable reforms. Before presenting our respondents with questions about the specific reforms discussed earlier in the chapter, we asked them an open-ended question that explored their own ideas about reform, hoping to uncover ideas that were novel or intriguing. We asked: "What kinds of changes would you like to see to improve your city's police department and police practices." Not surprisingly, many of the ideas were related to policing problems covered earlier in the questionnaire. People favored, for instance, stiffer punishment for misconduct, equal treatment of citizens regardless of race or class, curbs on police use of force, diversification of police departments, and ending racial profiling.[13] We report below only the responses that are distinct from and not redundant with other questionnaire items.

Some people offer fairly simple platitudes with respect to the changes they would like to see: such as more patrols in cars or on foot, faster response time, greater "professionalism," treating people with "common courtesy," psychological screening, background checks, better training, and so forth. Speeding cars is an issue for many whites and blacks, who want crackdowns on speeding in residential neighborhoods, but just as many say the police already put too much emphasis on speeding (writing tickets for going just a few miles over the speed limit) and other minor offenses, and should instead focus on "real crime" like murder and rape. Blacks and whites alike seem to think that the police spend a disproportionate amount of time on minor matters and need to redirect their efforts to target major crimes.

The qualitative data reveal some important racial differences in reform preferences. Most whites say one of three things: (1) they know too little to recommend changes; (2) no changes are needed, because there are no problems; or (3) all that is needed are changes that would fortify the department. They call for more resources and equipment (stun guns, dogs, high-powered weapons), want more officers hired and more street patrolling, and think cops should be paid more.[14] Higher pay is sometimes justified on the grounds that it will allow the department to recruit "better people" or to reduce turnover, but usually this is just asserted without explanation. Such boosterism fits well with the group-position tenet that dominant groups favor fortification of institutions of control, and see police as their allies in the fight against crime. Few whites, however, actually say that the police

---

[13] A national poll found that 7 out of 10 Americans feel that "police should be prohibited from taking race into account when targeting people as suspects" (Penn, Schoen, and Berland 2000).

[14] A majority of Americans (61 percent) believe that police officers are not paid enough for what they do; 27 percent feel they are paid the right amount and 3 percent think they are paid too much (CSR 2000).

should be strengthened or deployed in order to crack down specifically on minority offenders, although some do so: "Do something about the Section 8 [public] housing; those people are out of control" (LC white male, 49).

Many whites are *staunch champions of the police*. When asked if they desired changes in their city's police department, many saw absolutely no need for change. They felt that their police were doing a "fine," "great," and "excellent" job, and were "very happy," "very pleased," and "completely satisfied" with their police department. Consider the following declarations: "I believe they do an awesome job and we should all be thankful that there are dedicated men and women who want this job" (MC white female, 49); "The police seem to be doing a terrific job, so I wouldn't change a thing" (UMC white male, 19); and "Our police department is excellent. I see no need for my city's police department to change" (MC white female, 32). Few blacks and Hispanics used superlatives to describe their police department, and few were so satisfied that they had no ideas for improvement.

Troubled by critics of the police, some whites "condemn the condemners," one of Sykes and Matza's (1957) neutralization techniques for defusing attributions of deviant behavior. They redirect blame for problems from the police to citizens who cast aspersions on the police. This applies to belligerent citizens: "The public should have some education about manners. If a person screams and yells at a policeman, the policeman might have a harder time trying to be polite" (LC white female, 58). Blame is also directed at ignorant citizens, who do not understand the realities of police work yet feel free to criticize: "Let the complainers go on police patrol from 8 pm to 4 am" to understand how difficult and dangerous this work is (UMC white male, 74).

Also condemned by many whites are politicians, the media, community groups, minorities, and civil rights organizations – each of whom stands accused of meddling in police work. What is needed is "less interference from those outside law enforcement who have an agenda other than keeping the public safe" (LC white female, 68), and "let the police do their job and keep race out of it as well as politics" (MC white female, 62). We know from our version of the group-position thesis that dominant group members tend to jump to the defense of the police when they think the "race card" is being played, and they also associate minority groups with threats to law and order. Some whites express this position in a rather forthright manner: "I believe the over-all majority of police officers are doing a good job. The problem more lies with uneducated citizens who back criminals based solely on their race" (MC white male, 39).

Discontent with racial interference in policing was evident in a number of narratives, manifested in calls for "no racial quotas" in hiring and promotion and the removal of "politics" from hiring and promotion decisions, which should be strictly "based on merit." These views are expressions or reflections of the overall opposition among whites (see Figure 4.1) to giving minorities preferences in hiring.

The media are singled out for the harshest criticism. Americans are equally divided, according to a national poll, between those who believe that the media are "anti-police" and "pro-police."[15] Whites tend to see the media as anti-police. Portrayed as liberal, biased in favor of minorities and civil rights groups, and even coddling criminals, the net effect of media reporting, it is argued, is interference with law enforcement and an overall dilution of law and order:

> You hear so much bad news on TV about some cop gone bad or some blunder that happened, but you don't hear about the good cops, the one's who are out there every day putting their lives on the line to keep us safe. So maybe the media could play a role in honoring the millions of cops who do good. (MC white female, 40)

> Less media interference.... Unfortunately when an officer does something wrong the media is all over it and makes it a very large problem when it really isn't. (LMC white female, 64)

> We have a very good police chief. He should be allowed to work as he sees fit rather than have to bend to community groups who continually find fault with the police. Yes, the police department should be under some sort of scrutiny, but they need to be allowed to conduct investigations without interference from news media. They need to be able to keep some facts to themselves while investigating crimes and not have to be questioned on every little detail by news reporters. Let them do their jobs. (LC white female, 54)

---

[15] Thirty-six percent thought that the news media are generally anti-police, 38 percent thought the media were pro-police, and 14 percent volunteered that the media were balanced, neutral, or neither pro- nor anti-police (Fox/Opinion Dynamics 1997).

I see nothing wrong with police work. The changes that should be made are with the ultra-liberal media reporting on crime. In most cases the criminal is lovingly portrayed as having his civil rights violated and the police are usually termed as overstepping their bounds – whatever the hell that means. The police are doing a good job but the media along with the ACLU keep glorifying the criminal and handcuffing all law enforcement. I suggest the media should be made to detail all the facts so that an honest interpretation of every story can be revealed. (MC white male, 84)

This perspective puts the media in league with alleged opponents of the police, such as certain community groups, the ACLU, and "citizens who back criminals based solely on their race." Indeed, some white respondents seem to think these forces are aligned in a conspiracy to undermine the police. We have already established – from our survey question on exposure to media reports of police misconduct – that such exposure heightens dissatisfaction with, and demands for reform of, the police. For people who see the police as allies and view criticisms as a threat to law and order or to prevailing group-position arrangements, it is thus understandable that they would express strong disdain for the media, as revealed in the quotations above. Remarkably, *none* of our Hispanic or black respondents mentioned media representation of the police as a problem or thought that "reform" was needed in media reporting.

In fact, this critique of the media is fairly misguided. Although there certainly are times when the media do rush to judgment or frame stories in such a way that accused officers appear to be guilty, research indicates that, overall, news media reporting is biased in favor of police interpretations of events and only occasionally gives critics a voice. As an excellent study of media coverage of incidents of police brutality concludes, "the news media help to create and sustain the legitimacy of the police." Police are occasionally subject to critical scrutiny, but these critics "are generally not granted the same place in the news as those of police and other officials, and often are subtly undermined by the ways that reporters frame news stories" (Lawrence 2000:31). This is partly because of "reporters' professional unease with amplifying 'antipolice' voices" (Lawrence 2000:134) and partly a function of the ongoing symbiotic relationship between news organizations and police departments, where reporters depend on police sources for information on local crimes. Police and other officials are relied on in 80 percent of news stories related to police brutality, with the result that abuse is downplayed and individualized – framed as the work of a handful of "rogue" cops, rather than larger institutional problems (Lawrence 2000:43). Occasionally, however, the media do sensationalize an incident and provide a platform for critics of the police (e.g., Rodney King), and these exceptional reports may be what is feeding some of our white respondents' irritation with the media.

Not all whites are cheerleaders for the police. As indicated throughout this book, some take the view that police misconduct and racial bias are widespread in America and that much more accountability is needed. In addition, shocking events, highly publicized in the media, such as the beating of Rodney King, have been shown to sour white opinion of the police, although minority groups are even more strongly affected by such incidents (Tuch and Weitzer 1997; Weitzer 2002).

In addition, a number of white respondents are especially troubled by officers' authoritarian and condescending demeanor. They want officers to treat people with more respect, to presume citizens' innocence rather than guilt, and to behave like they are "human, not gods" above the law:

> Train them to treat everyone like a human being, not a perpetrator. (MC white male, 25)

> Most of the officers I encounter are arrogant, speak down to people, and generally act like everyone is a criminal and beneath them. (LMC white female, 41)

> Most of the police here think they are better than everyone else, when indeed they are not. A lot of them are liars, and will use excessive force if they can get away with it. (MC white male, 58)

Still, both criticisms and ideas for reform are scarcer among whites than favorable views. Whether the issue is overall satisfaction, police misconduct, racial discrimination, or reform, most whites give the police positive ratings, discount criticisms, and either reject or give lukewarm support to most of the reforms examined here. Although whites are not monolithic in their orientation toward the police, the *vast majority* are indeed champions of the police.

Few blacks and Hispanics give such unequivocal support to the police. Rarely do they call for fortifying the police department, or mention pay increases, hiring more officers, better equipment, and so forth. And those who do express favorable views of the police tend to temper or qualify their support with calls for both citizens and police to make concessions:

> I would like to see all police officers treat citizens with more respect, and the citizens [to] learn more about the officers and the daily problems they face so they could understand the officers more and respect them more. (MC black female, 56)

> [We need] change that promotes the idea of a police officer as a public servant first, a peacekeeper second, and then a law enforcer. If you believe you are a servant, you will not mishandle people who are different nor will you abuse them. If keeping the peace is your aim, you will not escalate situations. If you have to enforce the law you will do it with due diligence and not excessively use force. I am not naive to the police officers' role and responsibilities. I am thankful to them and am glad they take on the jobs they do. (MC black female, 48)

> More police officers with proper technical training, better equipment for officers to fight crime, and a system to weed out corrupt police officers, [because] they do so much damage to public trust. (MC Hispanic male, 58)

If they do not call for police fortification in the way whites do, many Hispanics and blacks clearly want more policing in their neighborhoods and cities. A common refrain among all three groups is that "more patrolling" and "more cops" are needed. The frequency of this demand among Hispanics and blacks (in both the qualitative data and as shown in Figure 4.5) is consistent with our argument that minorities are just as interested as whites in crime control, especially proactively via both more police patrols in cars, more surveillance, and more community policing. Many whites appear to view minorities as anti-police, consistent with group-position theory, but that is a gross distortion of blacks' and Hispanics' own orientation toward the police. They are indeed much more critical than whites, but they also are quite adamant about the need for more law enforcement.

In addition to advocating increased policing, what other reforms are popular among Hispanics and blacks? First, they see a need for

more accountability, because they think that police officers get away
with crime:

> A lot of police officers get away with things a citizen would not get
> away with. We need to crack down on police officers who commit
> crime just like citizens who commit those same crimes. (MC black
> female, 31)

> Officers who act contrary to public interest and the law are not fearful
> of [getting] caught. Law enforcement officials need to make an hon-
> est effort to catch them and fully punish them. (UMC black male, 39)

Second, minorities, and especially African Americans, support
changes that have the potential to reduce racial discrimination. As
one middle-class black woman stated, "Stop harassing innocent people because of the color of their skin and go after the real criminals."
Any reform that contributes to color-blind policing is supported – as
group-position theory holds – because it helps to advance the group
interests of the two minority groups, including their interest in seeing
fewer minority group members victimized by police.

Third, like some whites, Hispanics and blacks are bothered by police
demeanor in encounters with citizens, which they find demeaning.
Police were accused of talking to people "like they're street scum,"
of "thinking we must bow down to them," and giving "an impression
that they are better than the average citizen." Instead, they want to see
civility, sensitivity, and respectful treatment – including "learning how
to talk to people," showing that they "care about the people they are
supposed to be serving," and treating people politely:

> Most police do not live in the city and disdain city residents. They
> appear to have the mentality of "occupiers." . . . Police want to be
> treated as special whereas they are just like everyone else. If they
> treat citizens with respect, respect will be showed to them. (UMC
> black male, 45)

> They should have mock incidents where something would happen
> and have an officer . . . pretend to be a victim. Rate how the officer
> performs, the officer's "bedside manner," in order to determine if
> they need more customer service training. Any position that deals
> with the public should have some sort of "people handling training."
> (MC Hispanic male, 26)

Respect is a key concern, particularly for minority citizens. Not only do officers stand accused of treating people without respect, but they often unleash upon them verbally and physically. One elderly black man, for example, called the police a "gang" who like to "vent their frustrations" on members of the public. Several respondents felt that anger-management classes were needed to curb such conduct. Sensitivity training, not just for rookies but also throughout the officers' careers, is frequently called for especially by African Americans. The content of such training, according to our informants, should include both general human relations norms as well as more specific awareness of different cultures, races, and communities.

Fourth, Hispanics and blacks strongly favor community policing. The overwhelming support for community policing documented earlier in the chapter was also reflected in answers to two open-ended questions. One was the generic question asking respondents to volunteer ideas for desirable changes in their local police department. In response, many black and Hispanic respondents said that they wanted more police (1) interaction with neighborhood residents, (2) involvement in community programs, and (3) engagement with teenagers. These three related themes recur *very frequently* in the discourse of blacks and Hispanics and to a lesser extent among whites. There is a strong sense that police are alienated from the public, take little time to learn about neighborhoods and their residents, and are not invested in the city in which they work. This is why some people advocate requiring officers to live in the city in which they work – a policy mentioned by blacks and Hispanics but not whites.

The second open-ended question asked specifically about community policing. We first defined *community policing* as "police officers working with community members to address the causes of crime and to prevent crimes from occurring, rather than just responding to crimes after they have occurred." We then asked respondents who thought that police did not practice community policing in their neighborhood if they wished they did and, if so, why they felt this way.

First and foremost, community policing is seen as a way of reducing crime. Many people are frustrated with the reactive nature of traditional policing and want more effort placed on prevention:

> I see my police as being reactionary. Nothing is being done to stop crime before the fact. (UMC black female, 35)

> We are the eyes of the city, we are residents, the victims. We know where the offenders are. . . . And yet police do not listen to us; they show up 3–4 hours later; a person could be dead and buried by that time. I have lost faith in our city police. (LC Hispanic male, 45)

These individuals see community policing as a way of preventing crime and addressing larger problems that lead to crime, in part by opening a channel for community residents to convey to officers information about local problems:

> How else will they learn to prevent problems if they don't ask the people in my neighborhood what the problems are? They need to patrol the neighborhood and find out what is going on; ask questions, enforce obvious violations, confront loiterers, develop rapport with citizens, develop informants, and get to know the neighbors. (UMC Hispanic male, 73)

> Addressing the causes of crime seems to me to be the only true way of eradicating it. Responding after a crime is committed is only addressing the symptoms. (UMC Hispanic female, 43)

> Police would be committed to actually solving the problems in our neighborhood. They wouldn't just pass by, see the problem, and do nothing about it. (MC Hispanic female, 19)

Other benefits of community policing, according to our respondents, include deepening officers' understanding of a neighborhood (who belongs there, suspicious activities, etc.), which could only help in crime reduction; making residents feel safer by virtue of the visibility of officers in the neighborhood; and informing residents about crimes that had occurred in their area.

Second, community policing is valued because it will facilitate positive dialogue and help to promote mutual understanding and improved police-community relations:

> With this communication comes a better understanding and mutual respect between the residents and the police. (MC Hispanic female, 38)

Community policing is an excellent way to acquaint police officers with the people of a community, and vice versa. (MC black male, 33)

If we understood the practices and limitations of the police department, we would have more accurate expectations. (UMC white male, 49)

Third, some research has found that community policing can help to reduce the aggressive style of officers and curb the use of force (Greene 1999; Terrill and Mastrofski 2004), and several of our respondents agree:

Focus on the community, and less of the SWAT mentality. (LC white male, 15)

Community policing ... may help to ease fears of the police and stop some of the intimidating attitudes which the police have toward the people in the community. (UMC black male, 47)

One respondent, who sits on a police-community board, where officers and citizens meet monthly, noted that the board has succeeded in purging rogue cops from the department: "We have an open line with this police chief. He is getting corrupt officers off the beat and out of the force" (LC black female, 71).

Fourth, several individuals, especially in minority communities, singled out the possible benefits for neighborhood youth:

They will be able to know the children and teenagers. They can pinpoint when a teenager doesn't belong in the community and this could be an alarm system for them. They would be able to have a more bonding relationship with the youth in the community as it was in the fifties. (MC Hispanic female, 57)

It is a great way to teach children to respect and help police, and not fear and dislike them. (MC black male, 33)

Some of the kids in the neighborhood think poorly of police, that the officers are the bad guys. I realize that asking the police to do community policing is requiring a great deal from the police department, but if the manpower was there then kids could have someone else around as a role model. (LMC white female, 39)

Some mentioned specific programs for youth, and Hispanics in particular thought that such liaison with youth would help to combat gangs.

Interestingly, a number of our teenage respondents were also convinced of both the general value of community policing and the idea
that youth would benefit from it. They wanted the police to be more
involved with the neighborhood, and especially with young residents.
One girl wanted to see

> more involvement with children and teens, especially outside of
> school. Cops have come to my school in the past and they have done
> a good job, but they should come to neighborhoods more often.
> I've never had a cop talk to me in my neighborhood. (MC white
> female, 15)

Although broad support, across the three groups, for community
policing was documented earlier in the chapter, both the qualitative
and quantitative data show that blacks and Hispanics are more ardent
advocates than are whites – likely because their neighborhoods are
more afflicted with both crime and police misconduct. More than
any other group, blacks see community policing as a way of *reducing
tensions* between police and citizens – both improving police treatment
of residents and curbing residents' unruly behavior toward officers.
The notion that community policing would help *build confidence* in the
police was also frequently mentioned. It "will establish a relationship
of trust," with "the policeman not being viewed as the enemy" (LMC
black male, 63). Others elaborated:

> It would help deter the violent outbreaks that often result when the
> police respond to certain situations and someone ends up getting
> shot and killed. (UMC black female, 27)
>
> Community policing gives people a feeling of trust towards the police.
> At the same time it lets the police know more about the different
> types of people living in that neighborhood. The law officers will not
> be so fearful towards a certain race of people that live or visit that
> neighborhood. (MC black male, 57)

In a nutshell, the desire for genuine community policing is both
widespread and passionate, particularly in minority communities.

CONCLUSION

This chapter shows how race and other factors structure citizens' views on the issue of police reform. In the baseline race-only models, blacks and Hispanics are more likely than whites to endorse every type of reform with the exception of Hispanics' views of procedural justice, and blacks are more supportive than Hispanics of changes that would increase racial diversification, police accountability, and community policing.

The findings on reform generally support the African American–Hispanic–white racial hierarchy pattern we found for misconduct and racial bias. Police reform follows the same pattern in three of five cases – diversification, accountability, and community policing. Blacks are the most supportive of these policies, whites are the least so, and Hispanics are intermediate between the two.

To summarize our other findings: First, the perception that police misconduct is common in one's city or neighborhood increases support for reform in nearly half of the race-specific models. It seems logical that people who believe that police wrongdoing is a serious problem would tend to feel that a host of reforms are necessary to reduce it, and our findings tend to confirm this.

Second, citizens' experiences in encounters with officers is a fairly weak predictor when it comes to support for reform. We know that contact with the police is not a necessary condition for the formation of attitudes toward the police (cf. Brandl et al. 1994), a point that is borne out in popular evaluations of reforms. Reform preferences are instead shaped by assessments of larger policing problems, which largely transcend one's experiences with officers, with the exception of the indirect effects noted earlier in the chapter.

Third, the mass media play the same role in shaping public opinion on police reform as they do in shaping perceptions of misconduct and racial bias. Repeated exposure to media reports on police abuse is a strong predictor of citizens' support for a wide variety of reforms, net of other factors, in more than two-thirds of the race-specific models. Media effects are very robust especially for blacks and Hispanics – operating in 9 of 10 models. People who frequently hear or read about incidents of police misconduct, as transmitted by the media, are inclined to conclude that there are serious problems with their police department, problems that require sweeping changes – ranging from greater procedural justice and police accountability to racial diversification and community policing. Previous studies have documented the impact of single incidents of misconduct on lowering approval of the police in a particular city (such as the Rodney King beating in Los Angeles), and our results extend this finding to persons who are exposed to successive media reports over time.

Fourth, as with the other aspects of policing that we have examined, fewer factors shape whites' views than is the case for blacks and Hispanics. Overall, the path leading to views of reform is more varied for minorities. This may be because minorities have a more complex relationship with the police than is true for most whites (Bayley and Mendelsohn 1969).

Our research tests the assumption that there is widespread public support for changes that might improve policing. Findings indicate that there is indeed overwhelming agreement within the American population on some types of reform but also disagreement regarding the value of other innovations. Reforms that register the greatest approval – across the three groups – include the principle of matching the racial composition of a police agency to that of the host city; retaining the *Miranda* rule; requiring officers to explain to people the reasons for their actions; requiring officers to apologize to people whom they have stopped but subsequently found innocent of wrongdoing; greater citizen oversight of police behavior; and punishment of officers who abuse citizens.

The reforms discussed in this chapter cover most of the major types of changes, but these are not the only ones that have been proposed. One is hiring officers with college degrees, though there is little evidence that this makes much of a difference. Another is the independent auditor, an alternative to a civilian review board; examples include the Inspector General's office in Los Angeles, the Police Internal Investigations Auditing Committee in Portland, Oregon, and the Independent Police Auditor in San Jose, California. A relatively recent idea, the auditor model shifts the focus from individual officers to larger departmental practices that may invite misconduct (Walker 2005).

Most civilian review boards deal exclusively with complaints against specific officers, whereas auditors identify organizational problems, recommend remedies, and monitor their implementation. Auditors have investigated patterns and trends in citizen complaints, a department's internal review process, policies on officer use of force, the handling of domestic violence cases, community outreach practices, and so forth. The key question is: What happens after an auditor identifies a problem and makes recommendations? Does the police chief take the recommendations seriously? In at least one city, San Jose, the department has a good record of accepting and implementing most of the auditor's recommendations (Walker 2005).

Intensive sensitivity training for officers also has the potential to help improve police treatment of citizens. In our survey, sensitivity training was endorsed by 59 percent of whites, 75 percent of Hispanics, and 85 percent of African Americans. If implemented in a rigorous way, sensitivity training can pay off. To cite just one example: In two precincts in the Bronx, New York, where residents and police had a troubled relationship, complaints dropped substantially after precinct commanders retrained officers to ensure respectful demeanor toward citizens and instituted more robust monitoring of officers who received multiple complaints, backed up with meaningful sanctions for recidivists (Davis and Mateu-Gelabert 1999). A concerted overhaul of training and accountability helped improve police treatment of residents and resulted in significant improvement in police-community relations. Police themselves seem to think that sensitivity training makes a difference. In a study of 121 police departments in the United States, three-quarters of the officers believed that "training in human diversity or cultural awareness is effective at preventing abuse of authority" (Weisburd and Greenspan 2000:7).

Popular preferences may be useful in informing public policy. If the public overwhelmingly approves of a particular reform, this may be indicative of a problem that needs fixing, and our research findings on this issue have been conveyed to top police officials, such as the International Association of Chiefs of Police (Weitzer and Tuch 2004b). If implemented, reforms may pay dividends in several ways: They may help to *improve police practices* overall as well as *reduce specific kinds of abuse*. In this category, we would include community policing, sensitivity training, and procedural justice norms. Regarding the latter, it is important for police to understand the consequences of impolite or unfair treatment of civilians, in terms of souring their opinion of the police, which is only magnified when such bad experiences are communicated to friends and family members. When police explain their actions and treat people politely and respectfully, this encourages citizen cooperation with officers and satisfaction with the encounter (Wiley and Hudik 1974; Skogan and Hartnett 1997:217; Stone and Pettigrew 2000; Tyler and Huo 2002). Other types of innovations may substantially *enhance the legitimacy of the police* – such as a civilian review board, hiring more minority officers, and so on. Whether or not these kinds of reform actually change practices on the ground, they may be symbolically important to the public, with a resulting net improvement in public confidence and trust in the police.

But the bottom line is that most reforms will remain meaningless if not backed up with (1) sufficient resources, (2) a firm commitment from departmental leadership, and (3) genuine acceptance within the police subculture. The history of policing shows that many reforms, often implemented after a scandal, were either window dressing to begin with or were undermined or diluted by officers who refused to abide by the new policies. Whether we are talking about early warning systems, civilian review boards, independent auditors, mandatory data recording to curb racial profiling, or anything else – department leadership is crucial in ensuring that these changes are fully institutionalized and in encouraging rank-and-file cops to accept new norms. When the police brass as well as middle-ranking officers (sergeants, lieutenants) wholeheartedly embrace an innovation and convey its importance to street cops, reforms stand a better chance of truly improving police practice and of increasing popular confidence in the police department. At the same time, for a reform to "stick" among rank-and-file officers, it must become part of the organizational ethos. Increasing the percentage of minority officers in a department from, say, 10 percent to 35 percent is unlikely to have any effect on the police subculture. Increasing their presence to 60 percent may be more consequential. Community policing programs that are marginalized and piecemeal will have few positive results precisely because they are not integrated into the police culture, but when they guide the philosophy and practice of the entire department, a community orientation seems to improve matters significantly. Early warning systems and the recording of information on drivers stopped by cops are only as good as the supervisors who monitor these records. Once an "at-risk" officer is identified, further investigation or corrective action is called for. And when other officers learn that these oversight mechanisms are fully operational and have clear consequences for deviant cops, a more robust spirit of accountability may begin to spread within the police subculture, in turn improving police treatment of civilians.

CHAPTER FIVE

Conclusion: The Continuing Racial Divide

In the middle of the last century the Swedish economist Gunnar Myrdal, in his monumental book *An American Dilemma*, was one of the first scholars to analyze the role of police in oppressing blacks in a society in which racial prejudice and discrimination were deeply entrenched in all institutions. Police in the American South, in particular, were pillars in a system of white supremacy and virtually unrestrained in their coercive treatment of blacks (Myrdal 1944:535–545). But Myrdal's work was an exception; police-minority relations did not become a topic of serious investigation until the late 1960s.

Much of what was written in the 1960s and early 1970s painted African Americans and the police literally in black and white, as little more than enemies locked in conflict. The social commentator James Baldwin used dramatic language, describing the typical police officer as one who "moves through Harlem like an occupying soldier in a bitterly hostile country, which is precisely what and where he is." As for blacks' views at the time, police were hardly the friendly bobby on the beat: "Their very presence is an insult, and it would be even if they spent their entire day feeding gumdrops to children" (Baldwin 1962:67, 65). Baldwin's observations were confirmed by two blue-ribbon commissions. The President's Commission on Law Enforcement (1967:167) described white cops as an "army of occupation" despised in black neighborhoods, and the Kerner Commission (1968:206) concluded that, for many blacks, "police have come to symbolize white power, white racism, and white repression. And the fact is that many police do reflect and express these white attitudes." Academic articles published at the time tell the same story. Blacks' relations with the police were characterized in the strongest terms: "alienation," "antipathy," and "hostility" (Hahn and Feagin 1970). As one scholar wrote, "so deep is their hostility that many Negroes refuse to cooperate with the police," and "so intense is their resentment that many Negroes regard the police with outright contempt" (Fogelson 1968:225).

The same sweeping claims were made when comparing blacks and whites. As a leading study concluded, minorities and whites "live in completely different worlds" in relation to the police (Bayley and Mendelsohn 1969:141). The study, conducted in Denver in 1966, documented a substantial racial gap in citizens' views of many aspects of policing, as did a handful of other studies during this time. A 1968 survey of 15 cities found that two to four times more blacks than whites said they were the victims of officers' verbal or physical abuse and were between two and four times more likely to say this had happened to someone they knew (Campbell and Schuman 1968:42–43). This early research generally did not investigate variables other than race, such as divisions along class lines or media or contextual influences on citizen opinion. Even now, few researchers have studied the impact of macro-level forces.

Surveys of police themselves reveal a more variegated picture of their relations with the public in the 1960s, but one where blacks are still viewed in more adversarial terms than are whites. A 1967 poll of 437 officers in 11 cities, for instance, found that 29 percent thought that most blacks viewed the police as "enemies" (only 1 percent thought most whites felt this way), 34 percent thought that most blacks were "on their side," and 35 percent considered most blacks indifferent to the police (Groves 1968:106). The vast majority of officers (72 percent) thought that most whites were on the same side as the police. In other words, whites were generally regarded as allies whereas the majority of blacks were viewed either as enemies or indifferent to the police.

This book documents both continuity and change in minority and white perspectives on the police. In many respects, minority views have not improved much over the past four decades. Our research and other recent studies show that a substantial number continue to distrust the police and condemn a variety of police practices. Blacks and Hispanics are very concerned about the amount of police protection and other services in minority neighborhoods, the performance of local police in crime fighting, police brutality, racial discrimination, and, finally, the need for meaningful reforms in policing. We summarize our main findings here.

Race matters a great deal. Whites, blacks, and Hispanics differ on virtually every issue covered in this book, and, with the exception of overall satisfaction with police and some types of reform, these racial fault lines remain after taking other variables into account:

- Today, as in the past, African Americans hold the most critical views of the police.
- Hispanics are less likely than whites to hold favorable opinions of the police. On some issues, they are less likely than African Americans to view the police negatively, but on other issues, they tend to align with blacks. With regard to reform of the police, Hispanics and blacks are fairly closely aligned in supporting a whole host of reforms. With respect to police misconduct and racially biased policing, however, the two groups differ significantly. Here, Hispanics are less likely than blacks to hold negative views and, on some questions, they are *much* less likely to perceive problems. These results are especially noteworthy given the paucity of research on police relations with Hispanics. We now know much more about this group, and our findings show that it would be mistaken to assume that the pattern of Hispanic relations with the police is the same as the pattern for blacks. There are both similarities *and* important differences in each group's views of and experiences with the police – differences that are masked in writings that assume a single "minority group" perspective. Our racial hierarchy finding challenges this monolithic picture, highlighting important differences in the historical and contemporary experiences of each group – including differences in the incidence, scope, and severity of problems each faces. As noted in Chapter 1, the group position thesis implies that these differences will create different levels of alienation from social institutitons for blacks and Hispanics. Just as African Americans have a deeper and more crystallized sense of group subordination than is true for Hispanics, they also have a longer, more fractious, and more complex history with the police in America. This is one key reason why blacks' opinions are often more negative than Hispanics'.

- Whites, often in large numbers, express positive views of the police. Many reject the idea that police engage in misconduct and racial discrimination to any appreciable degree: Very few believe that the police frequently stop people without cause, abuse citizens verbally or physically, or engage in corruption. More than three-quarters believe that police treat individual Hispanics and blacks the same as they treat whites, and a majority believe that minority neighborhoods are treated the same as white neighborhoods.[1] That many whites are skeptical of charges of racially biased policing, seeing it as isolated and exceptional rather than widespread, is consistent with their views on racial discrimination elsewhere in American society, such as in education, housing, and employment. For most whites, racial discrimination in general, and racialized policing in particular, is not a serious problem in America – episodic rather than routine, isolated rather than institutionalized. If police racial bias and misconduct are exceptions to the rule, there is doubt about the need for reforms.

The race-only baseline models showed that blacks and Hispanics differ significantly from whites on virtually *every* issue we examined. When other variables are included in the models, race usually remains important. Net of controls for the set of non-racial variables we employed, blacks and Hispanics stand out in believing that all four types of police racial bias are serious problems; blacks remain more likely than whites to believe that every type of police misconduct is widespread in their city and neighborhood; and blacks and Hispanics remain more supportive of two or three reforms, depending on the group – namely, racial diversification, community policing, and intensified policing – whereas the three groups are in agreement on the value of procedural justice and accountability. In sum, we see that, compared to whites, blacks and Hispanics are particularly troubled by police misconduct and racially biased policing, but certain types of reform transcend racial divisions and are equally popular among all groups. This pattern makes sense for whites, who tend to deny racial discrimination

---

[1] The exception is the 70 percent of whites who think that racial profiling is widespread in the United States.

in other institutions as well, but at the same time are just as willing to accept certain types of reforms in the policies of those institutions.

Demographic factors were included in our models although we did not report their coefficients in tables. With the exception of race and, sometimes, age and income, these individual-level demographic factors played only a limited role in shaping citizen attitudes in each of the four main areas covered in this book. This finding is important, though not entirely unexpected. As noted in Chapter 1, some studies find that once certain macro-level conditions (such as the mass media or neighborhood context) or micro-level influences (such as personal contacts with officers) are factored into the equation, the effects of individual-level characteristics are reduced or eliminated. With one important exception, our findings are in line with these studies. The exception is the intersection of race, age, and gender, which produces *triple jeopardy* for young minority males who are more likely than same-age minority females and white males to experience both racial discrimination and other types of abuse by the police.

Neighborhood crime conditions have an impact on some types of attitudes and evaluations of the police. Where residents view crime as prevalent and feel unsafe walking in their neighborhoods at night, overall satisfaction with police declines and the awareness of police misconduct increases. Some other studies, cited in Chapter 1, also find that local crime conditions influence residents' views of the police (although fear of crime is a less consistent predictor), and our findings are in line with with this body of literature.

Neighborhood *concentrated disadvantage* sometimes amplifies citizens' negative views of the police, sometimes not. Despite these mixed results, it was important to incorporate this ecological factor into our analysis. Some analysts have shown that individual-level race differences alone cannot account for the heightened levels of cynicism toward the police that typify neighborhoods with high levels of socioeconomic deprivation. Our findings lend further credence to this argument. Although not significant in every model or for every racial group, concentrated disadvantage increases dissatisfaction toward the police among at least a segment of the American population. Other studies of the role of neighborhood context are limited because they are usually confined to a single city, with findings that cannot be generalized outside the study site. Because our sample is nationally representative, it is possible to draw broader generalizations. Nationwide, it is clear that the neighborhood conditions in which citizens live have at least some effect on their attitudes and experiences, just as some other studies have found.

Citizen experiences with police officers during face-to-face contacts strongly influence public opinion in two areas explored in the book. Negative experiences increase citizens' belief that police misconduct occurs frequently and that racially biased policing is widespread. Experience with police abuse has mixed effects, however, on overall satisfaction with the police (it depends on the racial group) and it does not predict support for reforms in policing. Reform preferences are shaped by larger views of the police (such as the belief that misconduct is widespread), which transcend one's experiences with officers. Unlike some other research, which focuses heavily or exclusively on personal experience, our findings suggest that it is an important but not exhaustive explanation of attitudes toward the police (see Brandl et al. 1994). Experience is a fairly robust predictor of beliefs about misconduct and racial bias, has mixed effects on overall satisfaction with police, and has no impact on assessments and preferences regarding reforms.

The *mass media* play a remarkable role in influencing public opinion about the police. In our research, repeated exposure to media reports on police abuse is a strong predictor of perceptions of police misconduct, views on racialized policing, and support for reforms. On many of these issues, media effects are evident for Hispanics, blacks, and whites alike, though in some cases whites are less affected. Previous studies have documented the impact of single incidents of misconduct in coloring the image of the police in a particular city, and our results extend this finding to persons who are exposed to separate, cumulative media reports over time.

Why does media coverage of police misconduct play such a strong role? Part of the explanation can be traced to a "negativity bias" that is well documented in the psychology literature. Negative experiences have greater cognitive and emotional salience and longevity than positive ones. Seeing a media story on an incident of police brutality, for instance, is less likely to be forgotten than a report on some positive accomplishment by an officer. Another part of the explanation is the well-documented tendency of the media to give prominent coverage to the most atypical instances of police deviance. Examples include the videotaped beating of Rodney King in Los Angeles in 1991, the gruesome assault on Abner Louima in a police station in New York City in 1997, and the killing of Amadou Diallo in a hail of 41 bullets fired by New York cops in 1999. Because each event was highly dramatic and repeatedly recounted in newspaper articles and on television newscasts, these stories have become part of the cultural repertoire with which people, and especially minority citizens, understand policing – as some of our respondents elaborated upon in their answers to open-ended questions. In other words, such events become larger-than-life narratives from which people draw global lessons beyond the specifics of the case in question. When the incident has been videotaped, this adds a visual and visceral dimension that only magnifies its effect on the hearts and minds of viewers. People are especially likely to recall seeing police slam a black man's head on the hood of a police car (videotaped in Los Angeles), seeing the repeatedly broadcast tape of Rodney King's beating, and other videotaped abuses. Some previous research indicates that such incidents have much more protracted "staying power" in the consciousness of minority citizens than is true for whites (Tuch and Weitzer 1997; Weitzer 2002).

It is surprising that media reporting on the police has received so little attention from scholars. It seems obvious that citizens' perceptions of the police would be influenced, at least to some degree, by media portrayals of the police – just as the media influence popular impressions of other institutions such as the criminal courts and prisons. The media's role may be an important dimension of any comprehensive explanatory framework of police-citizen relations, and we believe the media's impact deserves much more attention from researchers.

Our findings shed light on the question of why race matters in the study of police-citizen relations. As we noted in Chapter 1, most of the literature documents black-white differences but does not adequately explain them. Our data point to the role of several micro- and macro-level factors in perpetuating racial discord in group relations with the police. In sum, the greater tendency for blacks and Hispanics to hold critical views is largely a function of their adverse personal and vicarious contacts with police officers (which minorities disproportionately experience), their exposure to media reports of police abuse, and, to a lesser extent, their residence in high-crime and disadvantaged neighborhoods where police actions may be intrusive, aggressive, and contentious.

The findings also lend support to the group-position thesis. Our extension of this thesis holds that legal institutions in multiracial societies will function, or be perceived as functioning, to defend dominant group interests. As a general rule, dominant racial groups see the police as an institution allied with their interests, whereas minorities are inclined to view the police as a force that contributes to their subordination. The group-position thesis does not assume that all group members will subscribe to these views, but does forecast substantial polarization in the general orientations of dominant and subordinate racial groups. Our findings are quite consistent with this thesis:

- White Americans discount or minimize police wrongdoing, interpreting charges of misconduct as threats to law and order and, arguably, to whites' group interest in maximizing crime control. Blacks, by contrast, are much more inclined to believe that verbal abuse, brutality, unwarranted street stops, and corruption are widespread in their neighborhood, city, and throughout the nation, and many Hispanics share this view. On the question of excessive force, for instance, nearly half of African Americans and a third of Hispanics believe this happens often in their city, compared to only 13 percent of whites. This perceptual gap is wide enough to suggest that many whites and minorities are poles apart in their assessments of police misconduct in America.

- Whites tend to minimize or discount the existence of racially biased and discriminatory policing, and perhaps view such allegations as a threat to a revered institution. Some whites acknowledge disparate police treatment of members of different racial groups, but see this as "rational discrimination" insofar as officers target groups that are "crime prone." Others are completely color-blind; they may concede that police racial bias was a problem historically, but not today. Racialized policing is hardly a relic of the past for many African Americans, who see it as all too common today, and many Hispanics

share this view. On the question of whether police treat members of different racial groups similarly or differently, for instance,
fully three-quarters of whites believe all groups are treated equally,
whereas three-quarters of blacks and more than half of Hispanics
believe minorities are treated worse than whites.

- Group positions on the issue of police reform are more mixed. On
some kinds of reform, a majority of whites agree with blacks and Hispanics that a particular change is a good idea (e.g., video cameras in
cars, early warning systems, stiffer punishment for bad cops, more
sensitivity training). But many whites are skeptical that other types
of reforms are needed: If misconduct and other problems are only
minor or isolated, there is nothing in need of fixing. The qualitative
data indicate that whites' main concern is that officers are not aggressive enough in fighting crime or do not respond quickly enough
when called, but their idea of "reform" does not go much beyond
intensification of crime control. Most blacks and Hispanics, by contrast, overwhelmingly and enthusiastically favor changes designed to
reduce police abuse of citizens, and particularly of minority citizens,
who are disproportionately the recipients of mistreatment. Tighter
controls and more sensitive police practices are not only valuable
in principle but, we argue, would also help to advance blacks' and
Hispanics' group interests.

The contours of the group positions sketched above and illustrated
throughout the book are general patterns. Although it is not our inten-
tion to exaggerate the scope and intensity of minority discontent with
the police, a large critical mass of Hispanics and African Americans
are convinced that police misconduct is a serious problem, that racial
injustice is pervasive in American policing, and that major reforms are
long overdue. Assessments of the police are thus rooted in both group-
position arrangements and in real or perceived group vulnerability to
abusive police practices.

Finally, we wish to comment a bit more on one aspect of the study
that is particularly novel and that perhaps holds the greatest policy
implications: our exploration of popular support for reforms in policing. Almost all of the research on citizen perceptions focuses on general satisfaction or on particular policing problems, rather than on

corrective measures that might help to curb problems or improve policing more generally. Until now, little was known about the level of public support for specific kinds of reform or about the determinants of public evaluations of changes in policing. The book identifies a number of reforms that register broad public approval and which may be useful in informing public policy. Where popular acclaim for a specific change is widespread and intense, this may be symptomatic of a problem in need of fixing. If implemented, the reform may help to reduce the amount of police misconduct, reduce friction with citizens, or improve police practices more generally.

Some types of reform have the potential to improve the *behavior of officers during encounters*, and they are overwhelmingly endorsed by the population. Although it is not surprising that officer demeanor would be important to citizens, our findings document just how widespread support is for policies designed to improve police demeanor. Sensitivity training for officers is favored by a majority of whites and by most Hispanics (75 percent) and blacks (85 percent). More than 90 percent of our respondents feel that officers should be required to explain to citizens the reasons why they have been stopped; and more than three-quarters think that officers who stop and search people but find no evidence of wrongdoing should be required to apologize to the citizen for the inconvenience. More than 9 out of 10 people also want to retain the *Miranda* rights. These results confirm findings of prior studies about the importance people place on being treated fairly and respectfully, being told the reasons for officer actions, being informed of their rights, and receiving due process. Yet the intensity of support for these kinds of procedural justice is striking: Most whites, blacks, and Hispanics not only support but *strongly support* each of these policies.

Citizens' are not the only ones who have an interest in procedural justice. If the feeling that one has been treated unjustly or disrespectfully leads some citizens to act aggressively toward officers (possibly endangering them) or if it erodes basic trust in the police institution, it is clearly in the interests of the police themselves to ensure fidelity to procedural justice norms. Citizen behavior is influenced, at least to some degree, by officer behavior, and when officers communicate well and treat citizens with respect, citizens respond in kind. Police can do more to dispel beliefs that stops are racially motivated, for example, and also prevent altercations with citizens, by simply informing people why they have been stopped. Citizens are much more likely to cooperate with officers when they are given a reason for the stop, and people put a premium on officers being polite, listening to citizens, and explaining their actions. In short, both citizens and officers stand to gain from procedurally just policing.

Other reforms have less potential to influence face-to-face interactions, but they may still boost public trust and confidence in the police. Even if the reform does not change police practice, it may pay important symbolic dividends. For the most part, Americans value racial diversity in police departments and meaningful systems of accountability. In multiracial cities and communities, very few people want the police department to be populated by a single race or want only one type of officer working in their neighborhood. For the reasons discussed in Chapter 4, many people want cops to be "blue" rather than racially oriented. Similarly, few Americans believe that officers are sufficiently accountable for their behavior, which explains the widespread support for additional mechanisms to monitor officer conduct and stiffen punishment for those guilty of misconduct. One case in point is the civilian review board. Although such boards substantiate only a small fraction of complaints against officers, people strongly favor creating such boards in cities that do not have them. When it comes to accountability, external review boards enjoy a measure of symbolic capital greater than the frequency of the sanctions they mete out to wayward officers, with potentially important consequences: "Only an independent investigative body can allay public suspicions of the police" (Skolnick and Fyfe 1993:230).

* * * * *

Although all democratic societies aspire to treat citizens fairly and equitably without regard to race or ethnicity, none fully achieve this goal. In this book we have presented abundant evidence that in the United States, as in other multiracial societies, relations between police and members of minority groups are a persistent, troubling problem. We have argued that in order to address this long-standing dilemma between democratic principles and racial injustice we must better understand its causes, manifestations, and consequences. Accordingly, this book fills in some of the gaps in our knowledge of police-citizen relations.

As with other aspects of race relations in America, where it often appears that whites and minorities occupy different perceptual worlds, our analysis reveals a deep and continuing racial divide. Compared to whites, blacks and Hispanics see police treatment of minority individuals and neighborhoods as perpetuating deeply entrenched patterns of racial injustice. This is not to say, of course, that no progress has been made over the years in addressing the concerns of minority groups. Indeed, progress *has* been made, in the direction of greater justice, just as is true in other institutions – including education, economics, and politics. Since the beginning of the last century, when W. E. B. Du Bois (1903) made his now famous prediction that the problem of twentieth-century America would be the problem of the color line, to mid-century when Gunnar Myrdal (1944) wrote so eloquently about the persistence of discrimination in American society and of the contradiction it posed to American values of freedom and equality, race relations have undeniably improved. Yet, one hundred years after Du Bois and six decades after Myrdal, it is equally undeniable that race still matters. A wealth of material presented in this book – drawn from our own research and other studies – shows that, as we enter the twenty-first century, relations between police and minority citizens remain troubled.

Data and Methods

This book is based on a variety of information sources, but the primary data used here come from a national survey conducted by the authors between October and December, 2002 of 1,791 adults 18 years of age or older (619 whites, 565 blacks, and 607 Hispanics). Our sample also included 310 youths 13–17 years old, about 100 from each racial group. Although we occasionally quote some of our young interviewees, we do not systematically analyze the youth data due to small sample sizes. Only respondents who reside in metropolitan areas of at least 100,000 population (either cities or adjacent suburbs) were included in our sample because it is in such locales that policing is likely to be especially salient and, perhaps, contentious for residents – unlike in more rural areas (Weisheit, Falcone, and Wells 1995). Our sample is representative of citizens living in telephone households in areas that meet our population size criterion.

SAMPLING

The survey was conducted for the authors by Knowledge Networks, Inc., a Web-based survey research firm that combines probability sampling with the reach and capabilities of the Internet to yield representative samples of respondents without sacrificing data quality. Research comparing the quality of data yielded by Knowledge Networks' Web-based survey methodology with that of random digit dialed (RDD) telephone surveys has found that Knowledge Networks yields representative samples that produce parameter estimates very similar to the estimates of RDD samples (Krosnick and Chang 2001; Baker et al. 2003; Berrens 2003).

In drawing its sample, Knowledge Networks uses list-assisted RDD sampling techniques on a sample frame consisting of the entire United States telephone population. Any household with a telephone has the potential to be selected for the Knowledge Networks panel, including computer users and nonusers alike. In other words, unlike most other Web-based firms, Knowledge Networks recruits its initial sample of households by means of an RDD telephone survey. Telephone numbers are dialed up to 90 days, with at least 15 dial attempts on cases in which no one answers the phone, and 25 dial attempts on phone numbers known to be associated with households. Extensive refusal conversion is also performed.

In exchange for free Internet hardware (such as a television set-top box), connectivity (an Internet connection paid for by Knowledge Networks), and on-site installation, participants agree to complete a maximum of four surveys per month. Selected households remain on the panel for two to three years, at which time they are eligible for retirement. At retirement, households may keep their Internet equipment, but payments for Internet access are discontinued. As households retire, they are replaced with new recruits, assuring a balanced panel of consistent or growing size. Currently, Knowledge Networks has over 25,000 households in its Web-enabled panel.

To trigger a survey, e-mail messages are sent to those panel members who satisfy the screening criteria, if any, for the particular study. Knowledge Networks does not engage in any kind of surreptitious monitoring of respondents' use of the Internet; panel members provide all information voluntarily and with full informed consent. Each participant receives a password-protected e-mail account. Individuals are usually ready to begin taking surveys within two weeks after initial contact. Knowledge Networks maintains a call center to provide technical support and facilitate household cooperation.

PANEL REPRESENTATIVENESS

The Knowledge Networks panel is representative of and closely mirrors the U.S. population on key demographic, geographic, economic, and social characteristics. Tables A. 1 and A. 2 compare major demographic characteristics of the population with the Knowledge Networks panel. Table A. 1 compares the Knowledge Networks panel with population counts from the 2000 Census for the 25 largest metropolitan areas. The table shows that the Knowledge Networks panel closely mirrors Census counts. The most notable divergence is a slight underrepresentation in the panel of the New York–Northern New Jersey–Long Island MSA.

Table A. 2 compares the demographic characteristics of the Knowledge Networks panel with figures from the February 2002 Current Population Survey. As Table A. 2 shows, the Knowledge Networks panel closely reflects the U.S. population on gender, age, race, Hispanic ethnicity, employment status, marital status, education, household income, and region.

Four factors account for the representativeness of the panel. First, as noted above, the panel is selected using list-assisted RDD telephone methodology, providing a probability-based starting sample of telephone households.[1] Second, panel weights are adjusted to Census demographic benchmarks to reduce error due to noncoverage of households without telephones and to reduce bias due to nonresponse and other nonsampling errors. Third, samples selected from the panel for individual studies are selected using probability methods, and appropriate sample design weights are calculated for each study. Fourth, nonresponse and poststratification weighting adjustments are applied to the final survey data to reduce the effects of nonsampling error. The result is that the weighted demographic estimates from the Census and the Knowledge Networks panel differ only modestly across categories of gender, age, race, ethnicity, education, and region. Moreover, analyses of panel attrition indicate that no significant differences differentiate those who remain on the panel from those who do not (Dennis and Li 2003).[2]

---

[1] According to the 2000 Census, 98 percent of white households have telephone access, as do 94 percent of African American households and 95 percent of Hispanic households.

[2] A detailed demographic panel analysis is available at http://www.knowledgenetworks .com.

TABLE A.1. *Knowledge Networks and Census 2000 data for the top 25 metropolitan areas*

Top 25 MSAs	Knowledge Networks panel	U.S. Census 2000	Top 25 MSAs	Knowledge Networks panel	U.S. Census 2000
New York–N. New Jersey–Long Island	4.60%	7.57%	Phoenix–Mesa	1.57%	1.16%
Los Angeles–Riverside–Orange County	5.45%	5.85%	Minneapolis–St. Paul	1.57%	1.06%
Chicago–Gary–Kenosha	3.00%	3.27%	Cleveland–Akron	1.20%	1.05%
Washington–Baltimore	2.91%	2.72%	San Diego	.88%	1.00%
San Francisco–Oakland–San Jose	1.65%	2.51%	St. Louis	1.27%	.93%
Philadelphia–Wilmington–Atlantic City	2.49%	2.21%	Denver–Boulder–Greeley	1.22%	.92%
Boston–Worcester–Lawrence	2.01%	2.08%	Tampa–St. Petersburg–Clearwater	.88%	.86%
Detroit–Ann Arbor–Flint	1.94%	1.95%	Pittsburgh	1.10%	.84%
Dallas–Fort Worth	1.68%	1.86%	Portland–Salem	1.21%	.81%
Houston–Galveston–Brazoria	1.47%	1.67%	Cincinnati–Hamilton	.88%	.71%
Atlanta	1.89%	1.47%	Sacramento–Yolo	.78%	.64%
Miami–Fort Lauderdale	.98%	1.38%	Kansas City	.81%	.63%
Seattle–Tacoma–Bremerton	1.55%	1.27%			

Note: The Knowledge Networks panel was weighted by the selection probabilities in the stratified design for recruiting panel members over the telephone using RDD techniques. The data are weighted to reduce the effects of nonresponse and noncoverage.

TABLE A.2. *Demographic characteristics of Knowledge Networks panel*

		Knowledge networks panel	Adult U.S. population (February 2002 CPS)
Gender	Male	48.0%	48.0%
	Female	52.0%	52.0%
Age	18–24	11.2%	13.3%
	25–34	19.5%	18.0%
	35–44	22.1%	21.6%
	45–54	19.4%	18.9%
	55–64	14.0%	12.1%
	65 or over	13.9%	16.1%
Race	White	80.8%	83.1%
	Black/African-American	12.6%	12.0%
	American Indian or Alaska Native	3.6%	.9%
	Asian/Pacific Islander	2.6%	4.0%
	Other	.3%	n/a
Hispanic ethnicity	Hispanic	10.9%	10.9%
	Non-Hispanic	89.1%	89.1%
Employment status	In the labor force	65.3%	65.5%
	Working full time	53.5%	55.5%
	Working part time	11.8%	10.0%
	Not in the labor force	34.7%	34.5%
Marital status	Married	61.0%	57.1%
	Not married	39.0%	42.9%
Housing ownership	Own	65.6%	n/a
	Rent/other	34.4%	n/a
Level of education	Less than high school diploma	16.7%	16.7%
	High school diploma or equivalent	32.3%	32.3%
	Some college	20.8%	19.2%
	Associate's degree	6.2%	7.8%
	Bachelor's degree or beyond	23.9%	24.0%
Household income	Under $10,000	8.2%	7.4%
	$10,000–$24,999	18.2%	18.7%
	$25,000–$49,999	34.4%	29.2%
	$50,000–$74,999	21.1%	20.1%
	$75,000 or more	18.0%	24.7%
Census region	Northeast	19.3%	19.1%
	Midwest	22.6%	22.8%
	South	35.5%	35.6%
	West	22.6%	22.6%

Note: Estimates were calculated using CPS February 2002 microdata available on the http://www.census.gov Web site. The data are weighted using CPS final weights.

When using panels for survey research, potential sampling bias can occur at different stages. First, respondents consent to become panel members; this is referred to as the panel acceptance rate. At the time of this study, Knowledge Networks' panel acceptance rate was 40 percent, calculated by standards established by the American Association for Public Opinion Research (AAPOR).[3] Second, the within-survey completion rate – or percentage of panel members who completed our questionnaire among those who received it – was 67 percent. The margin of sampling error for our estimates was ± 2 percent for the total sample and ± 4 percent for each racial group.

Table A.3 presents means, standard deviations, mean difference tests, and the range of values on all study variables. The table shows that, as discussed at various points throughout this book, blacks are far more likely than whites to report negative views of and experiences with the police, and on most issues, Hispanics are intermediate between the two: more negative than whites but more positive than blacks.

INDEPENDENT VARIABLES

Despite some minor variation from chapter to chapter, we use a mostly uniform set of independent variables throughout the book:

Race. We use the term "race" in its broadest sense to include both racial and ethnic groups – whites, blacks, and Hispanics. Our sample consists of respondents who self-identify as African American, Hispanic American, or non-Hispanic white on Knowledge Networks' demographic profile of panel members. The Hispanic respondents were categorized by Knowledge Networks according to ancestry: Mexican, Puerto Rican, Cuban, Central or South American, and Caribbean or other Hispanic (among our Hispanic respondents, 50 percent were Mexican, 14 percent Puerto Rican, 3 percent Cuban, 13 percent Central or South American, and 20 percent Caribbean or other Hispanic). We examine whether nationality makes a difference in respondents' attitudes, but because the Ns for some of these groups are small, our intra-Hispanic analysis is necessarily limited and tentative. It is also for this reason that our primary analyses compare the three main racial groups rather than the Hispanic nationality groups.

[3] For a discussion of AAPOR response rates, see http://www.aapor.org.

TABLE A.3. *Descriptive statistics and mean difference tests on all study variables*

Variable	Range of values*	Total sample	Whites	Blacks	Hispanics
Satisfaction	2–8	6.47†(1.55)‡	6.64 (1.46)[a,b]	5.86 (1.64)[a,c]	6.17 (1.71)[b,c]
Unwarranted stops	2–8	3.93 (1.51)	3.61 (1.25)[a,b]	4.96 (1.85)[a,c]	4.51 (1.68)[b,c]
Verbal abuse	2–8	3.41 (1.51)	3.18 (1.30)[a,b]	4.30 (1.87)[a,c]	3.70 (1.76)[b,c]
Excessive force	2–8	3.68 (1.55)	3.39 (1.31)[a,b]	4.74 (1.79)[a,c]	4.12 (1.84)[b,c]
Corruption (1 = yes)	0–1	.22 (.41)	.16 (.36)[a,b]	.48 (.50)[a,c]	.28 (.45)[b,c]
Bias against individuals	0–8	5.17 (1.73)	4.70 (1.42)[a,b]	6.69 (1.82)[a,c]	5.95 (1.86)[b,c]
Bias against neighborhoods	0–4	2.79 (1.10)	2.56 (1.07)[a,b]	3.53 (.88)[a,c]	3.16 (1.02)[b,c]
Police prejudice	3–12	7.63 (2.45)	6.98 (2.16)[a,b]	9.80 (2.13)[a,c]	8.64 (2.52)[b,c]
Racial profiling	0–6	3.17 (1.82)	2.66 (1.61)[a,b]	4.88 (1.45)[a,c]	3.96 (1.81)[b,c]
Diversification	2–9	5.23 (1.95)	4.83 (1.83)[a,b]	6.46 (1.85)[a,c]	5.97 (1.92)[b,c]
Accountability	4–14	11.03 (2.35)	10.71 (2.29)[a,b]	12.23 (2.10)[a,c]	11.47 (2.45)[b,c]
Community policing	3–12	8.84 (2.20)	8.58 (2.12)[a,b]	9.80 (2.15)[a,c]	9.22 (2.37)[b,c]
Procedural justice	3–12	10.52 (1.69)	10.46 (1.59)	10.70 (1.98)	10.63 (1.83)
Intensified policing	3–12	8.24 (2.07)	8.02 (2.04)[a,b]	8.77 (1.97)[a]	8.79 (2.14)[b]
White-black police diffs (1 = yes)	0–1	.43 (.50)	.37 (.48)[a,b]	.65 (.48)[a,c]	.52 (.50)[b,c]
White-Hispanic police diffs (1 = yes)	0–1	.31 (.46)	.26 (.44)[a,b]	.47 (.50)[a]	.39 (.49)[b]
Education	1–9	4.12 (1.70)	4.25 (1.75)[a,b]	3.94 (1.48)[a,c]	3.66 (1.54)[b,c]
Income	1–17	10.07 (3.87)	10.50 (3.65)[a,b]	8.75 (4.20)[a,c]	9.22 (4.16)[b]
Gender (1 = male)	0–1	.51 (.50)	.52 (.50)	.47 (.50)	.47 (.50)
Age	18–91	45.44 (16.53)	48.55 (16.49)[a,b]	37.96 (14.57)[a]	37.49 (13.34)[b]

(continued)

TABLE A.3 (*continued*)

Variable	Range of Values*	Total Sample	Whites	Blacks	Hispanics
Population size (1 = 1 million+)	0–1	.55 (.50)	.52 (.50)^{a,b}	.67 (.47)^a	.60 (.49)^b
Residence (1 = city)	0–1	.69 (.46)	.67 (.47)^{a,b}	.76 (.43)^a	.77 (.42)^b
Region (1 = south)	0–1	.35 (.48)	.36 (.48)^b	.43 (.50)^c	.21 (.41)^{b,c}
Safety (day)	1–4	3.67 (.57)	3.76 (.48)^{a,b}	3.46 (.68)^a	3.45 (.75)^b
Safety (night)	1–4	3.26 (.77)	3.37 (.70)^{a,b}	3.01 (.84)^a	2.98 (.91)^b
Neighborhood crime	1–4	1.94 (.76)	1.85 (.70)^{a,b}	2.23 (.83)^a	2.13 (.85)^b
Media exposure	1–4	2.97 (.72)	2.90 (.68)^{a,b}	3.26 (.79)^{a,c}	3.04 (.79)^{b,c}
Personal experience with misconduct (1 = yes)	0–1	.27 (.44)	.21 (.41)^{a,b}	.46 (.50)^{a,c}	.37 (.48)^{b,c}
Vicarious experience with misconduct (1 = yes)	0–1	.22 (.41)	.16 (.37)^{a,b}	.40 (.49)^a	.32 (.47)^b
Personal experience with bias (1 = yes)	0–1	.15 (.36)	.04 (.20)^{a,b}	.52 (.50)^{a,c}	.33 (.47)^{b,c}
Vicarious experience with bias (1 = yes)	0–1	.13 (.33)	.04 (.19)^{a,b}	.42 (.49)^{a,c}	.28 (.45)^{b,c}
Police effectiveness	2–8	6.36 (1.37)	6.46 (1.33)^{a,b}	6.06 (1.46)^a	6.20 (1.45)^b
Community policing exists (1 = yes)	0–1	.56 (.50)	.56 (.50)	.54 (.50)	.54 (.50)
Perceptions of misconduct	7–28	13.04 (4.39)	12.08 (3.62)^{a,b}	16.60 (5.20)^{a,c}	14.40 (4.92)^{b,c}
Concentrated disadvantage	2.9–223.1	39.52 (36.63)	28.36 (21.07)^{a,b}	91.31 (55.06)^{a,c}	46.58 (33.43)^{b,c}

† mean; ‡ standard deviation.
* original metrics.
[a] The white and black means are significantly different, $p < .05$.
[b] The white and Hispanic means are significantly different, $p < .05$.
[c] The black and Hispanic means are significantly different, $p < .05$.

Perceived misconduct was measured as follows: (1) "How often do you think police officers stop people on the streets of [your neighborhood/your city] without good reason?" (2) "How often do you think police officers, when talking to people in [your neighborhood/your city], use insulting language against them?" (3) "When police officers use force against people, how often do you think they use excessive force (in other words, more force than is necessary under the circumstances) against people in [your neighborhood/your city]?" (Response options for these three questions are: never, on occasion, fairly often, or very often.) (4) "How common do you think corruption (such as taking bribes, involvement in the drug trade) is in your city's police department – not at all common, not very common, fairly common, or very common?" We standardized each of these questions and their sum to form a single measure of perceived misconduct (alpha = .89), with high scores indicating more perceived misconduct.

Experiences with police misconduct refer to these same four issues: unwarranted police stops, use of insulting language, use of excessive force, and corruption. Each question stipulates the site of misconduct as either the respondent's own neighborhood or elsewhere in his/her city (but outside the neighborhood), and with the exception of the corruption item, the questions examine both personal and vicarious experiences: (1) "Have you ever been stopped by police on the street without good reason?" (2) "Has anyone else in your household ever been stopped on the street by police without good reason?;" (3) "Have the police ever used insulting language toward you?" (4) "Have the police ever used insulting language toward anyone else in your household?" (5) "Have the police ever used excessive force against you?" (6) "Have the police ever used excessive force against anyone else in your household?" and (7) "Have you ever seen a police officer engage in any corrupt activities (such as taking bribes or involvement in drug trade)?"[4] All questions had yes/no response options. Combining neighborhood and city contexts, we summed

---

4 Although corruption takes many forms, the two parenthetical examples in our question are major. Accepting bribes has been designated as "the prototypical form of corrupt behavior," and the policing of drug crimes is "particularly prone" to corrupting the police (Newburn 1999:5, 26).

responses to the four misconduct questions and then dichotomized them to create two measures of experience with misconduct: personal experiences[5] and vicarious experiences (1 = experienced any type of misconduct, 0 = experienced no misconduct).

Media exposure. We asked the following question in order to gauge respondents' exposure to media accounts of police misconduct: "How often do you hear or read about (on the radio, television, or in the newspapers) incidents of police misconduct (such as police use of excessive force, verbal abuse, corruption, and so on) that occur somewhere in the nation?" Response options were "never," "rarely," "sometimes," and "often" on a 4-point scale coded so that higher scores indicate more frequent reported exposure.[6]

Police effectiveness in crime control. We summed and standardized responses to two questions about police effectiveness: "In your opinion, how effective are the police in [your neighborhood/your city] in fighting crime?" Response options are "very effective," "somewhat effective," "somewhat ineffective," and "very ineffective," with high scores indicating greater perceived effectiveness at crime control ($\alpha = .87$).

Race of officer. "In general in the United States, do you think there are differences in the way white officers and black officers act toward citizens?" A parallel question was asked comparing white and Hispanic officers (1 = yes, 0 = no).

Neighborhood conditions. We examine several neighborhood conditions. Local crime conditions are tapped via respondent assessments of personal safety and neighborhood crime. We measure *personal safety* by asking: "Overall, how safe do you feel being alone outside in your neighborhood [during the day/at night] – very safe, somewhat safe, somewhat unsafe, or very unsafe?" *Neighborhood crime* is measured with the following item: "How serious a problem is crime in your

5   Observation of police corruption is treated as a personal, rather than vicarious, experience because the actor has personally witnessed it, rather than learning of it from others.

6   Because our media exposure measure is based on respondents' self-reports, some caution is in order in interpreting media effects. There may be some self-selection involved in exposure to media reports regarding the police, with people who are particularly interested in the police being more attentive than others. The media variable is also fairly broad, asking about exposure to reports of police abuse anywhere in the country. An alternative measure would ask specifically about media coverage of incidents in the respondent's own city.

neighborhood – very serious, somewhat serious, not serious, or not a problem at all?" Responses to these questions are coded so that higher scores reflect more personal safety and more perceived crime. A second type of neighborhood condition is whether *community policing* is thought to exist in one's residential locale. This was measured with the following question: "Community policing involves police officers working with community members to address the causes of crime and to prevent crimes from occurring, rather than just responding to crimes after they have occurred. Based on this definition, do you think the police in your neighborhood practice community policing?" (1 = yes, 0 = no).

The third type of neighborhood condition is socioeconomic. Neighborhoods range from those marked by extreme affluence to those marked by extreme and multiple disadvantages. Following the literature, we label the latter "concentrated disadvantage" and examine its role in shaping citizen attitudes in our analyses throughout the book. Concentrated disadvantage is measured by a combination of specific ecological characteristics: *percent African American; percent unemployed; percent below the poverty line;* and *percent of female-headed families.* We standardized each of these items and their sum to form an overall index of concentrated disadvantage (alpha = .85). As is standard in the literature on neighborhood effects, we use census tracts as proxies for neighborhoods, recognizing that tracts are only rough approximations of neighborhood boundaries. Tract-level data for each of these variables was obtained from the 2000 Census.

Controls. We control on several demographic factors: *education,* measured on a 9-step ladder ranging from less than high school (coded 1) to doctorate degree (coded 9); *household income,* measured on a 17-step ladder ranging from less than $5,000 per year (coded 1) to $125,000 or more (coded 17); *gender* (1 = male, 0 = female); *age,* in years; *region* (1 = South, 0 = non-South); *place of residence,* measured with a dummy variable for city (coded 1) versus suburb (coded 0); and *size of place of residence* (1 = 1 million or more). For ease of presentation, we do not report the coefficients for the demographic factors in our multivariate models. As noted in Chapter 1, some studies find that the effects of individual-level demographic factors are reduced or eliminated after incorporating other factors such as neighborhood conditions, personal contacts with police, and so forth. Overall, our findings are consistent with these studies: the demographic factors usually had little impact on the dependent variables.

DEPENDENT VARIABLES

Question wording for all dependent variables is included in the chapters. In creating composite indices for the multi-item dependent measures, we initially factor analyzed the items using principal components analysis in order to verify the unidimensionality of each index. Subsequently, we standardized the items and their sum and created unit-weighted indices, calculating alpha reliability coefficients (also reported in the chapters) for each.

ANALYSIS OF QUANTITATIVE DATA

Throughout our quantitative analyses, we employ both univariate and multivariate statistical techniques. Our primary multivariate analytic tool is ordinary least squares regression analysis (OLS). We note that methods other than OLS regression are available for the analysis of hierarchically structured data such as ours. The idea underlying such multilevel models is that individuals in groups (in our case, census tracts) share certain characteristics with each other that they do not share with members of other groups. Because many of these characteristics are not measured, their effects are captured by the residual term in OLS models, causing correlated errors and, thus, violating OLS model assumptions. In addition, such homogeneity within groups results in an underestimation of the magnitude of standard errors of coefficients and an overestimation of significance. Multilevel modeling separates out variance due to individual- and group-level variables, making these techniques seemingly appropriate for our data. However, using multilevel models in situations where the ratio of level-1 to level-2 cases is nearly 1:1 is unnecessary because such models yield coefficients and standard errors that are comparable to pooled models (Raudenbush and Bryk 2002; Benson et al. 2004). Our full dataset (adults and youth) contains 2,101 respondents in 1,534 census tracts. 1,226, or 80 percent, of the tracts have a single respondent, yielding a level-1 to level-2 ratio of 1.5, nearly synonymous with a single-level data set. In such cases, multilevel modeling is unlikely to yield parameter estimates different from a single, pooled model. Thus, in our analyses, we use OLS or, in the case of one table in Chapter 2, binary logistic regression analyses.

ANALYSIS OF QUALITATIVE DATA

Although most response items in the survey were fixed-choice, several questions were followed up with open-ended questions, asking the respondent to elaborate or clarify his or her answer to the preceding question. Interviewees entered their responses to these questions in boxes on the survey instrument. If a respondent opted not to answer a particular open-ended question, they were prompted a second time for a response but they were not forced to answer any question. A number of respondents declined to answer at least one of the open-ended questions.

Two open-ended items were independent, not follow-up, questions: We asked people to tell us "what kind of changes you would like to see in your city's police department and police practices" and a parallel question regarding the respondent's own neighborhood. The purpose of these two questions, which were asked prior to our questions on specific kinds of reform, was the possibility of learning something novel about preferred changes in policing. In other words, we sought to gather spontaneous ideas about what people want from the police, rather than imposing a set of reforms on them. The results are presented in Chapter 4.

In the qualitative material quoted in the book, we use the following abbreviations to refer to respondents' social class position: LC = lower class, LMC = lower middle class, MC = middle class, and UMC = upper middle class. Class was measured by income level. Although we recognize that income is an imperfect measure, it provides at least a rough barometer of class position.

In keeping with our goal of examining how African Americans, Hispanics, and whites differ in their views of policing, we created class categories using unique income thresholds for each group rather than a common set of definitions applicable to the entire sample.

This procedure facilitated comparisons across groups. We divided the household income distributions for each racial group into quartiles, yielding the following categories: for whites, LC = $0–$24,999, LMC = $25,000–39,999, MC = $40,000–59,999, and UMC = $60,000 or more; for blacks, the respective income levels are $0–14,999, $15,000–29,999, $30,000–49,999, and $50,000 or more; and for Hispanics, $0–19,999, $20,000–34,999, $35,000–49,999, and $50,000 or more.

The qualitative data were analyzed with the help of the computer software program, Atlas/ti. This program allows for the organization, coding, and analysis of a large amount of qualitative data. Our principal strategy was to compare and contrast the group responses to each open-ended question – identifying both similarities across the three racial groups as well as differences in the frequency and content of their responses. This technique of "constant comparison" is standard in qualitative analysis (Strauss 1987).

It should be noted that the qualitative data are intended as both *illustrative* of findings derived from the quantitative analyses and *complementary* to the quantitative findings. The qualitative material help to provide a more nuanced understanding of issues than is sometimes apparent from the quantitative results, a window into the types of considerations people take into account in forming opinions, and a deeper appreciation of the ways people think about and experience policing.

References

Aberbach, Joel, and Jack Walker. 1970. "The Attitudes of Blacks and Whites toward City Services." In J. Crecine (ed.), *Financing the Metropolis*. Beverly Hills, CA: Sage.

Alex, Nicholas. 1969. *Black in Blue: A Study of the Negro Policeman*. New York: Appleton-Century-Crofts.

Alpert, Geoffrey, and William C. Smith. 1994. "How Reasonable Is the Reasonable Man? Police and Excessive Force." *Journal of Criminal Law and Criminology* 85:481–501.

Amnesty International. 2004. *Threat and Humiliation: Racial Profiling, Domestic Security, and Human Rights in the United States*. New York: Amnesty International.

Baker, Lawrence, M. Kate Bundorf, Sara Singer, and Todd Wagner. 2003. "Validity of the Survey of Health and Internet and Knowledge Network's Panel and Sampling." Unpublished manuscript: Stanford University.

Baker, Mark. 1985. *Cops: Their Lives in Their Own Words*. New York: Simon and Schuster.

Baldwin, James. 1962. *Nobody Knows My Name*. New York: Dell.

Barkan, Steven, and Steven Cohn. 1998. "Racial Prejudice and Support by Whites for Police Use of Force." *Justice Quarterly* 15:743–753.

Barlow, David, and Melissa Barlow. 2002. "Racial Profiling: A Survey of African American Police Officers." *Police Quarterly* 5:334–358.

Bayley, David, and Harold Mendelsohn. 1969. *Minorities and the Police*. New York: Free Press.

Benson, Michael, John Wooldredge, Amy Thistlethwaite and Greer Fox. 2004. "The Correlation between Race and Domestic Violence is Confounded with Community Context." *Social Problems* 51: 326–342.

Berrens, Robert. 2003. "The Advent of Internet Surveys for Political Research: A Comparison of Telephone and Internet Samples." *Political Analysis* 11:1–22.

Black, Donald. 1971. "The Social Organization of Arrest." *Stanford Law Review* 23:1087–1111.

Black, Donald, and Albert Reiss. 1967. "Patterns of Behavior in Police and Citizen Transactions." In President's Commission on Law Enforcement and Administration of Justice, *Studies in Crime and Law Enforcement in Major Metropolitan Areas*. Washington, DC: U.S. Government Printing Office.

Black, Joe. 2005. "Autopsy Clears Police in One Death." *Florida Times-Union*, January 2.

Blalock, Herbert. 1967. *Toward a Theory of Minority-Group Relations*. New York: John Wiley.

Block, Richard. 1970. "Support for Civil Liberties and Support for the Police." *American Behavioral Scientist* 13:781–796.

Blumberg, Mark. 1989. "Controlling Police Use of Deadly Force." In R. Dunham and G. Alpert (eds.), *Critical Issues in Policing*. Prospect Heights, IL: Waveland.

Blumer, Herbert. 1958. "Race Prejudice as a Sense of Group Position." *Pacific Sociological Review* 1:3–7.

Bobo, Lawrence. 1999. "Prejudice as Group Position." *Journal of Social Issues* 55:445–472.

Bobo, Lawrence, and Vincent Hutchings. 1996. "Perceptions of Racial Group Competition." *American Sociological Review* 61:951–972.

Bordua, David, and Larry Tifft. 1971. "Citizens' Interviews, Organizational Feedback, and Police-Community Relations Decisions." *Law and Society Review* 6:155–182.

Brandl, Steven, James Frank, Robert Worden, and Timothy Bynum. 1994. "Global and Specific Attitudes toward the Police." *Justice Quarterly* 11: 119–134.

Brown, Ben, and William Benedict. 2002. "Perceptions of the Police: Past Findings, Methodological Issues, Conceptual Issues, and Policy Implications." *Policing* 25:543–580.

Brown, Jodi, and Patrick Langan. 2001. *Policing and Homicide, 1976–1998*. Bureau of Justice Statistics. Washington, DC: U.S. Department of Justice.

Browning, Sandra, Francis Cullen, Liqun Cao, Renee Kopache, and Thomas Stevenson. 1994. "Race and Getting Hassled by the Police." *Police Studies* 17:1–11.

Bureau of Justice Statistics. 1999. *Criminal Victimization and Perceptions of Community Safety in 12 Cities, 1998*. Washington, DC: U.S. Department of Justice.

Bureau of Justice Statistics. 2001. *Contacts between Police and the Public: Findings from the 1999 National Survey*. Washington, DC: U.S. Department of Justice.

Bureau of Justice Statistics. 2004. *Law Enforcement Management and Administrative Statistics, 2000*. Washington, DC: U.S. Department of Justice.

Bureau of Justice Statistics. 2005. *Contacts between Police and the Public: Findings from the 2002 National Survey*. Washington, DC: U.S. Department of Justice.

Campbell, Angus, and Howard Schuman. 1968. "Racial Attitudes in Fifteen American Cities." In *National Advisory Commission on Civil Disorders, Supplemental Studies*. Washington, DC: U.S. Government Printing Office.

Cao, Liqun, James Frank, and Francis Cullen. 1996. "Race, Community Context, and Confidence in the Police." *American Journal of Police* 15:3–21.

Carter, David. 1985. "Hispanic Perceptions of Police Performance." *Journal of Criminal Justice* 13:487–500.

Cashmore, Ellis, and Eugene McLauglin (eds.). 1991. *Out of Order? Policing Black People*. London: Routledge.

Castro, Hecter. 2004. "Police Cars to Get Digital Cameras," *Seattle Post-Intelligencer*, December 18.

CBS News. 1995. CBS News Poll, September 5–6, Lexis-Nexis Public Opinion Online.

CCPEC [Chicago Community Policing Evaluation Consortium]. 2003. *Community Policing in Chicago: Years Eight and Nine*. Chicago: Illinois Criminal Justice Information Authority.

CCPEC [Chicago Community Policing Evaluation Consortium]. 2004. *Community Policing in Chicago: Year Ten*. Chicago: Illinois Criminal Justice Information Authority.

Chiricos, Ted, Michael Hogan, and Marc Gertz. 1997. "Racial Composition of Neighborhood and Fear of Crime." *Criminology* 35:107–131.

Chiricos, Ted, Kelly Welch, and Marc Gertz. 2004. "Racial Typification of Crime and Support for Punitive Measures." *Criminology* 42:359–389.

Christopher Commission. 1991. *Report of the Independent Commission on the Los Angeles Police Department*. Los Angeles: Author.

Cohn, Steven, and Steven Barkan. 2004. "Racial Prejudice and Public Attitudes about the Punishment of Criminals." In R. Miller and S. Browning (eds.), *For the Common Good*. Durham, NC: Carolina Academic Press.

Cordner, Gary, Brian Williams, and Alfredo Velasco. 2002. *Vehicle Stops in San Diego, 2001*. Report to the San Diego Police Department.

CSR. 2000. Center for Survey Research and Analysis Poll, University of Connecticut, February 17–March 2, Lexis-Nexis Public Opinion Online.

Dahlgren, Peter. 1988. "What's the Meaning of This? Viewers' Plural Sense-Making of TV News." *Media, Culture, and Society* 10:285–310.

Davis, Robert. 2004. *Assessing Police-Public Contacts in Seattle*. New York: Vera Institute of Justice.

Davis, Robert, Nicole Henderson, and Christopher Ortiz. 2005. *Can Federal Intervention Bring Lasting Improvement in Local Policing?* New York: Vera Institute of Justice.

Davis, Robert, and Pedro Mateu-Gelabert. 1999. *Respectful and Effective Policing: Two Examples in the South Bronx.* New York: Vera Institute of Justice.

Dean, Deby. 1980. "Citizens' Ratings of the Police: The Difference Contact Makes." *Law and Policy Quarterly* 2:445–471.

Decker, Scott, and R. Smith. 1980. "Police Minority Recruitment." *Journal of Criminal Justice* 8:387–393.

Dennis, J. Michael, and Rick Li. 2003. "Effects of Panel Attrition on Survey Estimates." Paper presented at the Annual Meeting of the American Association for Public Opinion Research, Nashville, TN.

Diedrich, John. 2005. "Police, Community Group Sign Pact." *Milwaukee Journal Sentinel*, May 26.

Dresner, Morris, Tortorello, and Sykes Research. 1981. *The State of Police-Community Relations.* Report to the Milwaukee Fire and Police Commission. Milwaukee, Wisconsin.

Du Bois, W. E. B. 1903. *The Souls of Black Folk.* Chicago: A. C. McClurg.

Enloe, Cynthia. 1980. *Ethnic Soldiers: State Security in Divided Societies.* Athens: University of Georgia Press.

Eschholz, Sarah, Brenda Blackwell, Marc Gertz, and Ted Chiricos. 2002. "Race and Attitudes toward the Police: Assessing the Effects of Watching 'Reality' Police Programs." *Journal of Criminal Justice* 30: 327–341.

Escobar, Edward. 1999. *Race, Police, and the Making of a Political Identity.* Berkeley: University of California Press.

Fagan, Jeffrey, and Garth Davies. 2000. "Street Stops and Broken Windows: *Terry*, Race, and Disorder in New York City." *Fordham Urban Law Journal* 28:457–449.

Flanagan, Timothy, and Michael Vaughn. 1996. "Public Opinion about Police Abuse of Force." In W. Geller and H. Toch (eds.), *Police Violence.* New Haven, CT: Yale University Press.

Fogelson, Robert. 1968. "From Resentment to Confrontation: The Police, the Negroes, and the Outbreak of the Nineteen-Sixties Riots." *Political Science Quarterly* 83:217–247.

Fogelson, Robert. 1977. *Big-City Police.* Cambridge, MA: Harvard University Press.

Fox News. 1997. National poll, conducted by Opinion Dynamics, August 20–21, Lexis-Nexis Public Opinion Online.

Frank, James, Steven Brandl, Francis Cullen, and Amy Stichman. 1996. "Reassessing the Impact of Race on Citizen's Attitudes toward the Police." *Justice Quarterly* 13:321–334.

Frank, James, Brad Smith, and Kenneth Novak. 2005. "Exploring the Basis of Citizens' Attitudes toward the Police." *Police Quarterly* 8:206–228.

Friedrich, Robert. 1979. "Racial Prejudice and Police Treatment of Blacks." In R. Baker and F. Meyer (eds.), *Evaluating Alternative Law Enforcement Policies*. Lexington, MA: Lexington Books.

Friedrich, Robert. 1980. "Police Use of Force." *Annals of the American Academy of Political and Social Science* 452:82–97.

Gallagher, Catherine, Edward Maguire, Stephen Mastrofski, and Michael Reisig. 2001. *The Public Image of the Police*. Alexandria, VA: International Association of Chiefs of Police.

Gallup. 1991. *The Gallup Poll: Public Opinion 1991*. Wilmington, DE: Gallup Organization.

Gallup. 1993. *The Gallup Poll Monthly*, No. 339. Princeton, NJ: Gallup.

Gallup. 1995. Gallup/CNN/*USA Today* poll, October 5–7, 1995, N = 1,225, Lexis-Nexis Public Opinion Online.

Gallup. 1999. Gallup poll, March 5–9, 1999, Lexis-Nexis Public Opinion Online.

Gallup. 2000. Gallup/CNN/*USA Today* poll, June 22–25, 2000, Lexis-Nexis Public Opinion Online.

General Accounting Office. 1998. *Information on Drug-Related Police Corruption*. Washington, DC: Author.

Gerbner, George, Larry Gross, Michael Morgan, and Nancy Signorielli. 1980. "The Mainstreaming of America: Violence Profile No. 11." *Journal of Communication* 30:10–29.

Glover, Scott, and Matt Lait. 2005. "LAPD Settling Abuse Scandal." *Los Angeles Times*, March 31: A1.

Goldsmith, Andrew, and Colleen Lewis (eds.). 2000. *Civilian Oversight of Policing*. Portland, OR: Hart.

Goldsmith, Andrew. 2005. "Police Reform and the Problem of Trust." *Theoretical Criminology* 9:443–470.

Goldstein, Herman. 1963. "Police Discretion: The Ideal Versus the Real." *Public Administration Review* 23:140–148.

Goldstein, Joseph. 1960. "Police Discretion Not to Invoke the Criminal Process: Low Visibility Decisions in the Administration of Justice." *Yale Law Journal* 69:543–588.

Greene, Judith. 1999. "Zero Tolerance: A Case Study of Police Policies and Practices in New York City." *Crime and Delinquency* 45:171–187.

Grinc, Randolph. 1994. "Angels in Marble: Problems in Stimulating Community Involvement in Community Policing." *Crime and Delinquency* 40:437–468.

Groves, Eugene. 1968. "Police in the Ghetto." In National Advisory Commission on Civil Disorders, *Supplemental Studies*. Washington, DC: U.S. Government Printing Office.

Hagan, John, and Celesta Albonetti. 1982. "Race, Class, and the Perception of Criminal Injustice in America." *American Journal of Sociology* 88: 329–355.

Hahn, Harlan, and Joe Feagin. 1970. "Riot-Precipitating Police Practices: Attitudes in Urban Ghettos." *Phylon* 31:183–193.

Harris, David. 1997. "'Driving While Black' and all Other Traffic Offenses: The Supreme Court and Pretextual Traffic Stops." *Journal of Criminal Law and Criminology* 87:544–582.

Harris, David. 1999. "The Stories, the Statistics, and the Law: Why Driving While Black Matters." *Minnesota Law Review* 84:265–326.

Harris, David. 2002. *Profiles in Injustice: Why Racial Profiling Cannot Work.* New York: New Press.

Harris. 1977. Louis Harris Poll, September 1977. In *Sourcebook of Criminal Justice Statistics.* Washington, DC: U.S. Department of Justice, 1978, p. 309.

Harris. 1992. Louis Harris Poll, October 1992.

Harris. 2002. Louis Harris Poll, February 13–19, 2002, Harris Interactive.

Harriston, Keith. 1993. "D.C. Police Chief Packs a High-Powered Agenda." *Washington Post*, February 15: A15.

Hepburn, John. 1978. "Race and the Decision to Arrest." *Journal of Research in Crime and Delinquency* 15:54–73.

Hochschild, Jennifer. 1995. *Facing Up to the American Dream.* Princeton, NJ: Princeton University Press.

Holmes, Malcolm. 1998. "Perceptions of Abusive Police Practices in a U.S.-Mexico Border Community." *Social Science Journal* 35:107–118.

Home Office. 2001. *Crime, Policing, and Justice: The Experience of Ethnic Minorities.* Research Study 223. London: Author.

Home Office. 2004. *Building Communities, Beating Crime: A Better Police Service for the 21st Century.* London: Author.

Hughes, Michael, and Steven Tuch. 2000. "How Beliefs about Poverty Influence Racial Policy Attitudes." In D. Sears, J. Sidanius, and L. Bobo (eds.), *Racialized Politics: The Debate About Racism in America.* Chicago: University of Chicago Press.

Human Rights Watch. 1998. *Shielded from Justice: Police Brutality and Accountability in the United States.* New York: Human Rights Watch.

Hurwitz, Jon, and Mark Peffley. 1997. "Public Perceptions of Race and Crime: The Role of Racial Stereotypes." *American Journal of Political Science* 41:375–401.

Ivkovic, Sanja. 2003. "To Serve and Collect: Measuring Police Corruption." *Journal of Criminal Law and Criminology* 93:593–649.

Jackson, Pamela Irving. 1989. *Minority Group Threat, Crime, and Policing.* New York: Praeger.

Jacob, Herbert. 1971. "Black and White Perceptions of Justice in the City." *Law and Society Review* 6:69–90.

Jacobs, David. 1979. "Inequality and Police Strength." *American Sociological Review* 44:913–925.

Jacobs, David, and Robert O'Brien. 1998. "The Determinants of Deadly Force: A Structural Analysis of Police Violence." *American Journal of Sociology* 103:837–862.

Jefferson, Tony. 1988. "Race, Crime, and Policing: Empirical, Theoretical, and Methodological Issues." *International Journal of the Sociology of Law* 16:521–539.

Jesilow, Paul, J'ona Meyer, and Nazi Namazzi. 1995. "Public Attitudes toward the Police." *American Journal of Police* 14:67–88.

Johnson, Miriam. 2003. *Street Justice: A History of Police Violence in New York City*. Boston: Beacon.

Kaiser Foundation. 1995. Kaiser/*Washington Post*/Harvard University Poll, July 20–September 28, 1995, Lexis-Nexis Public Opinion Online.

Kaiser Foundation. 2000. Kaiser/*Washington Post*/Harvard University Poll, May 2000.

Kaminski, Robert, and Eric Jefferis. 1998. "The Effect of a Violent Televised Arrest on Public Perceptions of the Police." *Policing* 21:683–706.

Kane, Robert. 2002. "The Social Ecology of Police Misconduct." *Criminology* 40:867–896.

Kennedy, Randall. 1997. *Race, Crime, and the Law*. New York: Pantheon.

Kerner Commission. 1968. *Report of the National Advisory Commission on Civil Disorders*. New York: Bantam Books.

Kinder, David, and Lynn Sanders. 1996. *Divided By Color: Racial Politics and Democratic Ideals*. Chicago: University of Chicago Press.

Klinger, David. 1997. "Negotiating Order in Police Work: An Ecological Theory of Police Response to Deviance." *Criminology* 35:277–306.

Kluegel, James, and Lawrence Bobo. 2001. "Perceived Group Discrimination and Policy Attitudes." In A. O'Connor, C. Tilly, and L. Bobo (eds.), *Urban Inequality: Evidence from Four Cities*. New York: Russell Sage.

Krivo, Lauren, and Ruth Peterson. 1996. "Extremely Disadvantaged Neighborhoods and Urban Crime." *Social Forces* 75:619–650.

Krosnick, Jon, and Lin Chiat Chang. 2001. "A Comparison of Random Digit Dialing Telephone Survey Methodology with Internet Survey Methodology as Implemented by Knowledge Networks and Harris Interactive." Paper presented at the Annual Conference of the American Association for Public Opinion Research.

Kubrin, Charis, and Ronald Weitzer. 2003. "New Directions in Social Disorganization Theory." *Journal of Research in Crime and Delinquency* 40:374–402.

Lasley, James R. 1994. "The Impact of the Rodney King Incident on Citizens' Attitudes toward the Police." *Policing and Society* 3:245–255.

Lawrence, Regina. 2000. *The Politics of Force: Media and the Construction of Police Brutality*. Berkeley: University of California Press.

Leiber, Michael, Mahesh Nalla, and Margaret Farnworth. 1998. "Explaining Juveniles' Attitudes toward the Police." *Justice Quarterly* 15:151–173.

Leinen, Stephen. 1978. *Black Police, White Society*. New York: New York Universtiy Press.

Leventhal, Gerald. 1976. "Fairness in Social Relationships." In J. Thibaut, J. Spense, and R. Carson (eds.), *Contemporary Topics in Social Psychology*. Morristown, PA: General Learning Press.

Levy, Burton. 1968. "Cops in the Ghetto." *American Behavioral Scientist* 11:31–34.

Liska, Allen, and Paul Bellair. 1995. "Violent-Crime Rates and Racial Composition." *American Journal of Sociology* 101:578–610.

Liska, Allen, and Jiang Yu. 1992. "Specifying and Testing the Threat Hypothesis: Police Use of Deadly Force." In A. Liska (ed.), *Social Threat and Social Control*. Albany: State University of New York Press.

Liska, Allen, Mitchell Chamlin, and Mark Reed. 1985. "Testing the Economic Production and Conflict Models of Crime Control." *Social Forces* 64:119–138.

Logan, John, and Brian Stults. 1999. "Racial Differences in Exposure to Crime." *Criminology* 37:251–276.

Los Angeles Times. 1988. Unpublished poll, no. 148, March 20.

Los Angeles Times. 2000. National Poll, Roper Center, June 22–25.

Markon, Jerry. 2004. "Ex-Officer in District Admits He Sold Drugs." *Washington Post*, August 5: B1, B5.

Mastrofski, Stephen, Michael Reisig, and John McCluskey. 2002. "Police Disrespect toward the Public." *Criminology* 40:519–551.

Mastrofski, Stephen, Jeffrey Snipes, and Anne Supina. 1996. "Compliance on Demand: The Public's Response to Specific Police Requests." *Journal of Research in Crime and Delinquency* 33:269–305.

McCombs, Maxwell, and Donald Shaw. 1972. "The Agenda Setting Function of the Mass Media." *Public Opinion Quarterly* 36:176–187.

Meehan, Albert, and Michael Ponder. 2002. "Race and Place: The Ecology of Racial Profiling African American Motorists." *Justice Quarterly* 19:399–429.

Mirande, Alfredo. 1981. "The Chicano and the Law." *Pacific Sociological Review* 24:65–86.

Mirande, Alfredo. 1987. *Gringo Justice*. Notre Dame, IN: University of Notre Dame Press.

Mollen Commission. 1994. *Report of the Commission to Investigate Allegations of Police Corruption*. New York: Mollen Commission.

Murty, Komanduri, Julian Roebuck, and Joann Smith. 1990. "The Image of the Police in Black Atlanta Communities." *Journal of Police Science and Administration* 17:250–257.

Myrdal, Gunnar. 1944. *An American Dilemma.* New York: McGraw-Hill.

National Research Council. 2004. *Fairness and Effectiveness in Policing: The Evidence.* Washington, DC: National Academies Press.

NBC. 1995. NBC News/*Wall Street Journal* poll, October 27–31, Lexis-Nexis Public Opinion Online.

New York Times. 1991. New York Times/CBS News Poll, April 1–3.

Newburn, Tim. 1999. *Understanding and Preventing Police Corruption: Lessons from the Literature.* Police Research Series Paper 110. London: Home Office.

Oliver, Mary. 1996. "Portrayals of Crime, Race, and Aggression in 'Reality-Based' Police Shows." *Journal of Broadcasting and Electronic Media* 38: 179–192.

Ousey, Graham, and Matthew Lee. 2002. "Examining the Conditional Nature of the Illicit Drug Market-Homicide Relationship." *Criminology* 40:73–102.

Packer, Herbert. 1968. *The Limits of the Criminal Sanction.* Stanford, CA: Stanford University Press.

Pate, Antony, and Lorie Fridell. 1993. *Police Use of Force: Official Reports, Citizen Complaints, and Legal Consequences.* Washington, DC: Police Foundation.

Penn, Schoen, and Berland Associates. 2000. National Poll, registered voters, June 10–13, 2000, Lexis-Nexis Public Opinion Online.

Pew Research Center. 1997. National Poll, fielded February 6–7, 1997, Lexis-Nexis Public Opinion Online.

Police Foundation. 2004. *Final Report: Biased Policing Project.* Washington, DC: Police Foundation.

Poulantzas, Nicos. 1973. *Political Power and Social Classes.* London: New Left Books.

President's Commission on Law Enforcement and Administration of Justice. 1967. *Task Force Report: The Police.* Washington, DC: U.S. Government Printing Office.

Princeton. 2000. National Poll conducted for *Newsweek* by Princeton Survey Research Associates, fielded June 29–30, 2000, Lexis-Nexis Public Opinion Online.

Punch, Maurice. 1985. *Conduct Unbecoming: The Social Construction of Police Deviance and Control.* London: Tavistock.

Quillian, Lincoln. 1995. "Prejudice as a Response to Perceived Group Threat." *American Sociological Review* 60:586–611.

Quillian, Lincoln, and Devah Pager. 2001. "Black Neighbors, Higher Crime? The Role of Racial Stereotypes in Evaluations of Neighborhood Crime." *American Journal of Sociology* 107:717–767.

Quinnipiac. 2005. "New Yorkers Approve of NYPD 3 to 1." Quinnipiac University poll, June 23, 2005.

Raudenbush, Stephen, and Anthony Bryk. 2002. *Hierarchical Linear Models.* Newbury Park, CA: Sage.

Reisig, Michael, and Meghan Chandek. 2001. "The Effects of Expectancy Disconfirmation on Outcome Satisfaction in Police-Citizen Encounters." *Policing* 24:88–99.

Reisig, Michael, and Roger Parks. 2000. "Experience, Quality of Life, and Neighborhood Context." *Justice Quarterly* 17:607–629.

Reisig, Michael, and Roger Parks. 2003. "Neighborhood Context, Police Behavior, and Satisfaction with Police." *Justice Research and Policy* 5: 37–65.

Reiss, Albert. 1971. *The Police and the Public.* New Haven, CT: Yale University Press.

Reitzel, John, Stephen Rice, and Alex Piquero. 2004. "Lines and Shadows: Perceptions of Racial Profiling and the Hispanic Experience." *Journal of Criminal Justice* 32:607–616.

Riksheim, Eric, and Steven Chermak. 1993. "Causes of Police Behavior Revisited." *Journal of Criminal Justice* 21: 353–382.

Rossi, Peter, and Richard Berk. 1997. *Just Punishments: Federal Guidelines and Public Views Compared.* New York: De Gruyter.

Rubenstein, Jonathan. 1973. *City Police.* New York: Farrar, Straus, and Giroux.

Sampson, Robert, and Dawn Jeglum Bartusch. 1998. "Legal Cynicism and (Subcultural?) Tolerance of Deviance: The Neighborhood Context of Racial Differences." *Law and Society Review* 32:777–804.

Sampson, Robert, and Janet Lauritsen. 1997. "Racial and Ethnic Disparities in Crime and Criminal Justice in the United States." In M. Tonry (ed.), *Crime and Justice,* vol. 22. Chicago: University of Chicago Press.

Scaglion, Richard, and Richard Condon. 1980. "Determinants of Attitudes toward City Police." *Criminology* 17:485–494.

Schafer, Joseph, Beth Huebner, and Timothy Bynum. 2003. "Citizen Perceptions of Police Services: Race, Neighborhood Context, and Community Policing." *Police Quarterly* 6:440–468.

Schuman, Howard, Charlotte Steeh, Lawrence Bobo, and Maria Krysan. 1997. *Racial Attitudes in America.* Cambridge, MA: Harvard University Press.

Sherman, Lawrence. 1978. *Scandal and Reform: Controlling Police Corruption.* Berkeley: University of California Press.

Sherman, Lawrence. 1983. "After the Riots: Police and Minorities in the United States." In N. Glazer and K. Young (eds.), *Ethnic Pluralism and Public Policy.* Toronto: Lexington.

Sigelman, Lee, and Susan Welch. 1991. *Black Americans' Views of Racial Inequality.* New York: Cambridge University Press.

Sigelman, Lee, Susan Welch, Timothy Bledsoe, and Michael Combs. 1997. "Police Brutality and Public Perceptions of Racial Discrimination." *Political Research Quarterly* 50:777–791.

Skogan, Wesley. 1994. "The Impact of Community Policing on Neighborhood Residents." In D. Rosenbaum (ed.), *The Challenge of Community Policing*. Thousand Oaks, CA: Sage.

Skogan, Wesley. 2005. "Citizen Satisfaction with Police Encounters." *Police Quarterly* 8:298–321.

Skogan, Wesley, and Susan Hartnett. 1997. *Community Policing, Chicago Style*. New York: Oxford University Press.

Skolnick, Jerome. 1966. *Justice without Trial*. New York: John Wiley.

Skolnick, Jerome, and James Fyfe. 1993. *Above the Law: Police and the Excessive Use of Force*. New York. Free Press.

Smalley, Suzanne. 2005. "Diversity Gap Seen in Police Upper Ranks." *Boston Globe*, November 17.

Smith, David. 1991. "The Origins of Black Hostility to the Police." *Policing and Society* 2:1–15.

Smith, Douglas. 1986. "The Neighborhood Context of Police Behavior." In A. Reiss and M. Tonry (eds.), *Crime and Justice*, vol. 8. Chicago: University of Chicago Press.

Smith, Douglas, Nanette Graham, and Bonnie Adams. 1991. "Minorities and the Police: Attitudinal and Behavioral Questions." In M. Lynch and E. B. Patterson (eds.), *Race and Criminal Justice*. New York: Harrow and Heston.

Smith, Douglas, Christy Visher, and Laura Davidson. 1984. "Equity and Discretionary Justice: The Influence of Race on Police Arrest Decisions." *Journal of Criminal Law and Criminology* 75:234–249.

Smith, Paul, and Richard Hawkins. 1973. "Victimization, Types of Citizens-Police Contacts, and Attitudes toward the Police." *Law and Society Review* 8:135–152.

Son, In Soo, Chiu-Wai Tsang, Dennis Rome, and Mark Davis. 1997. "Citizens' Observations of Police Use of Excessive Force and their Evaluation of Police Performance." *Policing* 20:149–159.

Sontag, Deborah, and Dan Barry. 1997. "The Price of Brutality: Police Complaints Settled, Rarely Resolved." *New York Times*, September 17: A1.

Stone, Vanessa, and Nick Pettigrew. 2000. *The Views of the Public on Stops and Searches*. London: Home Office.

Strauss, Anselm. 1987. *Qualitative Analysis for Social Scientists*. New York: Cambridge University Press.

Sun, Ivan, and Brian Payne. 2004. "Racial Differences in Resolving Conflicts: A Comparison between Black and White Police Officers." *Crime and Delinquency* 50:516–541.

Surette, Ray. 1998. *Media, Crime, and Criminal Justice.* Belmont, CA: Wadsworth.

Sviridoff, Michele, and Jerome McElroy. 1989. *The Processing of Complaints against the Police in New York City.* New York: Vera Institute of Justice.

Swickard, Joe. 2005. "Cop Suits Cost $44.7 Million: Misdeeds Added Up in 2002–2004." *Detroit Free Press,* July 5.

Swigert, Victoria, and Ronald Farrell. 1976. *Murder, Inequality, and the Law: Differential Treatment in the Legal Process.* Lexington, MA: Heath.

Sykes, Gresham, and David Matza. 1957. "Techniques of Neutralization." *American Sociological Review* 22:667–670.

Sykes, Richard, and John Clark. 1975. "A Theory of Deference Exchange in Police-Civilian Encounters." *American Journal of Sociology* 81:584–600.

Terrill, William, and Stephen Mastrofski. 2004. "Working the Street: Does Community Policing Matter?" In W. Skogan (ed.), *Community Policing: Can it Work?* Belmont, CA: Wadsworth.

Terrill, William, and Michael Reisig. 2003. "Neighborhood Context and Police Use of Force." *Journal of Research in Crime and Delinquency* 40: 291–321.

Thomas, George, and Richard Leo. 2002. "The Effects of *Miranda v. Arizona.*" In M. Tonry (ed.), *Crime and Justice,* vol. 29. Chicago: University of Chicago Press.

*Time/*CNN. 1995. National Poll, *Time/*CNN/Yankelovich Partners, September 13–14, 1995.

Trojanowicz, Robert. 1983. "An Evaluation of a Neighborhood Foot Patrol Program." *Journal of Police Science and Administration* 11:410–419.

Tuch, Steven, and Michael Hughes. 1996a. "Whites' Racial Policy Attitudes." *Social Science Quarterly* 77:723–745.

Tuch, Steven, and Michael Hughes. 1996b. "Whites' Opposition to Race-Targeted Policies: One Cause or Many?" *Social Science Quarterly* 77: 778–788.

Tuch, Steven, and Ronald Weitzer. 1997. "Racial Differences in Attitudes toward the Police." *Public Opinion Quarterly* 61:642–663.

Tyler, Tom. 1990. *Why People Obey the Law.* New Haven, CT: Yale University Press.

Tyler, Tom, and Yuen Huo. 2002. *Trust in the Law.* New York: Russell Sage.

Tyler, Tom, and Cheryl Wakslak. 2004. "Profiling and Police Legitimacy." *Criminology* 42:253–281.

U.S. Department of Justice. 2001. *Principles for Promoting Police Integrity.* Washington, DC: Author.

Velez, Maria. 2001. "The Role of Public Social Control in Urban Neighborhoods." *Criminology* 39:837–863.

Walker, Darlene, Richard Richardson, Oliver Williams, Thomas Denyer, and Skip McGaughey. 1972. "Contact and Support: An Empirical Assessment of Public Attitudes toward the Police and the Courts." *North Carolina Law Review* 51:43–79.

Walker, Samuel. 1999. *The Police in America.* New York: McGraw-Hill.

Walker, Samuel. 2001. *Police Accountability: The Role of Citizen Oversight.* Belmont, CA: Wadsworth.

Walker, Samuel. 2005. *The New World of Police Accountability.* Thousand Oaks, CA: Sage.

Walker, Samuel, Geoffrey Alpert, and Dennis Kenney. 2001. "Early Warning Systems: Responding to the Problem Police Officer." *Research in Brief.* Washington, DC: National Institute of Justice.

Wallach, Irving, and Colette Jackson. 1973. "Perception of the Police in a Black Community." In J. Snibbe and H. Snibbe (eds.), *The Urban Policeman in Transition.* Springfield, IL: Charles Thomas.

Washington Post. 1995. Poll, October 4–6, Lexis-Nexis Public Opinion Online.

Washington Post. 1997. Washington Post/ABC News poll, *Washington Post,* June 12.

Webb, Vincent, and Chris Marshall. 1995. "The Relative Importance of Race and Ethnicity on Citizen Attitudes toward the Police." *American Journal of Police* 14:45–66.

Weisburd, David, and Rosanne Greenspan. 2000. *Police Attitudes toward Abuse of Authority: Findings from a National Study.* Washington, DC: National Institute of Justice.

Weisheit, Ralph, David Falcone, and Edward Wells. 1995. *Crime and Policing in Rural and Small-Town America.* Washington, DC: National Institute of Justice.

Weitzer, Ronald. 1985. "Policing a Divided Society: Obstacles to Normalization in Northern Ireland." *Social Problems* 33:41–55.

Weitzer, Ronald. 1990. *Transforming Settler States: Communal Conflict and Internal Security in Northern Ireland and Zimbabwe.* Berkeley: University of California Press.

Weitzer, Ronald. 1995. *Policing under Fire: Ethnic Conflict and Police-Community Relations in Northern Ireland.* Albany: State University of New York Press.

Weitzer, Ronald. 1999. "Citizens' Perceptions of Police Misconduct: Race and Neighborhood Context." *Justice Quarterly* 16:819–846.

Weitzer, Ronald. 2000a. "Racialized Policing: Residents' Perceptions in Three Neighborhoods." *Law and Society Review* 34:129–155.

Weitzer, Ronald. 2000b. "White, Black, or Blue Cops? Race and Citizen Assessments of Police Officers." *Journal of Criminal Justice* 28:313–324.

Weitzer, Ronald. 2002. "Incidents of Police Misconduct and Public Opinion." *Journal of Criminal Justice* 30:397–408.

Weitzer, Ronald. 2005. "Can the Police be Reformed?" *Contexts* 4 (Summer): 21–26.

Weitzer, Ronald, and Charis Kubrin. 2004. "Breaking News: How Local TV News and Real-World Conditions Affect Fear of Crime." *Justice Quarterly* 21:497–520.

Weitzer, Ronald, and Steven Tuch. 1999. "Race, Class, and Perceptions of Discrimination by the Police." *Crime and Delinquency* 45:494–507.

Weitzer, Ronald, and Steven Tuch. 2002. "Perceptions of Racial Profiling: Race, Class, and Personal Experience." *Criminology* 40:435–456.

Weitzer, Ronald, and Steven Tuch. 2004a. "Race and Perceptions of Police Misconduct." *Social Problems* 51:305–325.

Weitzer, Ronald, and Steven Tuch. 2004b. "Public Opinion on Reforms in Policing." *Police Chief* (December): 26–30.

Welch, Susan, Lee Sigelman, Timothy Bledsoe, and Michael Coombs. 2001. *Race and Place: Race Relations in an American City*. New York: Cambridge University Press.

Werthman, Carl, and Irving Piliavin. 1967. "Gang Members and the Police," in D. Bordua (ed.), *The Police*. New York: Wiley.

Westley, William. 1970. *Violence and the Police*. Cambridge, MA: MIT Press.

White, M., T. Cox, and J. Basehart. 1991. "Theoretical Considerations of Officer Profanity and Obscenity." In T. Barker and D. Carter (eds.), *Police Deviance*. Cincinnati: Anderson.

Wickersham Commission. 1931. *Report on Lawlessness in Law Enforcement*. Washington, DC: U.S. Government Printing Office.

Wiley, Mary, and Terry Hudik. 1974. "Police-Citizen Encounters: A Field Test of Exchange Theory." *Social Problems* 22:119–127.

Williams, Brian. 1997. *Citizen Perspectives on Community Policing*. Albany: State University of New York Press.

Wilson, George, and Roger Dunham. 2001. "Race, Class, and Attitudes toward Crime Control." *Criminal Justice and Behavior* 28:259–278.

Wilson, James Q. 1972. "The Police in the Ghetto." In R. Steadman (ed.), *The Police and the Community*. Baltimore: Johns Hopkins University Press.

Wilson, William Julius. 1987. *The Truly Disadvantaged*. Chicago: University of Chicago Press.

Winton, Richard. 2005. "Video Cameras Urged for LAPD." *Los Angeles Times*, December 9.

Worden, Robert. 1996. "The Causes of Police Brutality." In W. Geller and H. Toch (eds.), *Police Violence*. New Haven, CT: Yale University Press.

Wortley, Scot, John Hagan, and Ross Macmillan. 1997. "Just Desserts? The Racial Polarization of Perceptions of Criminal Injustice." *Law and Society Review* 31:637–676.

Zauberman, Renee, and Rene Levy. 2003. "Police, Minorities, and the French Republican Ideal." *Criminology* 41:1065–1100.

Index

abuse, verbal, *see* verbal abuse
accountability, 37, 38, 51, 66, 106, 126, 129, 130–133, 138, 145–149, 152, 159, 161, 168, 173–175, 177, 181, 188
  monitoring, 137, 145
  sanctions, 188
  use of video cameras for, 131–132, 146
African American. *See* black
Alex, Nicholas, 98, 214
Amnesty International, 86, 88, 132, 205
Asians, perceptions of police, 121
auditor model, 174

Baldwin, James, 178
black, confidence in police, 1, 2
  criminality, 9, 11, 106
  experiences with police, 128, 183
  instruction in dealing with police, 19
  perceptions of police, 5–7, 12–21, 30, 189, 60–73, 96–126
  shared orientation with Hispanics, 16
black officers
  attitudes of, 32, 35
  recruitment of, 36, 37, 96
blue cops, idea of, 114
  position, 99, 114
bribery, 69
brutality, 1, 15, 20, 29, 64, 66, 71, 73, 130, 143, 161, 166, 183

Chicago's Alternative Policing Strategy (CAPS), 134
Christopher Commission, 5, 32, 76, 129
citizens, police treatment of, 3, 21

civilian review board, 130, 138, 146, 175
Commission on Accreditation for Law Enforcement Agencies, 133
Commission on Police-Community Relations, Milwaukee, 132
community policing, 38, 40, 44, 45, 58, 59, 64, 65, 71–73, 117, 126, 134, 135, 138, 149–150, 152, 153, 159, 161, 167, 169, 170–175, 181, 201
complaints against police, 25, 27, 47, 49, 107, 118, 130–132, 135, 138, 143, 175, 188
complaints process, 25
concentrated disadvantage, 22, 59, 64, 94, 153, 159, 160, 161, 182, 201
conflict theory, 9, 23
contacts, unpleasant versus positive, 17
COPS office, 131, 134
corruption, 1, 29, 30, 49, 51, 63–66, 69, 197, 209, 210, 212, 213, 214
  history of, 29
  rates of, 47
crime, neighborhood, 23, 40, 43, 44, 51, 60–65, 72, 73, 76, 89, 90–93, 121, 122, 134
  exaggeration of black involvement in, 10
  fear of, 24
  fighting, 45, 70, 150
  officially recorded, 24
  police response to, 79
  preventing, 170
  racial typification of, 10, 11
  residents' asssessments of, 24
  situation, 69
  street, 109, 139, 151

crime-control practices, 9, 160
criminal justice system, different
    perceptions of, 5, 9, 10, 78, 80
    racial bias in, 75, 106
criminal prosecution, as type of
    accountability, 130, 146–147
criminality, presumption of, 108

demographic factors, 182, 183
Diallo, Amadou, 1, 20, 148, 184
discrimination, 30, 31, 74, 75, 77–79, 80,
    84, 85, 94, 107–109, 120, 121, 143,
    153, 166, 168, 178, 181, 186, 189
    rational, 11, 106, 109, 185
    reverse, 107, 108
diversification, police department, 36,
    96, 126, 137, 139, 154, 197
    public assessments of, 127
diversity, police department, 96, 117, 127,
    141–143, 149, 152, 153, 159, 164,
    175, 188
dominant racial groups, perception of
    the police, 10
drinking while on duty, 66
driving while black, 27, 33, 34, 120
drug crimes, policing of, 66
due process, 136, 138

early warning systems, 138, 146
encounters, police-citizen, 13, 23, 38,
    118, 128
excessive force, 12, 28, 29, 49, 53–55, 62,
    64, 197
    frequency of use, 28, 49

force, excessive. See excessive force
    Supreme Court ruling on, 28
foot patrols, 149–150

gangs, 108, 135
General Social Survey, 10, 31
Graham v. Connor, 28, 49
group-position thesis, 8, 10, 12, 13, 15, 16,
    31, 47, 73, 75, 78, 89, 100, 105, 108,
    122, 123, 162, 163, 165, 167, 168,
    180, 185, 186

harassment, 4, 47, 57, 66
Hispanic populations, growth of, 9
    ancestry/nationality, 7, 193,
        196

Hispanics, anecdotal evidence on
    relations with police, 6
    lack of research on, 6
    perceptions of police, 60–63, 96–126,
        153, 189
    sharing of orientation with African
        Americans, 16

injustice, perceptions of, 10, 12
intensified policing, 136, 139, 150–153,
    158, 160, 161, 181
International Association of Chiefs of
    Police, 175

justice, group perceptions of, 10
    procedural. See procedural justice
    street, 5

Kerner Commission, 36, 178
King, Rodney, 1, 20, 73, 81, 102, 161, 166,
    174, 184, 211
Knapp Commission, 29
Knowledge Networks, 191–196, 211

language barrier, issue of, 105
    derogatory. See verbal abuse
law enforcement, inadequate, 14
Los Angeles Police Department
    (LAPD), 1, 20, 30, 161
    public confidence in, 1, 20
    Rampart Division of, 1
Louima, Abner, 20, 102, 148, 184

majority-group perspective, 7
mass media, 13, 17, 20, 73, 95, 102, 122,
    159, 160, 173, 182, 183
    reporting, 17, 20, 39, 164, 165, 166,
        184. See also misconduct, media
        coverage of, and police, media
        coverage of
    role in reform, 161, 173–174
minority-group perspectives, 7, 72, 119.
    See also black, Hispanic, Asians
Miranda, 137
Miranda rights, 128, 136, 137, 144, 174,
    187
misconduct, 25, 26, 39–73
    constraints on, 23
    discipline for, 22
    experiences of, 45, 53–55, 101,
        154–158, 160

forms of, 26, 30, 48
media coverage of, 1, 20, 45, 76, 89, 122
observations of, 65–70
opportunity for, 22
perceptions of, 2, 12, 15, 16, 24, 43–48, 50–65, 153, 159, 160, 173
prevalence in police departments, 46
sanctioning, 146
Mollen Commission, 7, 8, 9, 21, 29, 51, 67, 72, 212
Myrdal, Gunnar, 178

negative experiences, racial differences of, 18
neighborhood crime. *See* crime, neighborhood
disorganization, 24
socioeconomic status of, 21, 40
neighborhoods, differences in police practices in, 56
discrimination against, 31
influences on officer behavior, 109
minority, 6, 10, 34, 51, 56
misconduct in, 55
white versus black, 22, 23, 67, 115
neutralization techniques, 163
New York Police Department (NYPD), 1, 21, 29, 30, 67, 129, 213
nondemographic factors, research on, 17

Office of Community Oriented Policing Services, 131, 134
officers of different races, perceptions of, 98–111
order, maintenance of, 3

patrols, mixed race, 116
place, importance of, 34
police
behavior, 22, 187
communications, 32
corruption, lack of knowledge of, 50
effectiveness, 40
equanimity, white belief in, 78
lawsuits against, 2, 125, 129, 143
media coverage of, 13, 41
misconduct. *See* misconduct

prejudice, 32, 74, 80, 81, 89, 94, 121
racial bias, 32, 76, 89, 94, 95, 119, 121, 122, 153, 168
ratings on survey, 30
in reality shows, 20
satisfaction with, 39–45, 186, 187
subculture, 3–5, 105, 176, 177
surveys of, 179
unions, and civilian review boards, 146
police stops, 26, 48, 50, 51, 52–55, 197
in Britain, 57
citizen perceptions of, 27
legitimate versus unlawful, 27
racial differences in, 34, 57
police departments, improvement through racial diversity, 127
prevalence of misconduct in, 46
racial complexion of, 35, 96, 127
racial diversification of, 36, 38
Police Executive Research Forum, 96
Police Foundation, 4, 5, 14, 57, 96, 149, 213
police work, 3, 5
as a career, 74
low visibility of, 3
monitoring of, 146
politically motivated interference with, 125
public ignorance of, 163
public interference with, 37
public perceptions of, 153
routine, 22
police-citizen relations, 3, 5, 6, 21, 25, 122, 135, 174, 184, 189
police-community relations, 22, 23, 72, 132, 134, 141, 149, 151, 170, 171, 175
police-minority relations, 6, 7, 72, 119, 178
policing issues, convergence of minority and white interests, 14
policing, principles of, 37, 125
power-threat thesis, 8, 9
President's Commission on Law Enforcement (1967), 36
procedural justice, 17, 38, 126, 128, 137, 144, 145, 152, 159, 173, 174, 176, 181, 187
proportional representation, 96, 126, 140, 142, 143

public perceptions, media influences on, 20, 183–184
Puerto Ricans, 52
punishment, support for stronger, 148

race and class, interaction of, 105
racial bias, 13, 14, 27, 30–34, 74–76, 80, 82, 88, 94, 121, 122, 166, 173, 181, 183, 185
  discrimination, 31, 120, 121, 181
  diversification, 139–144
  groups, interests of, 10
  hierarchy, 7, 16, 55, 59, 72, 76, 88, 89, 106, 119, 121, 152, 173, 180
  perception of, 82, 86, 180–182
  prejudice, prevalence among officers, 80
  prevention of, 132
  profiling, 11, 20, 31, 33, 35, 74, 75, 77, 78, 80, 82, 83, 87, 88, 89, 94, 106, 108, 109, 118, 120, 122, 132, 133, 140, 143, 145, 146, 153, 162, 176, 181
  proportionality, principle of, 141
  typification, 11
racialized policing, 30, 74, 75, 77, 89, 95, 119, 121, 122, 181, 183
racial divide, 178–189
racially biased law enforcement, opposition to, 120
racism, institutionalized, 106
Rampart Division. *See* Los Angeles Police Department, Rampart Division
reform, potential of, 187
  public preferences regarding, 125, 139–174
  types of, 126, 161–162, 174–176

satisfaction, factors shaping general, 39–45
  variation by race, 41
selective enforcement, 3
sensitivity training, 169, 175, 188
sexual misconduct, 66, 70

social class versus race, 105
social disorganization theory, 23, 24
socioeconomic disadvantage, of neighborhood, 22
Spanish-English language differences, 105
speech, offensive, 49
stereotyping, 110
symbolic benefits, 118, 176

Terry v. Ohio, 26
theory, conflict, 8
theory, social disorganization, 23, 24
traffic violations, 34, 66, 77, 84

U.S. Department of Justice, 36, 75, 124, 127, 132, 133, 206, 207
  policy on racial diversification, 96
underenforcement of the law, 136
unequal justice, perceptions of, 75
use-of-force continuum, 28

verbal abuse, 27, 37, 49, 53–56, 61, 64, 197
Verbeke, Shawn, 67
vicarious experience, 43, 60–63, 90–93, 99, 121, 154–158, 198
victim, 2, 3, 4, 10, 21
  attitudes toward police, 24
Violent Crime Control Act of 1994, 134
violent crime, racial involvement in, 10

white officer mistreatment of blacks, 102
white privilege, 12
  perceptions of police by race, 96–126
  views of white officers, 103
white-black paradigm, 104
white-minority perception gap, 84
whites and racial profiling, 87
Whren v. United States, 27
Wickersham Commission, 29, 46, 218

youth, specific programs for, 171

The Criminal Career: The Danish Longitudinal Study, by Britta Kyvsgaard

Gangs and Delinquency in Developmental Perspective, by Terence P. Thornberry, Marvin D. Krohn, Alan J. Lizotte, Carolyn A. Smith, and Kimberly Tobin

Early Prevention of Adult Antisocial Behaviour, by David P. Farrington and Jeremy W. Cold

Errors of Justice, by Brian Forst

Violent Crime, by Darnell F. Hawkins

Rethinking Homicide: Exploring the Structure and Process in Homicide Situations, by Terance D. Miethe and Wendy C. Regoeczi

Understanding Police Use of Force: Officers, Suspects, and Reciprocity, by Geoffrey P. Alpert and Roger G. Dunham

Marking Time in the Golden State: Women's Imprisonment in California, by Candace Kruttschnitt and Rosemary Gartner

Economic Espionage and Industrial Spying, by Hedieh Nasheri

The Virtual Prison: Community Custody and the Evolution of Imprisonment, by Julian Roberts

Situational Prison Control: Crime Prevention in Correctional Institutions, by Richard Wortley

Prisoner Reentry and Crime in America, by Jeremy Travis and Christy Visher

Choosing White Collar Crime, by Neal Shover and Andrew Hochstetler

The Crime Drop in America, Revised Edition, edited by Alfred Blumstein and Joel Wallman

Police Innovation: Contrasting Perspectives, edited by David Weisburd and Anthony Braga

Policing Gangs in America, by Charles M. Katz and Vincent J. Webb

Third Party Policing, by Lorraine Mazzerole and Janet Ransley

Street Justice: Retaliation in the Criminal Underworld, by Bruce Jacobs and Richard Wright

What Works in Corrections: Reducing Recidivism, by Doris Layton MacKenzie

The Prison and the Gallows: The Politics of Mass Incarceration in America, by Marie Gottschalk